Backwoods Home Cooking

A *Backwoods Home Magazine* Anthology of Recipes

ISBN 978-0-9846222-7-6
Copyright 1989-2003

Backwoods Home Magazine
PO Box 712
Gold Beach, OR 97444

Drawings by Don Childers
Cover photo by John Silveira
Edited by Ilene Duffy

*This book is dedicated to Katherine Myers
in whose kitchen friends and family
have enjoyed countless meals.*

Acknowledgments

We would like to thank the writers who have contributed their articles and recipes during the past 14 years. Those included in this anthology of recipes are:

Richard Blunt, John Silveira, Jackie Clay, Alice Yeager, Katherine Dazazel, Pat Ward, Jo Mason, Jan Cook, Katherine Myers, Lucy Shober, Kristen Rogers, Mary Hembrow, Larry Cywin, Habeeb Salloum, Rodney Merrill, Charles A. Sanders, Thomas C. Tabor, Marcella Shaffer, Sandra L. Toney, Bonnie Gelle, Charles Bryant O'Dooley, Bill Palmroth, Darlene Campbell, Arthur Vernon II, Olivia Miller, Marjorie Burris, Tom Barth, Janine Hawley, Tricia Blunt, Tanya Kelley, Sharon Palmer, Linda Gabris, Sally Denney, Natalie McKnight Haugaard, Anne Westbrook Dominick, Joanie Rudolph, Jean Winfrey, Sharon Freeman, Jean Louis L'Heureux, William Shepherd, Sally Boulding, Kate Merrill, Sarah Blake, Edith Helmich, Jean Winfrey, Arline Tobola, Bonnie Maruquin, James Robertson, Jay Ansama, Tom R. Kovach, Leland Edward Stone, Tim and Anna Green, Sharon Thornbury, Rhoda Denning, Jeannette Kaner, Harriet Lussan, Gertrude Kenner, Dave Duffy, Annie Tuttle, Ilene Duffy, Nathele Graham, Muriel Sutherland, Lisa Nourse, Edwina Gower, Don Childers, Nancy Childers, Meaghan Silveira, Evelyn Leach, Oliver Del Signore

This cookbook would not have been possible without the hard work of our typists and proofreaders. Special thanks go to Lisa Nourse and Rhoda Denning.

Contents

Introduction

This is another in the line of *Backwoods Home Magazine's* anthologies and our first cookbook. The recipes are a compilation from our contributors, the staff, our families, and our friends. They include breakfasts, breads, quick dishes, main dishes, salads, desserts, pickles, jams, sauces, etc. Ingredients include beef, lamb, pork, chicken, wild game, fish and shellfish, vegetables, and a wide array of both common and uncommon herbs and spices.

Many of these recipes have been tested and tasted right here at *BHM*. Even in the early days of the magazine we ate well. The staff ate as I perfected my kale soup recipe and my egg thingies, O.E. MacDougal's baked curry was invented here, and when Richard Blunt (Butch to us) visited, he made some of the dishes that ultimately appeared in the pages of the magazine and now here in this cookbook.

Butch probably has had more to do with me turning into a decent cook than anyone else in my life. Whenever he gave me a recipe, I often found myself asking him why he did a step or added a certain ingredient. Each time, he gave me a clear and concise explanation of how a step or ingredient affected the final product's taste and appearance. For instance, I learned that salt is often added to a recipe not to make it taste salty, but to bring out the flavors: "Most of the time you add salt so the food doesn't taste flat. If you can taste the salt, you've added too much." He also explained why I should brown meat in small batches: "If you try to brown too much at once, you get too much liquid and you end up parboiling the meat." As I came to understand his recipes I began to learn how recipes go together and I've finally learned to improvise. Armed with knowledge I got from him, we ate fish we caught in the lake until it came out of our ears. He is the best cook I've ever known and you can benefit from his knowledge. Many of his best recipes are included here.

There are many other cooks represented here. Jackie Clay, the most prolific writer in the history of *BHM*, has many entries in the cookbook. And there are Alice Yeager's tasty recipes for the produce from her garden.

You can use this cookbook any way you want. Some of the recipes are quick and easy; others are exotic and will satisfy your desire to do gourmet cooking.

Whatever you do with this cookbook anthology, we are sure you, your family, and your friends will be as delighted as we have been at *BHM*.

— **John Silveira**

Appetizers

Dilled oyster crackers
By Alice Brantley Yeager

2 12-oz. pkgs. oyster crackers
1 cup canola oil or other light vegetable oil
2 tsp. dried dill weed
½ tsp. garlic powder

½ tsp. finely ground cayenne pepper
1 1.6-oz. package Ranch salad dressing, original flavor

Put the oyster crackers in a large mixing bowl. Thoroughly mix the last 5 ingredients together and pour a bit at a time over the crackers, stirring until the crackers are coated. Let stand covered at least 1 hour. Store them in an airtight container. They do not need refrigeration and they're good to use with soup, salads, and as snacks. It is not necessary to bake this recipe.

Deviled eggs
By Katherine Dazazel

6 eggs
mayonnaise
mustard

paprika
chopped chives (optional)
bacon bits (optional)

Hard-boil 6 eggs and set aside until they are cool enough to peel. When peeled, slice in half lengthwise and scoop the yolks out into a bowl. With the edge of a spoon, cut up the yolks until they are very finely chopped—don't mash them. Add a few generous spoonfuls of mayonnaise and a very small amount of mustard, until the mixture looks and tastes right.

Refill the eggs with the mixture. Be generous; there is now a lot more to put in than there was to take out. Sprinkle with a little paprika to decorate. You can also add a teaspoonful or so of chopped chives, or bacon bits.

Fresh cucumber delight
By Jackie Clay

3 qts. sliced cucumbers
¼ oz. mustard seed
½ lb. non-iodized salt
½ oz. celery seed

9 pints water
½ oz. black pepper
1 lb. brown sugar
1 qt. vinegar

Slice fresh medium-small cukes into thin slices. Place immediately into a solution of ½ lb. of salt and 9 pints of water. Let stand overnight. Next morning, drain, pack into jars, and cover with a cold, sweet liquid made up from the remaining ingredients. Seal tightly and store in the refrigerator. This recipe makes 3 qts.

Lazy housewife pickles
By Jackie Clay

4 qts. small cucumbers
1 cup dry mustard
1 cup sugar

1 cup salt
1 gallon vinegar

Wash the cucumbers, then pack them in glass jars. Mix the mustard, sugar, and salt together, then add the vinegar slowly, stirring well. Pour this over the pickles and seal the jars. Let the jars stand for at least a week in the refrigerator before using. The brine is not heated. Makes 4 qts.

Poor man's shrimp cocktail on perch
By Pat Ward

¾ cup ketchup
1 Tbsp. horseradish
2 tsp. Worcestershire Sauce

1 Tbsp. lemon juice
Tabasco to taste
about 2 lbs. filleted perch

Mix the ketchup, horseradish, Worcestershire, lemon juice, and Tabasco in a bowl and place the mixture in the refrigerator to let the flavors marry. Clean the perch by removing the heads and internal organs. Place the cleaned fish in a frying pan, in a single layer, with enough cold water to just cover them. Heat the fry pan over a high heat until the water just starts to boil, then remove the pan from the heat and let it sit for 1 minute. Pour off the hot water and rinse the fish under cold water until they are thoroughly cooled through. They should no longer be cooking. Skin and remove all the bones (a miserable job). Chill the fish in the refrigerator and serve with the cocktail sauce.

Crispy onion rings
By Jo Mason

4 or 5 medium-sized yellow
   onions
1½ cups flat beer
1¼ cups flour

¼ cup corn meal
shortening for frying
salt to taste

Combine flour, cornmeal, and beer. Cover bowl and let sit at room temperature for about 3 hours. Cut onions into ¼ inch slices. Separate into rings. Heat shortening in deep fryer or large heavy skillet. Using fork, dip onion rings into batter. Place in hot fat (375°). Fry until golden, turning if needed. Drain on absorbent paper. Salt to taste and serve immediately.

Appetizers

Corn chips
By Jo Mason

1 pkg. corn tortillas
shortening for frying
salt to taste

Using a sharp knife, cut each tortilla into about 6 "pie" sections, but do not slice all the way to the center. (This makes it easier to fry 6 chips at once.) Place shortening in heavy skillet (enough to cover tortillas). Dip each sliced tortilla into hot grease. Fry until golden, turning if needed.
Drain and salt to taste. Press center of each tortilla to break apart into chips.

David's deviled eggs
By Jan Cook

1 dozen eggs
1/8-1/4 cup cider vinegar

2-4 Tbsp. sugar
salad dressing or mayonnaise

Put eggs in pan and cover with cold water. Bring to boil, then cover and turn off heat. Allow eggs to stand for 20-30 minutes, then plunge into ice water for 10 minutes. Peel eggs, cut in half lengthwise and remove yolks, set whites aside. Mash yolks with fork, sprinkle with vinegar and sugar to taste. Moisten with salad dressing or mayonnaise and fill whites. Chill thoroughly, garnish with diced black olives or green onion tops.

Elissaburgettes
By Jan Cook

1 can buttermilk biscuits
1 lb. hamburger
1 medium onion, chopped
¼ cup ketchup

⅛-¼ cup mustard
1 cup shredded cheddar
cheese

Grease 10 cups of a muffin tin. Press 10 biscuits on the bottom and up the sides to form a biscuit cup. Fry hamburger and onion, drain. Combine ketchup and mustard with meat and onion and spoon into biscuit cups. Bake at 375° for 10-15 minutes. Top with grated cheese and bake for another 2-3 minutes until melted.

Hoe cakes
By Lucy Shober

a pot full of water
3 cups corn meal

1 tsp. salt
shortening

Put a pot of water on the stove to boil. Mix corn meal and salt in a large bowl. Slowly add boiling water until the batter becomes mushy but not stiff. Let this sit while you heat up some shortening in a skillet. When the shortening is hot but not smoking, drop several heaping tablespoons of the cornmeal mixture into the pan. Keep the corn "cakes" separate so they don't run together. Turn down the heat a little, then flip them over and cook the other side. They should be flat and crispy golden brown.

These are call HOE cakes because they were originally cooked over a fire on the flat part of a garden hoe.

Herbed cheese
By Kristen Rogers

6 oz. cream cheese
½ tsp. minced garlic
1 tsp. tarragon vinegar
4 tsp. milk

½ tsp. ground pepper
4 tsp. dried parsley
dash of salt to taste

Combine all of the ingredients and mix well. Serve on toast squares or crackers. This cheese improves with time, so try to wait 2 days before serving, and cover well in the refrigerator.

Hummus
By Richard Blunt

1 cup dried chick peas
1 tsp. baking soda
cold water
¼ tsp. salt plus ½ tsp. salt
2 cloves fresh garlic
⅓ cup sesame seed paste
(also known as tahani and
is available in most Middle
Eastern markets)

¼ cup fresh lemon juice
1 tsp. powdered cumin
¼ tsp. cayenne pepper
(more or less according to
taste)
3 Tbsp. water
1½ tsp. extra virgin olive oil
2 Tbsp. flat leaf parsley (for
garnish)

Mix the chick peas with 1 tsp. of baking soda and soak in 2 qts. of cold water overnight. The next morning rinse the chick peas several times in cold water and drain.

Place the peas in a medium saucepan with plenty of water and ¼ tsp. salt. Bring this to a boil and cook over medium heat until the peas are very soft (about 1½ hours).

While the peas are cooking, puree the garlic with the other ½ tsp. salt in a blender or food processor, add the sesame seed paste, lemon juice, cumin, cayenne pepper, and 3 Tbsp. of water. Blend until well mixed and smooth.

Drain the cooked chick peas and reserve the cooking liquid. Combine the chick peas with the garlic and sesame seed paste mixture. Process until well-blended and smooth. Thin to the consistency of warm cream cheese with a little of the reserved water from boiling the chick peas. Throw the rest of the water away.

Garnish with olive oil and chopped parsley, then serve at room temperature with warm or toasted pita bread.

Beverages

Old-fashioned hot chocolate
By Richard Blunt

2 cups whole milk
4 oz. bittersweet chocolate,
  chopped into pieces
2 Tbsp. granulated sugar
1/8 tsp. kosher salt
2 Tbsp. unsweetened, Dutch
  process cocoa powder

1½ cups coffee, hot
1 cup light cream
1 Tbsp. pure almond extract
fresh whipped cream

Combine milk and the chocolate pieces in a heavy-bottomed sauce pan over moderate heat. While stirring constantly with a wire whisk, heat the mixture until the chocolate is completely dissolved and the mixture is smooth.

Stir in the sugar, salt, and cocoa powder. Bring the mixture to a simmer and add the hot coffee and the light cream. Simmer the mixture for about 5 minutes.

Remove the cocoa from the heat, add the almond extract and serve immediately.

For an extra treat add a dollop of fresh whipped cream or a marshmallow. If you dare, add a little black pepper to taste.

Eggnog
By Larry Cywin

4 egg yolks
4 Tbsp. sugar
1 cup heavy or whipping
  cream

1 cup brandy (or whiskey or
  rum)
¼ cup wine
4 egg whites
grated nutmeg or cinnamon

Beat the egg yolks until light in color. Slowly beat in the sugar, cream, brandy, and wine. Whip the egg whites separately. Fold the egg whites into the other ingredients. Sprinkle with spices and serve.

Ginger beer
By Jackie Clay

4 oz. dried ginger root
1 gallon water
juice from 1 medium lemon

1 pkg. active dry yeast
½ lb. sugar

Pound or grind the ginger root, then boil it in ½ gallon of water for 20 minutes. Remove and set aside. Mix lemon juice and pkg. of dry yeast in a cup of warm water and add to the ginger root water. Pour in remaining water and let mixture sit for 24 hours. Strain out the root bits and stir in the sugar well. Bottle in sterilized glass bottles and place in refrigerator. Don't store at room temperature or bottles may explode. Makes ten 12-oz. bottles.

Moroccan mint tea
By Habeeb Salloum

4½ cups boiling water
3 tsp. green tea (if not available, Indian tea may be substituted)

½ cup of pressed fresh mint leaves with stalks (2 tsp. finely crushed dried mint leaves can be used if fresh mint is not available.)
3 tsp. sugar

Rinse out a teapot with hot water, then add tea. Pour in ½ cup boiling water, then, to remove bitterness, swish around in the pot quickly. Discard the water, but make sure not to throw away tea. Add mint, sugar and remainder of boiling water, then allow to steep for 3 minutes. Stir and taste, adding more sugar if necessary before serving. Note: For second helpings, leave mint and tea in pot; then add a teaspoon of tea, several mint leaves, and some sugar. Add again the same amount of boiling water. When mint rises to surface, the tea is ready. Stir and taste for sugar, then serve. Serves 4.

Southern mint julep
By Alice Brantley Yeager

4 sprigs fresh peppermint
1 tsp. sugar

cracked ice
1½ jigger bourbon whiskey

Crush mint leaves and sugar together in a 12-oz. glass. Fill with cracked ice and add the whiskey. Stir until glass is frosted. Garnish with a sprig of mint. This is the basic Mint Julep enjoyed by the old plantation owners.

Mint julep non-alcoholic
By Alice Brantley Yeager

5 lemons
1 bunch fresh peppermint
1½ cups sugar

½ cup water
3 qts. ginger ale
ice

Squeeze juice from lemons and strain to remove any seeds or pulp. Add lightly crushed mint leaves, sugar, and water and let stand 30 minutes. (Use a large stainless steel or glass bowl. Don't use aluminum.) Pour over a large piece of ice in a glass punch bowl and add ginger ale. Serve in small glasses. This is a recipe from the early 1900s.

Blueberry tofu frappe
By Rodney Merrill

1 cup fresh or frozen blueberries
½ cake Kingugoshi (soft
style) tofu
1 ripe banana

½ cup apple or white grape
juice
5 ice cubes

Put juice and tofu in a blender. Buzz at high speed until tofu is liquified. Continuing at high speed, add banana, then berries, then ice cubes. Frappe is finished when all ice has disappeared.

Lime freeze
By Jo Mason

2 scoops lime sherbet
1 scoop vanilla ice cream
juice of one lime

Place everything in a blender. Whirl until smooth. Serve in a tall glass with a straw and a long spoon.

Chocolate soda
By Jo Mason

2 scoops vanilla ice cream
chocolate syrup, to taste
carbonated water

Place ice cream in tall glass. Add syrup, then pour in carbonated water. Serve with a straw and a long spoon.

Breads

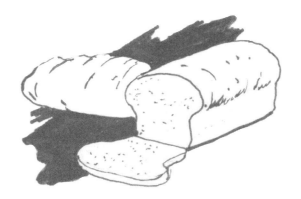

Pastoral bread
By Richard Blunt

2 pkg. active dry yeast
2 Tbsp. sugar
1/3 cup peanut oil
3 cups warm water (110°-115°)

5 cups hard wheat bread flour
2 tsp. kosher salt
4-5 cups additional bread flour as needed
shortening

Combine the yeast, sugar, peanut oil, and warm water in a bowl and mix with a wooden spoon or wire whisk. Set the mixture aside for the yeast to proof, about 15 minutes.

In a large bowl mix 5 cups of flour with the salt. Add yeast mixture and beat with a wooden spoon to form a heavy batter. Stir in additional flour, 1 cup at a time, until the mixture forms a stiff dough that does not stick to sides of bowl. Turn dough onto a floured surface, then knead until the dough is smooth, does not stick to the surface, and springs back into shape when poked with finger. This requires 15 minutes, minimum.

Coat the inside surface of a large mixing bowl with shortening, place dough inside, cover with a clean cloth, and allow dough to rise until triple in bulk. This will take about 1 hour.

Punch dough down and knead into a smooth ball. Coat the inside of the Dutch oven and lid with shortening. Place dough inside and put lid in place. Let dough rise until it touches the lid. Watch this rising carefully; you do not want the rising dough to lift the lid.

Place the loaf in a preheated 375° oven. Bake for 10 minutes, with the lid in place. Remove the lid and continue baking until the loaf sounds hollow when tapped. This will take between 35 and 50 minutes. Remove the fully-baked loaf from the pot and place it on a rack to cool.

Fail-proof white bread
By Jackie Clay

1 Tbsp. dry yeast
½ cup warm water
½ tsp. honey
4 cups hot water
3 Tbsp. shortening

1 Tbsp. salt
3 Tbsp. honey
8 cups unbleached flour
butter

Stir the yeast into ½ cup warm water and add the ½ tsp. of honey. Let sit until you are ready for it.

In a large bowl, add the hot water, shortening, salt, and the rest of the honey. Stir until honey is dissolved and the shortening has melted.

Sift 5 cups of flour into the liquid in large bowl and beat well with a whisk or wooden spoon. Let mixture cool to lukewarm and add yeast mixture. Again beat well. Add the remaining flour, 1 cup at a time. You want a dough that you can barely mix with a wooden spoon, held just above the spoon part.

Flour your kneading surface and dump the dough out onto the board. Flour your hands and begin kneading the dough. Add flour, as needed (no more than ½ cup at a time). If it is sticky, add more flour, a bit at a time, under the dough, and on your hands. When it seems more "workable," let it rest on the floured board while you wash out the mixing bowl with hot water. Dry it and return to your kneading.

Knead the dough ball until it feels alive and springy. Grease the bowl and rub the top of the ball in this grease, then turn it over so the top is nicely greased. Cover with a warm, damp kitchen towel and let rise in a warm place until doubled.

When the dough is ready (2 finger indentations on top remain for a minute), punch it down well. Grease 2 bread pans and form the dough into 2 loaves, leaving the tops smooth and the ends neatly tucked under. Again, cover with kitchen towel and let rise until nearly double. Preheat oven to 400°. Bake for 45 minutes until the top is nicely browned and sounds hollow when tapped with finger.

Remove the bread from the oven and butter the tops to soften them and give them a beautiful sheen. Remove from the pans and let them cool.

Corn bread
By Larry Cywin

½ cup cornmeal
1 cup flour
pinch of salt

4 eggs
2 Tbsp. milk
3 Tbsp. butter

Combine the dry ingredients in a bowl. Add the remaining ingredients and mix well.

Pour the batter into a greased 9 x 9 inch pan and bake at 375° for 15-20 minutes.

Persimmon bread
By Charles A. Sanders

1 cup persimmon pulp
2 cups flour
½ tsp. baking soda
½ tsp. salt
2 tsp. baking powder
1 tsp. cinnamon
½ tsp. nutmeg

½ cup milk
1 cup sugar
2 eggs
¼ cup butter or margarine
1 cup chopped walnuts,
  (optional)

Sift together the dry ingredients. Mix together the persimmon pulp, milk, eggs, and sugar. Add the flour mixture and the margarine. Mix until well-blended. Stir in chopped nuts. Pour batter into a well-greased 9 x 5 x 3 inch loaf pan and bake at 350° for 45 minutes.

Barmbrack

By Richard Blunt

¼ cup unsalted butter at room temperature
¼ cup whole milk
½ cup water
½ tsp. sugar
1 pkg. active dry yeast
1 egg (at room temperature) slightly beaten

3 cups all-purpose flour (approximately)
½ tsp. kosher salt
½ tsp. grated lemon peel
½ cup dried currants
¼ cup chopped mixed candied fruit

Heat the butter, milk, and water in a small sauce pan to 115°, then combine with the sugar and yeast. Stir the mixture to dissolve the yeast. Set the mixture aside and let the yeast proof.

Add the beaten egg to the proofed yeast mixture.

Combine the yeast mixture with 1½ cups of flour, the salt, and lemon peel and mix with a wooden spoon to combine.

Continue to stir in more of the remaining flour, ¼ cup at a time, until the dough forms a shaggy mass and pulls away from the sides of the bowl. (This means you may need more or less than the 3 cups of flour.) Lift the dough from the bowl and place it on a floured work surface.

Knead the dough for about 10 minutes or until it becomes smooth and elastic. Place the dough in a greased bowl, cover and set aside until the dough has doubled in bulk.

Punch the dough down, remove it from the bowl and knead the fruit into the dough.

Shape the dough into a loaf and place it into a standard bread pan. Cover it and set it aside to rise a second time. When the dough is just above the edge of the pan it is ready for the oven.

Bake in a preheated 350° oven for about 45 minutes or until the loaf sounds hollow when tapped on top. Remove the loaf from the oven and set on a rack to cool.

Challah
By Richard Blunt

2 pkg. active dry yeast
1 cup warm water (110° to 115°)
2 Tbsp. sugar
1/3 cup light vegetable oil
2 eggs, lightly beaten
4½-5 cups flour
1 tsp. salt
½ cup dried currants

Glaze ingredients:
1 egg (beaten slightly)
2 Tbsp. water
2 Tbsp. poppy seeds

Combine the yeast, warm water, sugar, and vegetable oil in a bowl. Stir until yeast is dissolved and set aside until yeast shows sign of activity.

Add egg to proofed yeast mixture.

Combine flour and salt. In a large mixing bowl combine 3 cups of the flour/salt mixture with yeast mixture and mix with a wooden spoon to form a sticky paste, then add the currants. Continue to add flour a little at a time until the dough pulls away from the sides of bowl.

Turn dough onto floured work surface and knead until it is smooth and elastic, about 10 minutes.

Place dough in a greased bowl, cover with a clean cloth, and set aside until it doubles in bulk.

Punch dough down and knead on a floured work surface for 1 minute.

Shape the dough into a 4-strand braid. When loaves are formed place them on a well-greased baking sheet.

Combine the remaining egg with the water and beat briskly with a fork until blended. Brush the egg glaze on the shaped loaf and sprinkle the loaf with poppy seeds.

Allow the loaves to proof, uncovered, until doubled in bulk, about 1 hour.

Place the loaves into a preheated 375° oven and bake until the loaves are done, about 40 minutes. Remove the loaves from the baking sheet and transfer them to a wire rack to cool.

Sally Lunn
By Larry Cywin

1 cups milk
2 Tbsp. shortening
½ oz. active dry yeast
3 cups flour

½ tsp. salt
1 egg
1 Tbsp. sugar

Combine milk and shortening and heat to scalding. Remove from heat and let cool.

Pour milk mixture into a bowl. Add the remaining ingredients and mix until smooth. Cover the bowl with a towel and let the dough rise for 60-90 minutes.

Punch down the dough and put in greased loaf pan. Let rise for another hour. Bake at 375° for approximately 45 minutes.

Pumpkin bread
By Larry Cywin

2 eggs
1 cup cooked, mashed
   pumpkin
2 cups flour

¾ cups sugar
½ tsp. grated nutmeg
1 tsp. baking soda

Mix eggs and pumpkin. Mix remaining ingredients into pumpkin mix. Mix well, pour into a buttered loaf pan. Bake at 350° for 1 hour.

Corn bread for a cajun/creole stew
By Richard Blunt

1 cup all-purpose flour
2½ cups yellow or white cornmeal
3 Tbsp. sugar
2 Tbsp. baking powder
1½ tsp. kosher salt
4 whole fresh eggs (slightly beaten)

1¾ cup buttermilk (any milk—whole, skim, or lactose free—will also work well)
½ cup melted butter or margarine

Combine and mix together the flour, cornmeal, sugar, baking powder, and salt in a large mixing bowl.

In a small bowl combine and mix the eggs, milk, and melted butter or margarine.

Gently fold the egg mixture into the dry ingredients using a spatula or wooden spoon. Do not overmix; a few lumps in the batter are OK.

Spoon the batter onto a 12 x 16-inch greased baking pan. Let the batter rest for 10 minutes.

Bake the corn bread in a preheated 425° oven for about 25 minutes or until it is nicely browned on top and a tooth pick comes out clean when inserted into the middle.

Parker House rolls
By Thomas C. Tabor

6-6½ cups flour
½ cup sugar
2 tsp. salt

2 pkg. active dry yeast
½ cup butter
1 egg

Combine in a large bowl 2¼ cups flour, sugar, salt, and yeast. In another bowl combine 2 cups hot water (130°-150°), ½ cup butter and 1 egg. When the butter is softened, pour the wet ingredients over the dry ingredients and beat 2 minutes, occasionally scraping the bowl. Fold in 1 cup of flour, or enough to make a thick batter. With a spoon, stir in the additional 2 cups of flour to make a soft dough. Turn the dough onto a lightly-floured surface and knead for approximately 15 minutes. Place the dough in a greased bowl and let rise for 1½ hours. Then punch the dough down and shape it into rolls. Let it rise until rolls have doubled in size. Bake in 375° oven for 18-20 minutes. This recipe makes about 3½ dozen.

Bannock
By Thomas C. Tabor

1½ cups flour
½ Tbsp. baking soda

½ Tbsp. salt
¾ cup water

Simply mix the dry ingredients thoroughly, then add the water. Knead until all lumps and dry spots have disappeared. Form into a patty and place in a hot, greased frying pan. Fry until it is cooked through. Bannock tastes best right out of the pan while still warm, but it's also good cold.

Corn bread
By Thomas C. Tabor

2½ cups cornmeal or stone
ground meal
½ cup flour
1 tsp. salt
2 tsp. baking powder
½ tsp. soda

2 Tbsp. melted margarine or
shortening
1 cup buttermilk (approximately)

Mix ingredients, adding enough buttermilk to make a thick batter.
Pour into greased baking pan. Bake in a 425°-450° oven for approximately 30 minutes or until brown. An iron skillet will help ensure
excellent results.

Gritted bread
By Thomas C. Tabor

2 cups gritted corn (see
below*)
½ cup sweet milk
1 tsp. sugar

1 tsp. salt
2 Tbsp. soft butter
½ tsp. baking soda
¼ cup flour

Mix ingredients together, adding flour as needed. Bake in greased
iron pan at 400° for approximately 25 minutes.
*Gritted corn is made by scraping ear corn with a grater. The corn
must be past roasting ear maturity, but not too hard. If a grater was
not available, homesteaders sometimes made one by puncturing a
piece of tin with a nail. This porous scraper was then used to grate
the corn while still on the cob.

Sourdough bread
By Thomas C. Tabor

Step 1
½ cup sugar
1 cup water
1½ cups flour

Step 2
⅓ cup sugar
½ cup vegetable oil
2 tsp. salt
1½ cups water
4 cups flour

Mix step 1 ingredients into your starter. (See below for starter.) Cover and let stand at room temperature for 10-12 hours. Remove 1½ cups and place in a covered jar in the refrigerator to replenish your stored starter.

Mix sugar, vegetable oil, salt, and water gradually with approximately 4 cups of flour or until a hearty dough is made. Knead thoroughly until no lumps remain. There is no such thing as "too much kneading"—the more the better. Place dough in an oversized, greased bowl and cover with a towel. The dough should be allowed to rise at room temperature. This is best accomplished overnight. The next morning, punch dough down and divide into loaves. This recipe will make about 3 normal-sized loaves. Place in greased baking pans and allow to rise again until size has doubled. Bake at 350° for 45 minutes. A little butter allowed to melt over the top of the loaves is the final stage and will add flavor.

Sourdough starter
By Thomas C. Tabor

1 Tbsp. active dry yeast
2½ cups warm water
2½ cups unbleached white
   flour

Dissolve the yeast in a glass bowl containing 1 cup of lukewarm water. Stir in the flour and remaining warm water and mix well. Cover and let stand 4-5 days in a warm place. Temperature should be between 75-90°. A windowsill is a great place, as long as it doesn't get too warm. If it gets too hot, the yeast will be killed. Until it's needed, the starter can be stabilized in the refrigerator.

Soda biscuits
By Thomas C. Tabor

2 cups flour
1 tsp. salt
3 tsp. baking powder

¼ tsp. baking soda
1/3 cup shortening
½ to ¾ cup buttermilk

Mix flour, salt, baking powder, and soda. Cut in shortening until thoroughly mixed. Add just enough buttermilk to make a soft dough. On a floured board, knead 6-7 times. Roll out and cut into biscuits. Melt about 2 Tbsp. of shortening in a baking pan. Put in biscuits and turn immediately to grease the tops. Bake for 10 minutes at 425° or until brown.

Fry bread
By Jackie Clay

4 cups flour
1 Tbsp. baking powder
1 tsp. salt

1½ cups and a little more
warm water
shortening or lard to deep
fry

Mix dry ingredients in a bowl. Add water and mix thoroughly. Knead, adding more water or flour as needed. Dough should end up elastic and soft but not sticky. Pinch off balls the size of a small peach. Pat back and forth in hands until about ½-inch thick.

Melt shortening in heavy frying pan or heavy deep fryer. Heat until hot but not smoking. Carefully fry each bread in hot fat, turning until each side is golden brown. Drain on paper towels and serve hot with warm honey.

Italian Christmas bread
By Richard Blunt

¼ cup warm milk (110-115°)
1 pkg. active dry yeast
½ tsp. brown sugar
¼ cup honey
4 Tbsp. unsalted butter
   (melted)
2 eggs (at room tempera-
   ture)
2 tsp. crushed anise seed

2-3 cups flour
½ tsp. kosher salt
¼ cup chopped mixed can-
   died fruit
1 Tbsp. pine nuts
¼ cup golden raisins
cornmeal
topping:
1 Tbsp. butter

Combine the warm milk, yeast, and brown sugar in a mixing bowl. Stir to dissolve yeast and set it aside to proof.

Combine honey, butter, eggs, and anise seeds in another bowl and beat with a wire whisk or fork until well-blended, then add yeast mixture.

Combine 1½ cups flour and the salt. Add liquid ingredients to flour and stir to make a soft sticky dough. Add the remaining flour ¼ cup at a time, continue to stir until the dough pulls away from the sides of the bowl.

Place the dough on a floured work surface and knead for 10 minutes or until the dough is smooth. Continue to add flour, while kneading, if the dough shows signs of being sticky.

Place dough in a clean bowl, cover with a clean cloth and set aside.

Mix together the candied fruit, pine nuts, and raisins.

Shape dough into a plump ball and pat down the top slightly to form an oval. Place half of the fruit mixture on top of the dough, fold dough over and knead fruit into the dough, then repeat with the rest of the mixture. Continue to knead dough until the fruits are well distributed.

Place the dough in a well-greased bowl, cover with a towel, and set aside to double in bulk, about 1 hour.

Remove the towel and punch dough down. Place dough on a floured work surface and shape dough into a plump round ball. Place the loaf on a well-greased baking sheet that has been lightly dusted with cornmeal. Cover the loaf with a clean light cloth and allow dough to rise for about 1-1½ hours or until double in bulk.

Preheat oven to 375°.
Cut a ½-inch deep cross all the way across the top of the loaf with a razor. Place loaf in oven on the middle shelf. Five minutes after loaf is in oven drop the final Tbsp. of butter on top of the loaf in the middle. Bake for about 40 minutes or until the loaf sounds hollow when tapped on the bottom. Allow loaf to cool completely before slicing.

Honey whole wheat bread
By Jackie Clay

½ cup warm water
2 Tbsp. dry yeast
½ tsp. honey
2 cups warm water
1 Tbsp. salt
2 Tbsp. honey
1 Tbsp. shortening

¼ cup chopped sunflower seeds
6 cups whole wheat flour
butter
sunflower seeds, chopped (optional)
sesame seeds (optional)

Stir ½ cup warm water, yeast, and ½ tsp. honey into a cup to proof. In large bowl, add 2 cups warm water, salt, 2 Tbsp. honey, and shortening. Beat until shortening has melted. Add the chopped sunflower seeds, then add 1 cup flour at a time until you have a medium batter. Add the yeast mixture. Add flour, while beating well. Stir the thickened dough with a wooden spoon until it is ready to knead, adding more or less flour, as needed. Turn out onto a floured board and knead for 10 minutes. Grease the top and place dough in a greased bowl and cover with a warm, damp towel until it rises to double in size. Punch down the dough and divide it into 2 loaves, or punch down the dough, and let it rise a second time for a finer loaf.
Place loaves in greased bread pans and let rise until nearly doubled. Preheat oven to 350°.
Bake bread about 45 minutes until tops are golden and sound hollow when tapped with a finger. When done, butter tops and sprinkle with chopped sunflower seeds or sesame seeds, if desired.

Irish soda bread
By Richard Blunt

2½ cups all-purpose flour	½ cup dried currants
½ cup sugar	1¼ cup buttermilk
1 tsp. salt	1 egg (slightly beaten)
½ tsp. baking soda	cornmeal
1¼ tsp. baking powder	**topping:**
1 Tbsp. caraway seeds	1 Tbsp. sugar
4 Tbsp. unsalted butter	1 tsp. water

There is no substitute for buttermilk in this recipe. The acid in the buttermilk is critical to the leavening action of the dough. However, you can use powdered buttermilk if you can find it.

Combine flour, sugar, salt, baking soda, baking powder, and caraway seeds in a mixing bowl. Cut in butter until mixture looks like coarse meal. Slowly stir in currants, buttermilk and egg. Mix all the ingredients thoroughly.

Scrape the mixture from the bowl onto floured work surface. Control the stickiness by sprinkling flour on the work surface and rolling the dough in the flour. This dough is not to be kneaded.

Shape the dough into a plump ball and place it on a well-greased baking sheet that has been lightly sprinkled with cornmeal. Pat down the top slightly and with a razor blade cut a ½-inch deep cross on the top.

Place loaf on middle rack of an oven that has been preheated to 375° and bake for about 45 minutes or until it is browned and has opened dramatically along the cuts.

Just before the loaf is ready to be removed from the oven, mix the sugar and water for the topping. As soon as you remove the loaf, brush the bread with this mixture.

Remove the finished loaf from the oven and place it on a rack to cool.

Spicy persimmon bread
By Marcella Shaffer

2 cups persimmon pulp
3 cups flour
1 tsp. salt
2½ tsp. baking powder
2 tsp. baking soda
2 tsp. ground cinnamon
1 tsp. ground nutmeg

pinch ground cloves
2 cups sugar
2 eggs
1¼ cups applesauce
½ cup raisins
1 Tbsp. vanilla

Sift dry ingredients into a bowl. In another bowl beat eggs and add persimmon pulp. Stir, then add applesauce and vanilla, mix well. Add dry ingredients and raisins to pulp mixture then stir until well-blended. Pour into greased loaf pans and bake for 50 minutes, (or until done) at 350°.

Half-time spoon rolls
By Jackie Clay

1 Tbsp. dry yeast
¼ cup warm water
pinch of sugar
¾ cup warm water
¼ cup shortening
¼ cup sugar

1 tsp. salt
½ cup cold water
1 egg
3½ cups unbleached flour
butter

Dissolve yeast in ¼ cup warm water. Add a pinch of sugar and stir well. In mixing bowl, add ¾ cup of very warm water, shortening, sugar, and salt. Mix well until shortening melts. Cool with ½ cup cold water and 1 egg. Mix well. When lukewarm, add yeast mixture, then stir in flour, a little at a time. The dough will be very sticky. You do not knead this dough.

Cover and let rise in a bowl until doubled. Grease muffin tins and using a greased ice cream scoop, knock down the risen dough and spoon 1 scoopful into each cup of the muffin tin. Let it rise, again, until they double in size and bake about 10 minutes in a 375° oven. Butter the tops and serve hot.

Corn tortillas
By Jackie Clay

2 cups masa harina de maize (corn flour, not cornmeal)

1 cup (more or less) water

In medium-sized bowl, mix enough water into the masa harina to make a very stiff dough. Add water slowly, mixing well with a fork. The dough will seem a bit dry, but will form a ball easily when worked by hand. You don't want any dry flour left, but the dough shouldn't be wet either. Let the dough rest for 10 minutes.

Dampen hands and pinch off a large walnut-sized piece and work into a ball. Repeat with the rest of the dough.

Using either a tortilla press, lined on both pads with waxed paper or plastic, or a pie plate and cutting board with waxed paper on the board and under the pie plate, sandwich a slightly flattened ball of dough between waxed paper and press flat. I've found that when using the tortilla press you need to turn the pressed tortilla around a half turn and press again to get a uniform thickness.

Some folks cut each tortilla into a perfect circle, using a bowl as a cookie cutter. But I don't mind irregular edges on the tortillas and dispense with the extra work.

Use a griddle or cast iron frying pan with no grease and heat it to a medium heat. Gently bake each tortilla about 30 seconds until edges seem dry, then gently turn and bake until it puffs slightly. Store in covered dish and use soon. This recipe makes 12 tortillas.

To make taco shells, heat ¼-inch of grease in heavy frying pan. Fry each baked tortilla until limp. With tongs, gently fold tortilla in half and continue frying, holding the edges apart. Cook 1½ minutes longer, turning once, until crisp. Drain on a paper towel.

To soften tortillas to fill, heat 2 Tbsp. grease in a small frying pan. Holding a baked tortilla with tongs, dip each one in oil until limp. Drain on paper towel. Repeat, adding oil, when necessary. Fill.

Hint: I often add spices, such as chili powder, garlic, and onion to the masa harina before adding the water for different flavors. We like them this way.

Flour tortillas
By Jackie Clay

2 cups flour
1 tsp. salt
1 tsp. baking powder

1 Tbsp. shortening
½-¾ cups quite warm water

In a medium mixing bowl, stir together the dry ingredients. Cut in the shortening well. Add warm water until the mixture forms a medium dough. Add more water if needed, but don't let it become a sticky dough. It needs to be able to be handled well. Let rest for 15 minutes; it rises some.

Divide the dough in half, then in halves again, eventually forming 12 pieces. On a lightly floured surface, roll each into a ball, then roll out into a 7-inch round. Again, some folks trim them into a perfect circle. We prefer the appearance of irregular tortillas; they have character.

I pat each tortilla a bit with my hands and lay it on an ungreased griddle over medium heat. Bake about 1½ minutes on each side until lightly speckled brown. Hold hot under a clean tea towel until ready to serve or fill.

Basic baking powder biscuits
By Jackie Clay

2 cups unbleached or whole
    wheat flour
2 tsp. baking powder

1 tsp. salt
¼ cup shortening
milk

Sift dry ingredients together in mixing bowl. Add shortening and mix in with a fork, until pieces of the mixture are the size of small peas. Add milk until you have a moist, but not sticky dough. Turn out onto floured surface and knead lightly. Pat down to about ½-inch thick. Cut biscuits out of this. (I use a greased canning jar ring.) Place biscuits on a greased cookie sheet touching each other in a rectangular pattern. Bake at 400° for about 10 minutes or until the tops are lightly browned.

You may add ½ cup grated cheddar cheese for cheese biscuits, topping the biscuits with more grated cheese after they have risen in the oven for a crispy cheesy treat.

Blueberry muffins
By Charles A. Sanders

2 cups all-purpose flour
½ cup sugar
2 tsp. baking powder
½ tsp. salt
¼ tsp. cinnamon
¾ cup milk
½ cup butter or margarine, melted

½ tsp. vanilla
1 egg, slightly beaten
1 cup fresh (or frozen, thawed and drained) blueberries
1 tsp. sugar

Heat the oven to 400°. Grease the bottoms only of 12 medium muffin cups, or line with paper baking cups. Mix the flour, ½ cup sugar, baking powder, salt, and cinnamon in a large bowl. Stir in the milk, butter, vanilla, and egg just until blended. Fold in the blueberries for a lumpy batter. Divide batter evenly among the muffin cups. Sprinkle each muffin with ¼ tsp. sugar. Bake for 25-30 minutes or until golden brown. Cool for 5 minutes; remove from pan. Makes 1 dozen muffins.

Zucchini pizza crust
By Sandra L. Toney

3 cups shredded zucchini (if frozen, thaw completely; discard the excess liquid)
2 eggs, beaten

½ cup grated mozzarella cheese
½ cup grated cheddar cheese

Preheat the oven to 400°.
Squeeze and drain any juice from the zucchini. Mix the eggs, zucchini, and cheeses together in a large bowl. Press out the mixture on a greased 12-inch pizza pan. Bake the crust at 400° for 10 minutes.
Add your favorite pizza toppings and sauce and bake the pizza for 10 minutes. Serves 6.

Pita bread
By Richard Blunt

1 pkg. active dry yeast
½ tsp. granulated sugar
1 cup warm water (110°-
115°)
4 Tbsp. extra virgin olive oil
1 tsp. salt

3⅓ cups bread flour
4-5 pieces of aluminum foil
cut about 8 inches square
cornmeal (for coating the foil
to prevent sticking)

Preheat oven to 450°.

Mix yeast with sugar and ½ cup warm water, set aside to proof (about 10 minutes).

Add remaining water and olive oil to proofed yeast mixture.

Combine flour and salt and add to the water mixture 1 cup at a time while mixing vigorously with a wooden spoon. If dough seems too sticky after all the flour has been incorporated, add more flour a little at a time until the dough feels soft and unsticky.

Knead dough for at least 10 minutes or until it becomes smooth and elastic.

Transfer dough to a shortening-coated bowl, cover with a towel, and let rise until it has doubled in bulk (about 1-2 hours).

Punch down dough and knead for 1 minute. Cover and allow to rest for 10 minutes.

Divide the dough into 4 or 5 equal-sized balls. Roll each ball with a floured rolling pin into 8-inch circles that are about ¼-inch thick. Don't worry about forming perfect circles; irregular shapes add to the character of the bread.

Transfer each rolled bread to a piece of aluminum foil that has been dusted with cornmeal. Place the sheets directly on oven racks and bake until puffed and very lightly browned (about 10 minutes).

Cool bread on wire racks, then seal in plastic bags to prevent bread from going stale.

Nana V's holiday corn bread
By Richard Blunt

8 oz. (raw weight) good quality smoked bacon
1 cup grated sharp cheddar cheese
2 cloves fresh garlic (chopped fine)
1 tsp. salt free butter
1 cup skim milk
2 pkg. dry yeast (not the rapid rise type)
1 Tbsp. honey

6 Tbsp. salt free butter
2 medium eggs (slightly beaten)
¾ cup buttermilk
3 Tbsp. maple syrup (real or artificially flavored)
3¾ cups bread flour
1¾ cups yellow cornmeal
2 tsp. kosher salt
a little reserved buttermilk
a few tsp. of cornmeal

Lay bacon slices on a cookie sheet and cook in 375° oven until crisp. Drain on paper towels. When cool, chop into bits and combine with shredded cheddar cheese.

Sauté the garlic in 1 tsp. butter over medium heat for about 60 seconds, cool and add to the cheese and bacon.

Heat skim milk over medium heat to 115° and blend with yeast and honey. Set aside for 5 minutes to proof.

Melt the remaining 6 Tbsp. butter over low heat and blend with eggs, buttermilk, and maple syrup. Add yeast mixture and cheese mixture and stir lightly. In a large bowl combine mixture with flour, cornmeal, and salt and blend with a wooden spoon. The batter will be rather stiff when mixed.

Divide dough into 2 medium 8 x 4 inch loaf pans, cover and let rise until dough is almost doubled in size.

Preheat oven to 375°. Brush tops of loaves with a little buttermilk and spinkle them with a few teaspoons of cornmeal. Bake for about 40 minutes. When tops are medium-brown and a thin bladed knife inserted into a loaf comes out clean and dry, remove the loaves from the oven. Remove loaves from pans and cool.

Milk starter
By Charles Bryant O'Dooley

1 cup milk
1 cup flour

¼ cup sugar
1 tsp. yeast

Mix together in a crock and let stand at room temperature uncovered for 2-4 days. Stir down 2 or 3 times a day.

To use the starter, take it out of the refrigerator at least 8 hours before using and add another cup of flour, cup of milk, and ¼ cup sugar.

Mix well and let stand in a warm place free from drafts. Save at least a cup of starter each time. If you want to bake several things and need more starter, you can double the recipe but let it sit out longer. If you are not going to use your starter for several months, it can be frozen to keep it.

Sourdough bread
By Charles Bryant O'Dooley

5-6 cups flour
3 Tbsp. sugar
1 tsp. salt
1 pkg. active dry yeast

1 cup milk
2 Tbsp. margarine
1½ cups starter (see recipe
   on this page)

To make dough, combine 1 cup flour with the sugar, salt, and undissolved yeast in a large bowl. Combine milk and margarine in a saucepan. Heat over low heat until liquid is warm. Gradually add to dry ingredients and beat 2 minutes at medium speed of electric mixer, scraping bowl occasionally. Add 1½ cups starter and 1 cup of flour or enough flour to make a thick batter. Beat at high speed 2 minutes, scraping the bowl. Stir in additional flour to make a soft dough. Turn out onto a lightly floured board. Knead until smooth and elastic, about 8-10 minutes. Place in a greased bowl and turn to grease the top. Cover and let rise in a warm draft-free place until doubled in bulk, about 1 hour. Punch down, turn out onto a lightly-floured board. Let rest 15 minutes. Divide dough in half. Shape loaf and place in greased loaf pans. Cover and let rise in a warm place until doubled in size. Bake in a hot 400° oven about 30 minutes or until done. Remove from pans and cool on wire rack. Makes 2 loaves.

Sourdough biscuits
By Charles Bryant O'Dooley

1 cup starter (see page 43
  for recipe)
1 cup flour
¼ tsp. baking soda

2 tsp. baking powder
½ tsp. salt
¼ cup shortening

Sift dry ingredients into bowl. Cut in shortening as for pastry.
Add starter and mix lightly using all dry mixture. Knead 5 times.
Cut into thick biscuits. Let rise awhile. Bake at 425° for 10-12 minutes.

Special bread
By Charles Bryant O'Dooley

6 cups milk (can use part
  yogurt, sour milk, buttermilk)
1 stick butter or margarine
1 Tbsp. salt
6 Tbsp. sugar
¾ cup warm water
1 Tbsp. sugar
3 pkg. dry yeast
1-2 cups soy flour

2/3 cup unprocessed bran
1/3 cup wheat germ
1½ cups whole wheat flour
4 cups or more unbleached
  white flour
1 handful each: cornmeal
  and oatmeal
2 handfuls of your favorite
  wheat cereal, crushed

Heat milk, butter, salt, and 6 Tbsp. sugar together to scald, and
cool to lukewarm. Mix together warm water, 1 Tbsp. sugar, and
yeast, and allow to proof. Add yeast to milk in large bowl, and mix in
grains, adding enough white flour to make a smooth dough. Knead
well (10-15 minutes) and let rise until doubled in a greased bowl.
Punch down, shape into loaves, and let rise again until nearly doubled. Bake for about 1 hour at 350°. Makes 6 loaves.

Sourdough corn bread
By Charles Bryant O'Dooley

1 cup sourdough starter (see
   page 43 for recipe)
1½ cups evaporated milk
1½ cups yellow cornmeal
2 Tbsp. sugar

2 whole eggs, beaten
¼ cup warm melted butter
½ tsp. salt
½ tsp. soda

Mix starter, milk, cornmeal, sugar, and eggs; stir thoroughly in a large bowl. Stir in melted butter, salt, and soda. Turn into a 10-inch greased frying pan and bake in a hot 450° oven for 20 minutes or until they test done.

Note: Buttered corn stick pans may also be used for a delightful, colorful hot bread for a table. Fill each cup 2/3 full. Bake in a hot 450° oven for 20 minutes or until they test done.

Sourdough French bread
By Charles Bryant O'Dooley

1 cup starter (see page 43
   for recipe)
½ cup lukewarm milk
1 Tbsp. sugar

2 Tbsp. melted shortening
2 tsp. salt
2½ cups flour

Mix ingredients together in the order given, working in the flour well. Let the dough rise in a greased bowl until it has doubled in bulk. Knead again and form into a long French loaf. Cut slashes across top of loaf and let rise again. Bake at 325° for 35-40 minutes. Take from oven and brush the top with butter. (If your starter does not seem lively, add a teaspoon of dry yeast to starter and mix in before you begin.)

Sourdough wheat bread
By Charles Bryant O'Dooley

2 cups starter, warmed overnight (See page 43 for
starter recipe)
1 cup whole wheat flour

1 cup all-purpose white flour
2 Tbsp. sugar
1½ tsp. salt

Combine ingredients and mix well with a fork. The sponge will be
soft and sticky. Cover with a cheesecloth and set in a warm place
for 2-3 hours. Turn out on a warm, well-floured board. Knead 1½
cups white flour into dough for 5-10 minutes. Shape into a round
loaf and place in well-greased pie pan. Grease sides and top of loaf.
Cover with towel and let rise until doubled in bulk (about 1 hour).
Bake at 450° for 10 minutes. Reduce heat to 375° and bake 30-40
minutes. Remove, brush top with butter.

Sourdough herb bread
By Charles Bryant O'Dooley

1½ cups water
1 cup cottage cheese
¼ cup honey
3 Tbsp. oil
6-6½ cups whole wheat flour
1 cup starter (see page 43
for recipe)

2 Tbsp. dry yeast
1 egg
2 tsp. dill
3 Tbsp. chopped onion
2 Tbsp. chopped fresh parsley

Heat first 4 ingredients in a medium saucepan, until very warm
(110° to 120°). Combine warm liquid with 3 cups flour and the
remaining ingredients in a large bowl. Beat 2 minutes. By hand, stir
in remaining flour to make a stiff dough. Knead dough until it is
smooth and elastic, about 5 minutes. Place in a greased bowl and
turn around to grease all sides. Cover and let rise in a warm place
until double in size. Punch down and divide into 2 balls. Shape each
ball into loaves and place into 2 greased loaf pans. Let rise again
until double in size. Bake 40-45 minutes in 350° oven.

Dill-onion bread
By Charles Bryant O'Dooley

1 Tbsp. dry yeast
½ cup warm water
1 beaten egg
½ cup cottage cheese
⅓ cup finely chopped onion
1 Tbsp. butter
2 cups whole wheat flour
⅓ cup whole bran cereal

½ cup wheat germ
1 Tbsp. honey
1 Tbsp. dillseed
1 tsp. kelp, optional
¼ tsp. baking soda
1 cup starter (see page 43 for recipe)

Soften yeast in warm water. Combine egg, cottage cheese, onion, and butter; mix well. In another bowl stir together the flour, cereal, wheat germ, honey, dill, kelp, and soda. Add cottage cheese and starter and yeast mixture, stirring well. Cover and let rise until double in size, about 1 hour. Stir dough down. Knead on a lightly-floured surface 1 minute. With a greased hand pat into a well-greased 9-inch round baking pan. Cover; let rise until doubled in size, about 1 hour. Score top in a diamond pattern. Bake 40 minutes at 350°. Remove from dish and place on rack to cool.

Sourdough banana bread
By Charles Bryant O'Dooley

⅓ cup margarine
1 cup sugar
1 egg
1 cup mashed bananas
1 cup starter (see page 43 for recipe)

2 cups sifted flour
1 tsp. salt
1 tsp. baking powder
½ tsp. soda
¾ cup chopped nuts

Cream together margarine and sugar; add egg; stir until blended; stir in banana and starter. Sift flour, salt, baking powder, soda and add to first mixture; stir in nuts. Bake in greased loaf pan 350° for 1 hour.

Breads

Huckleberry muffins
By Bonnie Gelle

1½ cups fresh or frozen
  huckleberries
½ cup orange juice
½ cup rolled oats
2 cups flour
½ cup sugar

1½ tsp. baking powder
½ tsp. salt
½ tsp. soda
½ tsp. cinnamon
1 slightly beaten egg
½ cup oil

Wash and drain the huckleberries. Pour the orange juice over the rolled oats. Stir. Let stand while you mix the dry ingredients in a separate bowl.

To the oatmeal and juice add the egg and oil. Stir in the dry ingredients. Add the huckleberries.

Fill greased muffin cups 2/3 full of batter. Bake at 350° about 25 minutes or until tops look light brown.

Pilgrim's bread
By Charles Bryant O'Dooley

½ cup yellow cornmeal
1/3 cup brown sugar
1 Tbsp. salt
2 cups boiling water
¼ cup oil
2 pkg. dry yeast

½ cup warm water
¾ cup whole wheat flour
½ cup rye flour
4¼-4½ cups unbleached
  white flour

Combine cornmeal, brown sugar, and salt in a bowl. Stir cornmeal mixture gradually into boiling water. Add the oil. Cool to lukewarm. In a separate bowl, dissolve yeast in ½ cup warm water. Add yeast to cornmeal mixture. Beat in wheat and rye flours. Stir in white flour by hand.

Turn onto lightly-floured surface. Knead until smooth and elastic. Place in a lightly-greased bowl, turning once to grease surface. Cover and let rise in warm place until double. Punch dough down; turn out onto lightly-floured surface. Divide in half and knead a second time for 3 minutes. Shape dough into 2 loaves and place in greased pans. Cover and let rise again in warm place until double. Bake at 375° for 45 minutes.

Three-flour bread
By Charles Bryant O'Dooley

2 pkg. dry yeast
1 cup warm water
1 Tbsp. salt
¼ cup vegetable oil
¼ cup honey or molasses
3 cups warm water
1 cup dry milk powder

1 cup rye flour
¼ cup soy flour
¼ cup wheat germ
4 cups whole wheat or graham flour
5 or more cups white flour

Dissolve yeast in 1 cup of warm water and stir in salt, vegetable oil, honey or molasses, and 3 more cups of warm water. Mix in milk powder, flours, and wheat germ.

Turn out on floured surface and knead until smooth, adding more flour if needed. Place in greased bowl, turning once. Cover and put in warm place to rise until doubled, about 2 hours. Turn out onto floured surface, knead, and place in 3 greased 9 x 5 inch pans. Let rise until almost double. Place in a cold oven and set at 450° for 10 minutes. Turn down to 350° and bake 25-30 minutes. Makes 3 loaves.

Soya-carob bread
By Bill Palmroth

2 Tbsp. dry yeast
1 cup lukewarm water
3 cups warm water
½ cup vegetable oil

½ cup powdered milk
¼ cup raw honey
10-12 cups soya-carob flour
1 Tbsp. salt

Dissolve yeast in 1 cup lukewarm water and wait for bubbles. Meanwhile, mix honey, oil, and 3 cups warm water in mixing bowl. Add salt, powdered milk, and then add proofed yeast and enough flour to make kneadable dough. Knead on floured board until no longer sticky. Place in oiled bowl, let rise until doubled. Punch down, let rise again. Punch down, shape into 3 loaves. Let rise in well-oiled bread pans until dough reaches at least the tops of pans. Bake in preheated 375° oven until the loaves sound hollow on the bottom (about 1 hour).

Classic white bread
By Richard Blunt

1 pkg. (¼-oz.) dry yeast	4 Tbsp. melted margarine
1½ Tbsp. white sugar	5-6 cups bread flour
2 cups warm water (110°-115°)	⅓ cup non-fat dry milk
	2 tsp. salt

Mix yeast and sugar with 1 cup of warm water and set aside to proof.

Melt butter or margarine and allow to cool.

Combine 4 cups of bread flour with non-fat dry milk and salt. Blend this mixture.

Combine proofed yeast with remaining cup of warm water and melted margarine or butter. Do this in a bowl large enough to mix in the flour. With a wooden spoon, stir flour mixture into yeast 1 cup at a time until all 4 cups are mixed in. Continue adding the remaining 2 cups of flour until the dough becomes firm. The flour not used at this time will be used during the kneading process.

Sprinkle some of the remaining flour onto work surface and remove dough to this surface.

Knead until dough no longer feels sticky and has developed an elastic texture. Continue to add flour to the work surface to prevent sticking. Knead until dough is not sticky and has developed a smooth and elastic texture.

Transfer dough to a well-oiled bowl, cover and allow to rise until it's doubled in bulk. Depending on the temperature, this will take from 1-2 hours.

When the first rising is complete, punch dough down to remove the air. Transfer dough to a lightly-floured work area and knead for 5 minutes.

Divide the dough into 2 equal-sized balls and allow them to rest for 5 minutes. Shape these balls into loaves and place them into 2 well-oiled 9 x 5 x 3 inch loaf pans. Cover and allow to rise until double in bulk.

Bake at 375° for 40-45 minutes or until each loaf sounds hollow when tapped with knuckles.

When loaves are done and removed from the pans, set them onto wire racks to cool. Do not cut the loaves while they are hot.

Whole wheat bread
By Richard Blunt

2 pkg. (¼-oz. each) dry yeast
2 tsp. sugar
2 cups warm water (110-115°)
3 Tbsp. melted butter or margarine

2½ cups whole wheat flour
2½-3 cups bread flour
2 tsp. salt
½ cup non-fat dry milk
1 Tbsp. honey
1 Tbsp. molasses

Combine yeast, sugar, and warm water. Set aside to proof.
Melt butter or margarine and mix with honey and molasses.
Combine whole wheat flour with 1½ cups of bread flour, salt, and non-fat dry milk.
Combine proofed yeast mixture with melted butter or margarine mixture in a bowl large enough to mix in the flour.
With a wooden spoon, stir flour mixture into yeast, 1 cup at a time, until it is completely mixed in. Continue adding remaining 1 cup of bread flour until dough becomes firm. Use what is left during the kneading.
Remove dough to a floured work space and knead until dough no longer feels sticky and has developed an elastic texture.
After kneading, transfer dough to a well-oiled bowl, cover and allow to rise until it doubles in bulk.
When completely risen, punch dough down and knead for 5 minutes more. Then cut dough into 2 equal-sized balls and allow to rest another 5 minutes.
Shape balls into loaves and place them into two 9 x 5 x 3 inch loaf pans. Cover and allow to rise again until double in bulk.
Bake at 375° for 40-45 minutes until each loaf sounds hollow when tapped with knuckles. Remove loaves from pan and place back into the oven for a couple of minutes. This will add color and crispness.
Set bread aside on wire racks to cool.

Mixed grain bread
By Richard Blunt

1½ cups regular oatmeal (uncooked)
⅓ cup Wheatena (uncooked)
2 tsp. salt
2½ cups boiling water
2 Tbsp. melted margarine or butter
½ cup molasses
¼ cup honey
2 pkg. (¼-oz. each) dry yeast
½ tsp. granulated sugar
1 cup warm water
4 cups bread flour
2½ cups whole wheat flour
⅓ cup non-fat dry milk

Combine oats, Wheatena, and salt in a bowl then mix in boiling water. Set this mixture aside to thicken for about 10 minutes. When the cereal has absorbed the water and has become thick, add butter or margarine, molasses, and honey. Set this aside to cool to about 115°.

When cereal mixture has cooled, combine yeast, sugar, and warm water. Mix and set aside to proof.

In a separate bowl, combine 3 cups of the bread flour with 2½ cups of whole wheat flour and non-fat dry milk.

After yeast has proofed, combine with cooled cereal in a bowl large enough to mix in the flour.

Mix the blended flour into the yeast cereal mixture, 1 cup at a time, until completely incorporated. Continue to add part of the remaining 1 cup of bread flour, a little at a time, until the dough becomes firm. Use remaining flour during kneading.

Knead dough until it's smooth and elastic and not sticky.

Transfer the dough to a well-oiled bowl, cover and allow to rise until it doubles in bulk. When the first rising is complete, punch down the dough, remove it from the bowl and knead it for another 5 minutes.

Divide the dough into 2 equal-sized balls and allow them to rest for 5 minutes.

Shape the dough into 2 loaves and place each into well-oiled 9 x 5 x 3 inch loaf pans. Cover pans with a clean cloth and allow them to rise until they double in bulk.

Bake in a 350° oven for about 1 hour or until bread sounds hollow when tapped with knuckles.

Mayonnaise biscuits
By Darlene Campbell

2 cups self-rising flour
1 cup milk
3 Tbsp. mayonnaise

Place flour in medium-sized bowl. Stir in mayonnaise and milk. Knead dough lightly, adding additional flour if necessary. Roll out on a floured board and cut with a medium-sized biscuit cutter. Bake at 450° until lightly brown.

Angel biscuits
By Darlene Campbell

1 cup buttermilk
4 cups all-purpose flour
2 tsp. baking powder
1 tsp. salt
1 pkg. dry yeast

½ cup warm water (105-115°)
5 Tbsp. shortening
2 Tbsp. sugar
2 Tbsp. butter or margarine, melted

Heat buttermilk in a small pan until bubbles form around edge, careful not to overheat as buttermilk will curdle. Cool to lukewarm. While milk is cooling, sprinkle yeast over warm water in a small bowl. Add sugar to yeast mixture. Stir in lukewarm buttermilk. Into a large bowl sift flour with baking powder and salt. Cut shortening into flour mixture with a pastry blender until mixture resembles coarse cornmeal.

Make a well in the center of the flour mixture and pour buttermilk and yeast mixture into it all at once. Stir with a wooden spoon to mix well. Dough will be stiff. Knead as you would for bread until smooth. Roll out with a rolling pin to ½-inch thickness. Cut with a floured 2-inch cutter. Place 1 inch apart on greased cookie sheet, cover with a kitchen towel and let rise in a warm place free from drafts until double in bulk. Brush tops with melted butter and bake ar 400° 10-12 minutes.

Boston brown bread
By Darlene Campbell

1½ cups yellow cornmeal
2 cups all-purpose flour
2 tsp. baking soda
1 tsp. salt

1⅓ cups milk
1⅓ cups buttermilk
¾ cup molasses
1 cup raisins

Sift cornmeal, flour, baking soda and salt into a large bowl. In a small bowl, combine the molasses, milk and buttermilk. Slowly add the molasses milk mixture to the flour mixture. Mix with a spoon. Stir in raisins. Spoon dough into well-greased coffee cans, filling ⅔ full. Cover the cans with foil and place on a rack in deep kettle. Add boiling water to the kettle to come halfway up sides of cans. Cover the kettle and steam 2½-3 hours, adding more water as needed. Remove loaves from cans and cool on a rack.

English muffin bread
By Darlene Campbell

2 pkg. dry yeast
2 Tbsp. sugar
1 cup warm water
small amount of cornmeal
1 tsp. salt

5 cups flour (approximate)
1½ cups warm milk
½ tsp. baking soda dissolved
in 1 Tbsp. water

Combine yeast and sugar with warm water (about 110°) in a large bowl and let stand for several minutes until puffy. Using an electric mixer, slowly beat while adding alternately into the yeast mixture the salt, 3 cups of the flour, and 1 cup warm milk. Beat well after each addition. Add soda-water mixture and beat well to blend.

With a wooden spoon, beat in remaining ½ cup milk and enough remaining flour to make a stiff dough. Dough should be too sticky to knead with hands. Spoon the dough into coffee cans that have been greased and sprinkled with cornmeal on the inside. Top with their lids. Place in a warm spot to rise until the lids pop off, about 45-60 minutes. Carefully remove lids.

Bake the cans upright on a rack in the oven at 375° for 25-30 minutes or until loaves are well-browned on top and sides and bottoms are golden. Slide loaves out of cans and stand upright on wire racks to cool. Slice in rounds and toast to serve.

Whole wheat sponge bread
By Jan Cook

3 cups scalded milk
½ cup honey plus 1 Tbsp.
¼ cup warm water
1 pkg. yeast
1 Tbsp. molasses

8-9 cups whole wheat flour
(substitute 2-3 cups white
flour for a lighter loaf)
¼ cup oil
1 tsp. salt

Scald milk, let cool slightly and add ½ cup honey. Dissolve yeast in ¼ cup warm water with 1 Tbsp. honey and 1 Tbsp. molasses. Let sit until milk has cooled to body temperature. Blend yeast mixture with milk and honey. To make the "sponge" add half the flour, mixing each cup thoroughly before adding the next. Beat the batter for a minute or two and let stand in a warm place until bubbly and frothy.

Add oil and salt, then add remaining flour a cup at a time, kneading until the dough does not stick to board (or mixing bucket). Place in a well-greased earthenware bowl, and cover with a damp cloth. Let set in a warm, non-drafty place until double (about 1 hour). Punch down, cut in half with knife to make 2 loaves. Place in well-greased bread pans, set in warm place until dough doubles (½-1 hour). Cut tops with 3 slits to let steam escape. Brush tops with water. Bake at 350° for 1 hour. Top of bread should sound hollow when tapped. Let pans cool for a few minutes before turning out loaves.

Beer biscuits
By Mary Hembrow

2 cups sifted all-purpose
  flour
3 tsp. baking powder
¾ tsp. salt

2 Tbsp. sugar
1/3 cup plus 1 Tbsp. shortening
16 oz. can of beer

Preheat oven to 350°. Grease an 8-muffin tin. Put dry ingredients in a medium-sized mixing bowl, and mix well. Cut in shortening with a fork or pastry knife until mixture resembles fine bread crumbs. Add just enough beer (about 2/3 can) so the dough leaves the spoon with a little coaxing. (Exact amount varies with type of flour used.) Stir only enough to moisten dry ingredients. Spoon into muffin cups. Bake until golden, about 20 minutes.

Paul Bunyan corn bread
By Rodney Merrill

1 cup cornmeal
1 cup flour
1 Tbsp. baking powder
1 tsp. salt
1 tsp. cumin
1 tsp. chili powder
1 medium-large egg
1 cup milk
1 17-oz. can cream style
  corn

1 medium onion, chopped
¼ cup chopped green chilies
¼ cup chopped pimento
¼ cup butter or margarine
1 cup shredded cheese
  (near equal parts cheddar,
  jack, and mozarella works
  best)

Preheat oven to 400°. Combine all dry ingredients (including spices) in bowl and mix well. In a separate bowl, beat egg and milk together, then stir in creamed corn.

Melt butter or margarine in a cast iron skillet. Sauté onion, chilies, and pimento until onion is softened.

Pour milk mixture over dry ingredients, add cheese, then add sauté mixture. Smear oil residue over inside of skillet with baker's brush or thickly folded paper towel (careful to avoid burning fingers).

Stir corn bread batter until just mixed. (Avoid overmixing.) Pour into hot skillet and place in oven for 35-40 minutes. Toothpick inserted in center should come out slightly moist but not doughy.

Cornmeal sour cream biscuits
By Arthur Vernon II

1 cup unbleached all-pur-
pose flour
1 cup cornmeal
1 Tbsp. sugar
1½ tsp. baking powder
1 tsp. baking soda
¾ tsp. salt
4 Tbsp. (½ stick) cold unsalted butter, cut in ¼-inch
pieces
¾ cup sour cream
¼ cup milk or as needed

Preheat oven to 425°. Put flour, cornmeal, sugar, baking powder, baking soda, and salt into a large mixing bowl. Toss with hands to combine. Using a wire pastry blender, add butter and cut into the dry ingredients until mixture is crumbly. (This can also be done in a food processor). Combine sour cream and milk in a large measuring cup. Make a well in the dry ingredients and add sour cream mixture all at once. Stir gently, just until the dough coheres. If the dough seems dry, add a little more milk.

Dust the dough, your hands, and a work surface with a little white flour. Scrape dough out onto the work surface and knead it gently about 10 times. Pat out to an even thickness of ¾ inch. Cut out biscuits with a biscuit cutter or a floured water glass; place on a lightly-greased baking sheet.

Bake biscuits about 15 minutes, rotating the baking sheet front to back about halfway through the baking time (to brown evenly). The biscuits are done when the tops and bottoms are golden. Serve hot with sweet butter.

Sourdough pancakes
By Jackie Clay

1 cup starter
2 cups flour
2 cups + 1 tsp. warm water
1 tsp. baking soda
2 egg yolks

1/3 cup milk
2 Tbsp. sugar
2 Tbsp. melted butter
2 stiffly beaten egg whites

Mix the starter, flour, and 2 cups of water and let stand overnight in crock or glass bowl. Add 1 tsp. soda in 1 tsp. warm water, 2 egg yolks, 1/3 cup milk, 2 Tbsp. sugar, 2 Tbsp. melted butter. Beat well, then fold in 2 stiffly beaten egg whites. Let stand 10 minutes, then fry on griddle.

Sourdough starter:
2 cups flour, mixed with 2 cups lukewarm water and 2 tsp. of dry yeast. Place the mixture in crock or glass bowl—no metal. Let it stand in warm place 48 hours. When very bubbly, cover and store in the fridge. Cover loosely with wax paper so it doesn't dry out, but so it can breathe a bit. To use, set out at room temperature about 18 hours. Each time you use any, add equal amounts of water and flour and you will keep it going for years.

Canning

Pickled nopalitos
By Jackie Clay

4 lbs. de-spined, sliced fresh
   nopalitos
mustard seed
dill seed (if dill flavoring is
   desired)

garlic cloves, halved
dry red hot peppers
5 cups white vinegar
5 cups water
½ cup salt

Rinse the sliced nopalitos in cold water. Pack them into pint jars. For each pint jar, add ½ tsp. whole mustard seed, ½ tsp. dill seed (optional), 1 clove garlic, peeled and halved, and a small dry red hot pepper.

Combine vinegar, water, and salt in saucepan and heat to boiling. Pour the boiling solution over nopalitos, filling to within ½ inch of top of jar. Wipe the jar rims clean, place hot, previously-boiled lids on the jars, and screw the ring down firmly tight. Process in hot water bath for 5 minutes, counting from the time the water in the canner reaches a full rolling boil after the jars have been added. Cool. Store for at least 2 weeks to allow the flavor to develop. Refrigerate the jar before serving and serve icy cold.

Pickled peppers
By Jackie Clay

1 gallon mixed hot peppers
   of your choice
1½ cups salt

1 gallon water
1 cup water
5 cups vinegar

Wash and drain fresh peppers. Cut 2 small slits in each pepper. Dissolve the salt in the gallon of water. Pour over the peppers and let sit over night. Drain and rinse. Drain again.

Add 1 cup water to 5 cups vinegar. Simmer 5 minutes. Pack peppers into hot, sterilized jars. Heat the water-vinegar mixture to boiling and pour over peppers to within ½ inch of the top. Wipe the rims. Place lids on and screw the rings on firmly tight. The jars will seal as they cool.

Fresh-pack dill pickles
By Jackie Clay

18 lbs. of 3-5 inch cukes
1½ cups plus ¾ cup salt
2 gallons plus 9 cups water
6 cups vinegar
¼ cup sugar
7 small dry pods hot pepper

2 Tbsp. pickling spice
⅓ cup mustard seed
7 cloves garlic
21 heads of dill (or 1 cup dill
    seed)

Thoroughly wash, rinse, and drain the cucumbers. Cover them with a brine made of 1½ cups salt and 2 gallons cold water and let stand overnight. Rinse and drain the cukes. Mix the vinegar, 9 cups of water, the remaining ¾ cup salt, sugar, mixed spices (tied in a cloth bag), and heat to a boil. Keep hot. Pack cucumbers to within ½ inch of the top of quart jars. Put 2 tsp. mustard seed, 1 clove peeled garlic, 3 heads of dill (or 1 Tbsp. dill seed) and 1 pod of pepper in each jar. Cover cucumbers with hot pickling liquid. Wipe rim. Put on hot, previously-boiled lid and screw down ring firmly tight. Process 20 minutes in boiling water bath. Makes 7 qts.

Sweet cuke slices
By Jackie Clay

10 lbs. medium cukes
1 cup salt
2¼ qts. white vinegar

2 Tbsp. Sucaryl solution
½ cup mixed pickling spices

Wash and slice cukes ¼-inch thick. Mix cukes with salt and enough ice water to barely cover. Let sit overnight, covered. In morning, drain and rinse with cold water. Combine vinegar, liquid Sucaryl and spices. Boil 1 minute. Add cukes and bring to full boil. Immediately pack cukes into clean, hot, sterile jars to within 1 inch of top. Fill jars with hot, spiced vinegar to within ½ inch of top. Wipe rim and seal. Makes about 12 pints.

Salsa
By Jackie Clay

40 medium tomatoes
5 cups finely chopped
onions
4 cups finely chopped celery
2 cups finely chopped jalapeños (may use other pep-
pers, to taste)

½ cup lemon or lime juice
½ cup finely chopped cilantro
5 Tbsp. salt

To peel tomatoes, dip in boiling water a few at a time for 30 seconds, plunge into cold water, then slip the skins off. Chop the veggies finely; add other ingredients in large pot. Bring to boil. You may
add sugar to taste, if desired. Pour into hot jars, seal. Process pints
25 minutes at 10 lbs. pressure. (Adjust the pressure, if needed, due
to altitude.)

Fermented dill pickles
By Olivia Miller

50-60 smooth small cucum-
bers
1 oz. whole mixed spices
dill

1 lb. pure salt
1 gallon water
1 pint cider vinegar

Place a layer of dill in the bottom of a clean, 4-gallon crock. Add
½ oz. whole mixed spices. Pack cucumbers to within 3 inches of top
of crock. Then add another ½ oz. whole mixed spices and a layer of
dill.

Make a cold brine of the salt, water, and vinegar. Pour brine over
cucumbers. Cover with a china plate. Weight the plate down to keep
cucumbers below surface of brine. Cover top of crock with cloth.

Remove any scum that forms on surface of liquid.

Just as soon as bubbling ceases and active fermentation stops,
place pickles in standard canning jars. Pour brine over pickles,
screw on lids firmly tight, and immerse in a kettle of tap-temperature
water. Bring to a boil and boil for 15 minutes. When jars are cooling,
you can tell when each one vacuum-seals because the lid will click
down into a little indentation. Store in a cool, dry, dark place.

Ruth's old-fashioned zucchini pickles
By Richard Blunt

7 lbs. zucchini or yellow
  summer squash
1 large sweet red pepper
4 large white onions
1/3 cup coarse sea salt or
  kosher salt

ice water to cover
2 cups cider vinegar
3½ cups sugar
1 tsp. turmeric
1½ tsp. celery seed
2 Tbsp. mustard seed

Wash squash and pepper in plenty of cold water and drain. Slice squash on the diagonal into ½-inch pieces. Cut pepper in half, remove seeds and slice into pieces that are 1 inch long by ¼ inch thick.

Peel onions, cut in half, and slice lengthwise into ¼-inch strips.

In a large stainless steel bowl, mix squash, pepper, and onions with salt. Add just enough ice water to cover vegetables. Let vegetables stand for 3 hours, then drain.

In a sauce pan, mix together cider vinegar, sugar, turmeric, celery seed, and mustard seed. Bring this mixture to a boil over medium heat while stirring constantly. Remove from heat as soon as it starts to boil.

Combine hot liquid with drained vegetables in a large sauce pan and bring mixture to a boil once again. Turn off heat as soon as the boil starts.

With a slotted spoon, fill jars with hot vegetables to ½ inch from the top. Divide hot pickling brine evenly among the jars without exceeding the ½-inch head space. Remove any trapped air from the jars by running the narrow blade of the spatula down the sides of the jar. Carefully wipe the rim of the jar with a clean cloth that has been wet with boiling water to remove any traces of food. Set the sealing lid on the rim of the jar and screw on the band until it is firmly in place. Do not force or over-tighten the band. Put jars in the canner. As you are placing the jars in the canner, set them so they are not touching each other or the side of the canner.

Add enough boiling water to the canner to cover the jars with 2 inches of water. Do not compromise this step; proper processing requires at least a 2-inch covering of rapidly boiling water. Less water may cause the whole procedure to fail. Process the jars in the hot water bath for 10 minutes. Store the pickles in a cool dark place for 3-4 weeks.

Pickled chili peppers
By Richard Blunt

Brine:
2 lbs. (1 gallon) fresh, ripe, chili peppers
1 gallon water
2 cups of sea or kosher salt
Marinade:
1 cup water
5 cups white vinegar (5% acidity)
2 Tbsp. sugar
1 tsp. dried thyme
10 whole allspice
1 tsp. whole coriander seeds
12 black peppercorns
12 white peppercorns
1 tsp. whole mustard seeds
2 juniper berries
6 whole cloves
Herb oil garnish:
4 dried bay leaves
12 whole, unpeeled, garlic cloves (parboiled for 2 minutes)
2 carrots, parboiled for 2 minutes and sliced into 1/8-inch coins
6 peeled shallots
12 Tbsp. virgin olive oil

Wash peppers, trim stems to a stub and prick each pepper twice with a fork on opposite sides.

Bring water to a boil, immediately remove from the heat, and dissolve the salt in it to make a brine. Let cool.

Combine washed peppers and cooled brine in a glass, plastic, stainless steel, or other non-reactive container. Place a china plate on top of peppers to hold them down in the brine. Use 2 if necessary. Soak peppers in brine for a minimum of 12 hours.

Combine all marinade ingredients in a heavy-bottomed stainless steel sauce pan. Bring this mixture to a boil, then reduce heat to low and simmer, uncovered, for 10 minutes.

Wash and sterilize 8-12 pint-sized canning jars and lids. In each sanitized, hot jar place 1/4 of a dried bay leaf, 1 garlic clove, several carrot slices, 1/2 of a shallot and 1 Tbsp. olive oil, then pack peppers into jars. Pour marinading liquid into each jar leaving at least 1/2-inch of head space from the top of the liquid to the rim.

Use a boiling water bath method to seal the jars and process the peppers for 5 minutes. Store jars in a cool, dark place for 3-4 weeks before using. Refrigerate unused portions after opening a jar.

Old World apple chutney
By Richard Blunt

40 oz. cider vinegar
1½ lbs. brown sugar
1½ tsp. kosher salt
1 Tbsp. ground ginger
2 tsp. ground cinnamon
1 Tbsp. pickling spice

6 whole cloves and 1 bay
leaf tied in a spice bag
4 lbs. fresh-picked underripe
apples
2 lbs. Spanish onions
2 fresh garlic cloves, minced
1 lb. golden raisins

Combine vinegar, brown sugar, kosher salt, ground ginger, ground cinnamon, pickling spice, and spice bag in an 8-qt. sauce pot. Mix and bring to a slow boil over medium-low heat for 30 minutes.

While sugar syrup is cooking, peel, core, and coarsely chop the apples. Peel and coarsely chop onions, and mince garlic clove. Uniformity is not necessary; this chutney is meant to be chunky.

Combine apple, onion, and garlic in cooked syrup and cook mixture over low heat for 1½ hours, stirring occasionally to prevent scorching.

While chutney is cooking, carefully wash jars, screw bands, and lids in hot soapy water and rinse with plenty of hot water. Fill clean jars with boiling water and cover with a clean towel. Place screw bands and lids in a bowl and cover with boiling water. Let stand this way until ready to fill them. Time this process so that the boiling water will not cool below 160° or remain in the jars for more than 10 minutes.

Arrange all necessary utensils so that you will be able to fill, seal, and cap the jars efficiently.

Fill canner to ½ of its capacity with water, place racks on the bottom, and start heating to a boil. Have an additional kettle of boiling water available to add more boiling water to the canner after the filled jars have been put into place.

Fill jars with hot chutney to ½ inch from top, using a wide-mouth funnel to minimize spilling. Remove any trapped air from the jars by running the narrow blade of the spatula down the sides of the jar. Carefully wipe the rim of the jar with a clean cloth that has been wet with boiling water to remove any traces of food.

Set sealing lid on rim of jar and screw on band until it is firmly in place. Put jar in canner. As you are placing the jars in the canner, set them so they are not touching each other or the side of the canner.

Add enough boiling water to canner to cover the jars with 2 inches of water. Do not compromise this step; proper processing requires at least a 2-inch covering of rapidly boiling water.

Process filled jars for 15 minutes in rapidly boiling water.

To compensate for altitude add at least 2 minutes of processing time for every 1000 feet above sea level.

When processing is complete, turn off heat. Using jar lifter, carefully remove jars from canner and set on a towel-covered flat surface to cool. It is important not to disturb the jars during the next 24 hours. During this period the jars will cool and the vacuum-sealing will occur. With the modern Mason jars the vacuum created during the cooling period will pull down the dome in the center of each lid to make the air tight seal. If the seal does not happen, just store chutney in the refrigerator and eat within a few days.

Stewed tomatoes
By Alice Brantley Yeager

1 gallon ripe tomatoes
2 cups onions, coarsely
 chopped
1 cup celery, coarsely
 chopped
1 cup sweet peppers,
 coarsely chopped
1 Tbsp. sugar
2 tsp. salt

Wash all vegetables before using. Scald tomatoes in boiling water about 1 minute so that skins may be removed easily. Quarter tomatoes and then measure to be sure of correct amount. Mix all ingredients together in a stainless steel or porcelain pot. (Do not use aluminum.) Bring to a boil and simmer 10 minutes. Stir occasionally to prevent sticking. Pour mixture into hot, sterilized jars and process in canner. Pints require 15 minutes and quarts 20 minutes at 10 lbs. pressure. (More time may be needed depending on your altitude.)

Remove jars from canner, cover them with a light cloth, and let stand in draft-free place for several hours or until cool. Check to see that all lids are down or stay down when pressed. Jars with lids that have not sealed should be put in refrigerator and contents used within a few days.

Green tomato relish
By Alice Brantley Yeager

2 gallons green tomatoes,
   cut in bite-sized chunks
½ gallon sweet peppers,
   coarsely chopped (use
   both green and red)
½ gallon white onions,
   coarsely chopped
10 jalapeño peppers, cut in
   rings (optional)

¾ cup salt
8 cups sugar
½ gallon apple cider vinegar
1 Tbsp. crab boil OR
   pickling spices
1 tsp. whole cloves

Put vegetables in a large stainless steel or porcelain container. (Do not use aluminum.) Sprinkle with salt and let stand about 3 hours. Drain well. Do not rinse.

Dissolve sugar in vinegar and bring to a boil. Put spices in a clean cloth bag or large stainless steel tea ball and add to vinegar. Add drained vegetables and simmer until all are hot throughout and onions are clear. Remove spices. Pack mixture into hot, sterilized jars and seal. Cover hot jars with a light cloth and let stand in a draft-free place for several hours or until cool.

Fermented mustard pickles
By Olivia Miller

50-60 smooth small cucum-
   bers
1 gallon vinegar

½ lb. (16 Tbsp.) dry mustard
1 cup salt

Wash cucumbers, pack into sterilized jars. Work the mustard into a paste using a little of the vinegar, then dissolve it in the rest of the vinegar. Pour cold solution over cucumbers to within ½ inch of the jar top. Put on the cap, and screw the band firmly tight. When fermentation (bubbling) has stopped, process in boiling water bath 15 minutes. Makes 3 gallons.

Fresh kosher-style dill pickles
By Olivia Miller

30-36 cucumbers (3-4 inches long)	6 Tbsp. salt
3 cups vinegar	fresh or dried dill
3 cups water	½ to 1 clove garlic, sliced
	½ tsp. mustard seed

Wash cucumbers. Make a brine of the vinegar, water, and salt. Bring to a boil. Place a generous layer of dill, garlic, and mustard seed in the bottom of 6 pint jars. Pack the cucumbers in the jars. Fill the jars to within ½ inch of the top with the boiling brine. Put lids on jars, screw bands firmly tight. Process 20 minutes in boiling water bath. Pickles will shrivel after processing, but will plump up in the sealed jars, so don't panic and open the jars. Yields 6 pints.

Bread-n-butter pickles
By Olivia Miller

16 cups cucumber, sliced ¼-inch thick (4 lbs.)	5 cups cider vinegar
6 cups thinly sliced onions	1½ tsp. turmeric
½ cup salt	1½ tsp. celery seed
5 cups sugar	1½ tsp. mustard seed

In a large (7-qt.) kettle, mix cucumbers, onions, and salt. Cover with cold water and 3 trays of ice cubes. Let stand 3 hours. Drain, rinse well, and drain again. Set aside. In another large kettle, mix sugar and remaining ingredients. Over high heat, heat to boiling. Reduce heat and simmer uncovered 30 minutes, or until syrupy, stirring often. Get jars ready (wash and have hot), add cucumbers and onions to syrup over high heat, heat almost to boiling, stirring some, but don't boil. Ladle hot mixture into hot jars. Leave ½-inch head space. Wipe jar tops, put on rings and lids and process in boiling water 15 minutes. Cool. Makes 6 pints. For a Christmas variation, add 2 cups of sliced red sweet peppers.

Icicle pickles
By Olivia Miller

cucumbers
celery
pickling onions

1 qt. cider vinegar
1/3 cup pickling salt
1 cup sugar

"Icicle" pickle refers to the shape of the cucumber pieces, a lengthwise cut resulting in long slivers shaped like icicles. Cucumbers cut in this fashion can be dilled, sweetened, or fermented.

Cut large cucumbers into 4-8 pieces lengthwise. Let stand in ice water 8 hours or overnight. Pack into hot sterilized jars.

Fill the center of each jar with 2 pieces of celery and 6 pickling onions. Combine the vinegar, salt, and sugar. Heat to a boil. Fill jars and seal in water bath 10 minutes.

This is the basic recipe, and you make as much vinegar/sugar/salt solution as you need. I save unused portions in the refrigerator for the next day's pickles during canning season, or pour it over sliced cucumber, green bell pepper, and onion for a salad. This salad is best when chilled a few hours.

Piccalilli
By Marjorie Burris

1 qt. chopped cabbage
1 qt. chopped green tomatoes
2 sweet red peppers, chopped
2 sweet green peppers, chopped
2 large onions, chopped

1/4 cup salt
1½ cups vinegar, 5% acidity
1½ cups water
2 cups firmly packed brown sugar
1 tsp. each dry mustard, turmeric, celery seed

Mix chopped vegetables with salt and let stand overnight. Next morning, line a colander with cheesecloth, pour vegetable mixture into colander, let drain, then bring edges of cheesecloth up over mixture and squeeze until all liquid possible is removed. Boil vinegar, water, sugar, and spices 5 minutes. Add vegetable mixture. Bring to a boil. Pour into sterilized jars to within ½ inch of top. Put on cap. Process in boiling water bath 5 minutes. Yield: 6 pints.

India relish
By Marjorie Burris

12 large green tomatoes
4 large sweet green peppers
4 large sweet red peppers
6 cucumbers (6 inches long)
2 large onions
6 Tbsp. salt
2 cups chopped cabbage
2 small hot peppers
2½ cups sugar

3 cups vinegar, 5% acidity
½ tsp. ground mace (or nutmeg)
1 tsp. cinnamon
2 tsp. ground ginger root
1 tsp. turmeric
3 Tbsp. mustard seed
3 bay leaves

Remove seeds from peppers. Put peppers, tomatoes, cucumbers, and onions through food chopper, using coarse blade. Stir salt into vegetables. Let set overnight. Next morning, line a colander with cheesecloth, pour vegetable mixture into colander, let drain, then bring sides of cheesecloth up over mixture and squeeze until all liquid possible is removed. Chop cabbage very fine. Combine all the vegetables. Add sugar, vinegar, and spices. Mix well and heat to boiling. Boil 3 minutes. Pack into sterilized jars to within ½ inch of top. Put on cap. Process in boiling water bath 5 minutes. Yield: 8 pints.

Green tomato kosher dill pickles
By Marjorie Burris

small, firm green tomatoes
celery stalks
sweet green peppers, cut
    into fourths
garlic

1 qt. vinegar, 5% acidity
2 qts. water
1 cup pickling salt
dill

Pack tomatoes into sterilized quart jars. To each jar add 1 stalk celery, 1 green pepper, and a bud of garlic. Make a brine of the vinegar, water, and salt. Boil with the dill for 5 minutes. Pour hot brine over vegetables to within ½ inch of top of jar. Put on cap. Process in boiling water bath 15 minutes. This amount of liquid fills 6 quarts. These pickles will be ready for use in 4-6 weeks.

Chow-chow
By Marjorie Burris

1 peck (12½ lbs.) green
  tomatoes
8 large onions
10 green bell peppers
3 Tbsp. pickling salt
6 hot peppers, seeded and
  chopped
1 qt. vinegar, 5% acidity

1 Tbsp. ground cinnamon
1 Tbsp. ground allspice
¼ tsp. ground cloves
3 Tbsp. dry mustard
4 bay leaves
1¾ cups sugar
½ cup horseradish (optional)

Remove seeds from peppers and chop with the tomatoes and onions. Stir in salt and let stand overnight. Next morning, line a colander with cheesecloth, pour mixture into colander, and let drain. Bring edges of cloth up over mixture and squeeze to remove all liquid possible. Put in a large kettle. Tie the spices in a cheesecloth bag and add to the mixture along with the vinegar and sugar. Allow to boil slowly until tender, about 15 minutes. Add horseradish, return to boil. Remove spice bag. Pack into sterilized jars within ½ inch of top. Put on cap. Process in boiling water bath 5 minutes. Yield: 10 or 11 pints.

Green tomato pickles
By Marjorie Burris

4 qts. thinly sliced green
  tomatoes
4 small onions, thinly sliced
4 green bell peppers, seeded, cut into strips
½ cup pickling salt

1 qt. vinegar, 5% acidity
¾ cup pickling salt
1 Tbsp. each black pepper,
  mustard seed, celery
  seed, cloves, allspice, and
  cinnamon

Sprinkle ½ cup salt over vegetables, let set overnight. Next morning, drain well but do not squeeze dry. In a large kettle, mix vinegar, ¾ cup salt, and spices. Bring to boil. Add vegetables. Boil 20 minutes, pack into sterilized jars. Put on cap. Process in boiling water bath 5 minutes. Yields approximately 8 pints.

Green tomato sweet pickles
By Marjorie Burris

1 gallon green tomatoes (16
   cups sliced)
¼ cup pickling salt
1½ tsp. powdered alum
3 cups vinegar, 5% acidity
1 cup water

4 cups sugar
1 Tbsp. mixed pickling spices
½ tsp. ground cinnamon
1 Tbsp. celery seed
½ tsp. ground allspice
1 Tbsp. mustard seed

Sprinkle salt over sliced tomatoes and allow to stand overnight. Next morning drain well, but do not squeeze dry. Mix alum with 2 qts. boiling water and pour over tomatoes. Let stand 20 minutes. Drain and cover with cold water, then drain well, rinsing alum away. Tie spices in a cheesecloth bag. Combine spices with vinegar and 1 cup of water. Add sugar and bring to a boil. Pour solution over tomatoes, let stand overnight. On the third morning, bring the pickles and the solution to a boil. Remove spice bag. Pack into sterilized jars to within ½ inch of top. Put on cap. Process in boiling water bath 5 minutes. Yield: 8 pints.

Green tomato mincemeat
By Marjorie Burris

3 qts. coarsely ground green tomatoes
3 qts. peeled, cored, coarsely ground apples
1 cup ground suet
1 lb. seedless raisins
2 Tbsp. each grated orange and lemon rind
5 cups well-packed dark brown or raw sugar

¾ cup vinegar
½ cup fresh lemon juice
½ cup water
1 Tbsp. ground cinnamon
¼ tsp. ground cloves
¼ tsp. ground allspice
2 tsp. salt

Combine all ingredients in large kettle, bring to boiling, stirring frequently. Reduce heat and simmer until dark and thick, about 2½ hours, stirring occasionally. Use a pad under kettle to help prevent scorching. Pour boiling hot into pint jars to within ½ inch of top. Process in a boiling water bath 25 minutes. Makes 8 pints, enough for 8 eight-inch pies. Pressure processing is not needed for this recipe because of the very long cooking time.

Green tomato mincemeat #2
By Marjorie Burris

6 lbs. green tomatoes
6 lbs. apples, cored and peeled
6 lbs. raisins
1 lb. suet
1½ Tbsp. salt

6 tsp. ground cinnamon
3 tsp. ground cloves
3 tsp. ground nutmeg
1½ cups lemon juice
3 lbs. brown sugar

Grind apples, tomatoes, and suet. Put into large kettle with other ingredients. Cook until dark and thick, about 2½ hours, stirring occasionally. Watch closely to prevent scorching. Pour into sterilized jars to within ½ inch of top. Put on cap. Process in hot water bath 25 minutes. Yields 7 qts.

Clara's beef stew with vegetables
By Jan Cook

4-5 lbs. beef stew meat
2 qts. sliced small carrots
  (about 16)
3 cups sliced celery
3 cups chopped onions
3 qts. peeled potatoes,
  cubed

2 Tbsp. salt
2 tsp. rosemary or thyme
1 tsp. coarsely ground black
  pepper
1 tsp. garlic salt

Cut meat into 1½ inch cubes (about 2 qts.) and brown in a small amount of fat. Combine meat, vegetables, and seasonings; cover with boiling water. Pack, hot, into hot quart jars, leaving 1 inch head space. Tighten caps to just hand-tight. Process ONLY in pressure canner for 1 hour and 15 minutes at 10 lbs. according to pressure canner manufacturer's directions. If you prefer to use pints, processing time is 1 hour. Yield 7 qts.

Vegetable soup
By Jan Cook

1½ qts. water
2 qts. peeled, cored,
  chopped tomatoes (about
  12 large)
1½ qts. peeled potatoes,
  cubed (about 6 medium)
1 qt. green beans
1 qt. cut corn, uncooked
  (about 9 ears)

1½ qts. ¾-inch sliced carrots
  (about 12 medium)
2 cups 1-inch sliced celery
2 cups chopped onion
4 cloves garlic, crushed
2 tsp. coarsely ground black
  pepper
salt

Add water to vegetables; boil 5 minutes. Pour, hot, into hot quart jars, leaving 1 inch of head space. Add ½ tsp. salt to each quart. Tighten caps to just hand-tight. Process ONLY in pressure canner for 1 hour and 25 minutes at 10 lbs. according to pressure canner manufacturer's directions. If you prefer to use pints, processing time is 55 minutes. Yield 7 qts.

Kosher dill pickles

By Katherine Myers

1 lb. 2-3 inch pickling cucumbers
fresh dill
1 tsp. mixed pickling spices
1 tsp. dill seed
1 tsp. mustard seed

½ tsp. celery seed
½ clove garlic, diced
kosher coarse salt
boiling water
use 1 Tbsp. salt to each cup
  of water

Wash cukes and drain. In sterilized canning jar put sprigs of fresh dill and half of each of the spices and garlic. Fill jar (not quite full) with cukes and then add the rest of the spices and garlic and more sprigs of fresh dill. Pour boiling salted water to cover pickles to within ½ inch of top of jar. Seal jar immediately.

Casseroles

Bean-beef casserole
By Tricia Blunt

1 lb. ground beef
1 large can baked beans
1 medium onion
½ cup brown sugar
2/3 cup ketchup

2-3 slices bacon
2 Tbsp. butter
salt
pepper

Brown ground beef in butter with salt and pepper. Layer as follows: ground beef, beans, onions, ketchup, and brown sugar. Repeat for a second layer. Top with bacon strips. Bake at 350° for 30-40 minutes. Serves 4-6.

Red flannel hash
By Rodney Merrill

2 cups chopped turkey,
corned beef, or ham
2 cups diced leftover baked
potatoes
1 cup diced onions
1 cup diced beets

1 cup sliced mushrooms
2 Tbsp. chopped or dried
parsley
2 Tbsp. Parmesan cheese
1 Tbsp. basil
1 tsp. pepper

Preheat oven to 350°. Put all ingredients in a large bowl and toss gently until ingredients are mixed evenly. Lightly grease inside of 2-quart baking dish (a large old-fashioned cast iron frying pan works best and imparts natural iron to the dish). Pour all ingredients into pan. Bake for 15 minutes or until lifting with a spatula shows a crust has formed. Serves 4.

Serving suggestion: For an old-time hardy breakfast, serve Red flannel hash with home-baked biscuits. They also take about 15 minutes to bake, so you get double duty from the oven.

Jerusalem artichokes with brown rice
By Richard Blunt

4 Tbsp. extra virgin olive oil
1 medium carrot, peeled and
　diced small
1 small red onion, peeled
　and diced small
¼ cup fresh mushrooms,
　diced
2 cloves garlic, minced fine

3 cups Jerusalem arti-
　chokes, scrubbed and
　diced medium
¼ cup long grain brown rice
½ cup fresh chicken stock
1 Tbsp. lemon juice
1 Tbsp. fresh mint, diced fine
kosher salt and freshly
　ground black pepper to
　taste

Heat the oil in a large skillet. Add the carrots, onion, mushrooms, and garlic and sauté for about 5 minutes. Add the Jerusalem artichokes and continue to sauté until the artichokes are just tender.

In oven casserole combine vegetable mixture with rice, chicken stock, lemon juice, and mint. Add kosher salt and freshly ground pepper to taste. Cover casserole and bake in a preheated 350° oven for about 20 minutes, or until the rice is tender.

Emergency casserole
By Jan Cook

3 lb. yellow squash, sliced
2 medium onions, chopped
2 carrots, slivered
½ pint sour cream
2 cans cream of chicken
　soup
1 jar pimentos

1 pkg. herb-seasoned dress-
　ing mix
1 stick butter or margarine,
　melted
1 whole, cooked chicken
salt and pepper to taste

Cook first 3 ingredients in a small amount of salted water and drain.

Remove chicken from bones and cut in small pieces.

Combine cooked vegetables and chicken, sour cream, soup, and pimentos. Add butter to dressing mix.

Alternately layer vegetable-chicken mixture with dressing, beginning and ending with dressing mix.

Bake at 350° for 30 minutes or until heated through. Serves 8-10.

Root vegetable casserole
By Richard Blunt

2 cups medium parsnips
(peeled and diced medi-
um)
1½ cups medium carrots
(peeled and diced medi-
um)
1½ cups white turnip (peeled
and diced medium)
3 Tbsp. unsalted butter

¼ cup onion (diced fine)
1 Tbsp. flour
1 cup hot milk
¼ tsp. freshly grated nutmeg
kosher salt to taste
½ cup grated cheddar
cheese
bread crumbs to top casserole

Cook parsnips, carrots, and turnips separately in lightly-salted boiling water until tender. Drain and combine in a greased oven casserole.

Melt butter in a heavy-bottomed pan over medium heat and saute
onion until it's translucent. Stir in flour and cook mixture over medium heat for 5 minutes while stirring constantly to prevent burning.
Add hot milk and stir mixture over low heat until sauce is thickened
and smooth. Add nutmeg, salt, and grated cheese and stir until
cheese is melted.

Pour sauce over vegetables, coat with toasted bread crumbs, and
place in 400° oven for about 5-10 minutes. Serve hot.

Ham and sausage jambalaya
By Tom Barth

½ tsp. salt
½ tsp. black pepper
½ tsp. white pepper
½ tsp. cayenne pepper
½ tsp. paprika
½ lb. chicken breast (¾-inch dice)
3 Tbsp. vegetable shortening
2 onions, chopped
3 (or more) cloves garlic, minced

1 rib celery, chopped
1 tomato, diced
1 cup raw, long grain rice
1½ cups chicken stock
¾ lb. smoked sausage, such as Kielbasa, sliced thin
1 lb. cooked ham, diced
8 green onions, chopped
¼ cup minced parsley

In a bowl, mix salt, peppers, and paprika and coat chicken with mixture.

In a large, heavy pot with a tight-fitting lid, heat shortening. Add chicken and sear on medium heat until brown, about 3 minutes. Set aside.

Add onions, garlic, and celery to pot and sauté until soft, about 2 minutes. Add tomatoes and blend. Add rice and cook until it is golden, about 2 minutes.

Add stock, reserved chicken, sausage, and ham. Bring to a boil, stirring. Lower heat and cover. Cook over low heat for 30 minutes. Check rice for tenderness. If it seems too dry, but rice is not yet tender, add a little more stock, cover, and continue cooking. When rice is done add green onions and parsley and toss lightly to combine.

Yields 4 servings.

Terrific tamale pie
By Janine Hawley

1 cup chopped onion
1 cup chopped green pepper
1 lb. ground beef
2 8-oz. cans seasoned tomato sauce
1 12-oz. can whole kernel
  corn, drained
1 cup chopped ripe olives,
  drained
2 cloves minced garlic
1 Tbsp. sugar

1 tsp. salt
1 Tbsp. chili powder
dash pepper
1½ cups shredded sharp
  cheddar cheese
Topper:
¾ cup cornmeal
½ tsp. salt
2 cups very cold water
1 Tbsp. margarine

Sauté onion and green pepper in a little hot oil until just tender. Add meat and brown lightly. Add tomato sauce, corn, olives, garlic, sugar, salt, and chili powder. Simmer 20-25 minutes until thick. Add cheese and stir until melted. Pour into greased 10 x 6 x 1½ inch baking dish.

For cornmeal topper, stir corn meal and salt into cold water. Cook and stir until thickened. Add margarine and mix well. Spoon strips of cornmeal topper over hot meat mixture.

Bake in 375° oven for about 40 minutes. Makes 6 servings.

Zucchini casserole
By Pat Ward

2 lbs. zucchini
1 large onion, chopped
1/3 cup raw long grain rice
1 can cream of mushroom
  soup

2 beaten eggs
2 Tbsp. butter or margarine
grated cheddar cheese

Cook zucchini and onion until tender, drain.

Add rice, soup, eggs, and butter or margarine. Mix and pour into a 2-quart casserole. Top with lots of grated cheddar cheese. Bake 1 hour at 350°.

Old-fashioned meat pie casserole
By Richard Blunt

Ingredients:

1 4-5 lb. roasting chicken or stewing hen
2 cups lowfat, low-salt canned chicken broth
1 medium carrot, diced
1 medium onion, diced
3 celery stalks, cut into ½-inch pieces
2 bay leaves
1 cup pale dry sherry or other dry white wine
5 Tbsp. butter or margarine, room temperature
5 Tbsp. all-purpose flour

1¼ cups frozen baby carrots, diced medium
1¼ cups frozen pearl onions
1¼ cups frozen sugar snap peas
kosher salt to taste
freshly ground black pepper to taste

Topping ingredients:

1½ cups all-purpose flour
½ cup cake flour
1 Tbsp. double-acting baking powder
1 tsp. salt
¼ cup shortening
¾ cup whole milk

After washing the chicken in cold water and removing the giblets, cut chicken into quarters with a sharp knife.

Combine chicken stock, carrot, onion, celery, bay leaves, wine, and quartered chicken in a heavy-bottomed stockpot and stew chicken over medium-low heat until chicken is cooked completely, about 1 hour. Remove chicken from stock and set aside to cool.

Strain stock and discard vegetables and bay leaves.

Combine softened butter or margarine with flour and stir mixture into a smooth paste.

Return strained stock to stove and bring to a slow boil over medium heat. Slowly stir flour paste into hot stock with a whisk to make a thickened sauce. Slowly cook this sauce for about 5 minutes.

Add frozen vegetables, salt and pepper to taste, and continue to cook mixture for another 5 minutes. Remove mixture from heat and set aside to cool.

Remove chicken from bones and cut large pieces into 1-inch chunks. Add boneless chicken to sauce, place mixture into a 10 x 10 x 2 inch casserole. Cover the casserole and refrigerate overnight.

Biscuit topping:

Sift the 2 flours, baking powder, and salt together in bowl.

Blend shortening into flour with a pastry blender, 2 knives, or your fingers until mixture resembles grains of rice or smaller.

Using a heavy fork, stir milk into flour until all of the milk is incorporated and a slightly sticky dough is formed.

Turn dough onto a floured surface and lightly turn dough until stickiness is gone. Add a little more flour to the working surface if necessary.

Preheat oven to 450°.

Lightly roll dough to fit snugly on top of casserole.

Remove chilled casserole from refrigerator and let warm, at room temperature, for a few minutes.

Fit the biscuit topping onto the casserole and place in the oven. Cook casserole at 450° for 15 minutes, then turn oven down to 350°. Continue to cook until the casserole reaches serving temperature, about 30 minutes.

Fruit compote
By Aunt Harriet Lussan

1 pkg. (¾ lb.) prunes
dried apricots
dried peaches
raisins
dates

1 large can pineapple
    chunks, drained
¾ cup pineapple juice
¾ cup sherry wine
1 can cherry or apple pie
    mix

Soak dried fruit in warm water to rehydrate. (Any mixture of dried fruit works with this recipe. You'll want enough to cover the bottom of a 9-inch baking dish.)

Take fruit out of water and place in the bottom of baking dish. Pour pineapple and pineapple juice over fruit. Pour wine on top. Then spoon pie filling over all. Bake uncovered at 350° for 1 hour. (This can be prepared a day in advance without baking it, refrigerated, then baked before serving. It goes well on Thanksgiving served with turkey.)

Cookies

Persimmon cookies
By Charles A. Sanders

1 cup persimmon pulp
¾ cup shortening
1 cup sugar
1 egg
1 tsp. baking soda
2 cups flour
1 tsp. baking powder

dash of salt
1 Tbsp. vanilla
1 tsp. cinnamon
¾ cup chopped nuts
¾ cup coconut
¾ cup raisins (optional)

Simply mix all the ingredients together well and drop onto a cookie sheet by the spoonful. Bake in a 350° oven for 15-20 minutes. These are even better on the second day... if there are any left.

Dark moons
By Tanya Kelley

1 cup butter (not margarine)
1 cup confectioner's sugar
2 tsp. vanilla
1½ cup flour

½ tsp. baking soda
1 cup rolled oats
1 7-oz. chocolate bar, milk
   or dark chocolate

Cream butter and sugar until fluffy. Add vanilla and rolled oats. Sift flour and baking soda together and add to mix. Mix thoroughly. Shape dough in a 2-inch roll and chill in refrigerator for 1 hour. Slice in ¼-inch slices. Bake on an ungreased cookie sheet at 325° for 25 minutes, until the cookies are lightly browned. When the cookies are cool, melt the chocolate until it can be stirred smooth. Dip the side of each cookie in the chocolate, rotating it to make a crescent moon shape.

Hamentaschen
By Richard Blunt

Cookie dough:
2 cups all-purpose flour
2 tsp. baking powder
1/3 cup sugar
1/2 lb. margarine
2 Tbsp. honey
2 eggs
grated rind of one orange
1/2 cup finely ground pecans
2 Tbsp. Lairds Applejack or
    brandy

Filling:
1 cup poppy seeds
4 Tbsp. raisins
3/4 cup apple juice
3 Tbsp. honey
4 Tbsp. sugar
1 Tbsp. grated lemon rind
1 1/2 Tbsp. margarine
1 Tbsp. Lairds Applejack or
    brandy
1/3 cup finely ground pecans

Dough:

Combine flour, baking powder, and sugar in large bowl. Stir with wire whisk to blend ingredients.

Using a pastry blender or 2 knives, cut margarine into flour until mixture resembles coarse oatmeal.

In separate bowl, blend honey, eggs, grated orange rind, ground pecans, and applejack. Gently stir mixture into flour. Continue stirring only until all ingredients are incorporated.

Shape dough into ball, dust lightly with flour, wrap loosely in waxed paper and place in a gallon-sized ziplock plastic bag. Refrigerate dough for at least 6 hours.

Filling:

In a heavy-bottomed sauce pan, combine poppy seeds, raisins, and apple juice. Simmer mixture over low heat until seeds start to soften and mixture starts to thicken, about 10 minutes.

Add honey, sugar, grated lemon rind, margarine, and applejack. Continue to simmer mixture for another 5 minutes. Remove pan from heat, stir in ground pecans and set mixture aside to cool. When cool, place filling in an airtight container and refrigerate along with dough.

Assembling and baking the cookies:

Preheat the oven to 350°.

Remove the dough and the filling from the refrigerator and let both set at room temperature for 30 minutes. To make rolling the dough easier, divide it into 2 equal-sized pieces.

On a lightly-floured surface, gently roll the first half of the dough to a thickness of approximately 1/8 inch. Using a 3-inch cookie cutter, cut as many circles as you can, about 18. Place 1 rounded teaspoon of filling in the center of each cookie. Form triangular pyramids with each cookie by folding the edges of the dough up on 3 sides of the circle. Gently shape the raised edges up over the filling to form a pocket. Pinch the points of the newly formed pyramid to prevent the sides from falling during baking.

Place cookies on lightly-greased baking sheet and bake until lightly browned, about 15 minutes.

Dishpan cookies
By Darlene Campbell

4 cups all-purpose flour	2 cups oil
2 tsp. baking soda	4 eggs
1 tsp. salt	2 tsp. vanilla
2 cups brown sugar	1½ cups quick-cooking oats
2 cups granulated sugar	4 cups cornflakes

In a large bowl or pan combine sugars, oil, eggs, and vanilla. Mix well. Blend and sift flour, soda, and salt. Add flour mixture to sugar mixture, mixing thoroughly. Blend in the oats and cornflakes. Drop by spoonful onto greased cookie sheets. Bake 8-10 minutes at 325°. Makes 9-12 dozen cookies.

Basic biscotti cookie
By Richard Blunt

Ingredients for egg wash:
1 egg
2 Tbsp. milk
Ingredients for cookies:
¼ cup unsalted butter
½ cup sugar, divided
1 tsp. almond extract

2 large eggs
1½ cups all-purpose flour
½ tsp. baking powder
¼ tsp. kosher salt
½ cup whole blanched
almonds (lightly toasted,
cooled, and chopped fine)

Preheat oven to 375°.

Prepare egg wash by combining 1 egg with 2 Tbsp. milk and stir with a fork.

To prepare cookies, use an electric mixer to combine butter with ¼ cup sugar and almond extract until mixture is light and fluffy. Beat in eggs, one at a time, making sure that each one is incorporated before adding another.

Sift flour together with baking powder and salt.

Fold dry ingredients into creamed mixture, stir in nuts, and form mixture into a round ball. Cover dough with plastic wrap and place in refrigerator for 30 minutes.

Divide dough in half. Sprinkle half of remaining sugar on a work surface and roll 1 piece of dough through the sugar to form a 12-inch long log, about 1½ inches in diameter. Transfer log to a greased baking sheet. Repeat process with remaining half of dough.

Brush logs with egg wash and bake in oven for 20 minutes or until lightly golden. Cool logs for 20 minutes. Do not turn the oven off after removing logs.

Transfer logs to cutting board and cut diagonally into ½-inch thick slices. Lay slices, cut side down, on a cookie sheet. Return cookies to oven and bake for an additional 20 minutes, or until golden brown.

Pecan twerps or sand tarts
By Alice Brantley Yeager

½ lb. butter or shortening
4 heaping Tbsp. powdered
sugar
2 cups flour

pinch of salt
2 tsp. vanilla mixed with 1
Tbsp. water
2 cups chopped pecans

Cream butter and sugar together until smooth. Mix in flour and salt and add vanilla. Add pecans and stir until all ingredients are thoroughly mixed.

Hand roll bits of dough into date-size pieces and place about ½ inch apart on an ungreased cookie sheet. Bake at 250°, about 50-55 minutes or until very lightly browned. When cookies have cooled, roll them in powdered sugar.

This should make about 55-60 pecan twerps.

Earth's greatest cookies
By Darlene Campbell

2 sticks margarine (1 cup)
1 cup sugar
1 cup brown sugar
1 egg
1 cup vegetable oil
1 cup rolled oats

1 cup crushed cornflakes
1 cup shredded coconut
1 cup pecans
3½ cups all-purpose flour
1 tsp. soda
1 tsp. vanilla

Preheat oven to 350°. Cream margarine and sugar until light and fluffy. Add egg; mixing well after each addition. Add oats, cornflakes, coconut, and nuts. Blend well. Form into balls the size of a walnut and place on ungreased cookie sheet. Flatten with the bottom of a glass dipped in sugar, and bake until lightly browned.

**Instructions for Cookies in a Jar
(See the next 4 recipes)**

These are great for gift-giving during the holidays or anytime!
Here are some general instructions for assembling these jars:

✳ Start with a CLEAN quart-sized glass canning jar, lid, and
seal.
✳ Spoon layers in carefully, then slightly pack so there is a defi-
nite line of demarcation.
✳ Select decorative fabric and cut a 6-inch circle.
✳ Center fabric over canning seal and place canning lid on top
of fabric and seal.
✳ Handwrite or print the individual cookie instructions on coor-
dinating colored paper.

Rainbow chip cookies in a jar
By Sharon L. Palmer

Layer the following ingredients in a glass jar in this
 order:
½ cup white sugar
½ cup brown sugar
2 cups all purpose flour

½ tsp. salt
¾ tsp. baking soda
⅓ cup peanuts
¾ cup mini colored baking
 chips

Cookie instructions:
Preheat oven to 350°. In a medium bowl, cream ¾ cup margarine,
2 eggs, and 1 tsp. vanilla. Add entire contents of jar and mix well.
Drop by heaping teaspoonfuls on ungreased cookie sheet. Bake
10-12 minutes until lightly golden.

Chocolate chip walnut cookies in a jar
By Sharon L. Palmer

Layer following ingredients in
   a glass jar in this order:
½ cup white sugar
½ cup brown sugar
2 cups all purpose flour
½ tsp. salt
¾ tsp. baking soda
½ cup chopped walnuts
¾ cup chocolate chips

Cookie instructions:
Preheat oven to 350°. In a medium bowl, cream ¾ cup margarine, 2 eggs, and 1 tsp. vanilla. Add entire contents of jar and mix until combined. Drop by heaping teaspoonfuls on ungreased cookie sheet. Bake for 10-12 minutes.

Country oatmeal cookies in a jar
By Sharon L. Palmer

Layer following ingredients in
   a glass jar in this order:
½ cup sugar
½ cup brown sugar
1 cup rolled oats
1 cup all purpose flour
¼ tsp. salt
½ tsp. baking soda
½ tsp. cinnamon
1 cup raisins

Cookie instructions:
Preheat oven to 350°. In a medium bowl, cream ½ cup margarine, 1 egg, and 1 tsp. vanilla. Add entire contents of jar and mix until combined. Drop by heaping teaspoonfuls on ungreased cookie sheet. Bake for 12-15 minutes until lightly golden.

Ranger cookies in a jar
By Sharon L. Palmer

Layer following ingredients in
a glass jar in this order:
½ cup white sugar
½ cup brown sugar
1 cup rolled oats
½ cup crispy rice cereal

1 cup all purpose flour
½ tsp. baking soda
½ tsp. baking powder
½ tsp. salt
¼ cup coconut
½ cup chocolate chips

Cookie instructions:
Preheat oven to 350°. In a medium bowl, cream together ½ cup margarine, 1 egg, and 1 tsp. vanilla. Add the entire contents of the jar and mix until combined. Drop by heaping teaspoon on ungreased cookie sheet, and flatten with fork. Bake for 10-12 minutes, until lightly golden.

Blonde brownies
By Rhoda Denning

½ cup butter (no substitutes)
2 cups lightly packed brown
sugar
2 eggs
1 tsp. vanilla

2 cups flour
2 tsp. baking powder
½ tsp. salt
1 cup chopped pecans,
toasted

Melt butter in saucepan, remove from heat. Stir in sugar. Add eggs and vanilla. Stir in dry ingredients then add nuts. Spread into greased 13 x 9 inch pan. (Mixture will be thick.) Bake for 20-25 minutes in a preheated 350° oven.

Lunchbox cookies
By Rhoda Denning

¾ cup butter
¼ cup shortening
1 cup sugar
1 cup brown sugar
2 eggs
1 tsp. vanilla

2 cups flour
2 tsp. baking powder
¾ tsp. cinnamon
½ tsp. salt
1 cup oats
1½ cups raisin bran

Preheat oven to 350°. Cream together butter, shortening, and sugars. Add eggs and vanilla. Add all dry ingredients, mixing well. Stir in oats and raisin bran. Bake on an ungreased cookie sheet for 8-10 minutes. (I sometimes add a cup of raisins, if the raisins are sparse in the cereal.)

Chocolate crinkles
By Rhoda Denning

½ cup butter
1²/₃ cup sugar
2 tsp. vanilla
2 eggs
2 1-oz. squares semi-sweet
    chocolate, melted

2 cups flour
2 tsp. baking powder
½ tsp. salt
1/₃ cup milk

Mix butter, sugar, vanilla, eggs, and chocolate together. Add dry ingredients alternately with the milk. Chill dough in refrigerator for 3 hours. Roll into 1-inch balls then roll balls in powdered sugar. Bake on a greased cookie sheet for 10 minutes at 350°.

Old-fashioned ginger snaps
By Rhoda Denning

¾ cup cooking oil
1 cup brown sugar
¼ cup dark molasses
1 egg
2¼ cups flour

2 tsp. baking soda
1 tsp. ground ginger
1 tsp. ground cinnamon
½ tsp. ground cloves
¼ tsp. salt

Beat oil, sugar, molasses, and egg. Combine dry ingredients and add to beaten mixture. Form into 1-inch balls. Roll in granulated sugar and place balls 2 inches apart on an ungreased cookie sheet. Bake in a 375° oven for 8-10 minutes. Makes 48.

Desserts

Bread pudding
By Marjorie Burris

2 cups cubed dry bread
4 cups milk, scalded
1 Tbsp. butter
¼ tsp. salt
¾ cup sugar

4 eggs, beaten
1 tsp. vanilla
½ cup raisins
nutmeg

Use the butter to grease a 2-quart baking dish. Beat the eggs in the dish. Set aside. Scald the milk in a sauce pan. Soak the bread in the hot milk, add salt, sugar, vanilla, and raisins. Pour over eggs in baking dish, stir lightly. Sprinkle generously with nutmeg. Bake at 350° until firm, about 50 minutes. Cover tightly the last 10 minutes if it starts to get too brown on top. This will puff up, then settle back down in the dish. Good hot or cold.

Tetsukabuto squash pie
By Alice Brantley Yeager

1 9-inch unbaked pie shell
2 cups mashed or pureed
  cooked pulp of
  Tetsukabuto squash
½ tsp. vanilla
10 oz. evaporated milk

¼ cup brown sugar
2 Tbsp. unbleached flour
½ tsp. nutmeg
½ tsp. ginger
⅓ cup chopped pecans

Thoroughly mix pulp, vanilla, and milk. Mix sugar, flour, nutmeg, and ginger together and stir into the wet mixture. Pour into the pie shell and bake in 375° oven until the middle of pie is almost firm but still sticky. Remove from the oven and sprinkle with pecans. Continue baking until a straw inserted in the center comes out clean. Entire baking time takes 40-45 minutes.

Desserts

Glazed spiced mocha brownies
By Richard Blunt

Ingredients:
soft shortening
5 oz. bittersweet chocolate
6½ oz. unsalted butter
⅛ tsp. kosher salt
½ tsp. powdered, instant
espresso coffee
½ tsp. freshly ground black
pepper
¼ tsp. freshly grated nutmeg
½ tsp. pure vanilla extract

1 cup dark brown sugar,
firmly packed
3 large eggs
¾ cup sifted all-purpose
flour
1 cup pecans, broken into
large pieces
**Ingredients for semisweet
chocolate glaze:**
4 oz. semisweet chocolate
2 oz. sweet butter

Brownies:

Prepare a 12-inch square baking pan by coating sides and bottom with soft shortening. Place a piece of waxpaper, cut to fit, on bottom of pan. Coat wax paper with soft shortening, dust with flour, and shake off excess. Set prepared pan aside.

Place bittersweet chocolate in a double boiler over medium heat. When chocolate is melted, stir with a wire whisk until smooth and set aside to cool slightly.

Cream butter in large bowl of an electric mixer. Add salt, instant coffee, black pepper, nutmeg, vanilla extract, and brown sugar. Beat mixture until all of the ingredients are blended. Add eggs, 1 at a time, beating mixture just enough to incorporate each egg. Scrape bowl with a rubber spatula after incorporating each egg.

With mixer on low speed, add melted chocolate, then flour to mixture. Stir using a rubber spatula to get mixture away from sides, then continue mixing, at low speed with the electric mixer, until all ingredients are incorporated.

Remove bowl from mixer and stir in nuts, using a wooden spoon.

Turn mixture into pan, smooth the top, and bake for about 30 minutes or until a toothpick inserted into middle of brownie comes out slightly moist. It is critical not to overbake this brownie. Doing so will give it a dry crumbly texture.

Remove brownie from oven and let cool in pan for 30 minutes. Place a cake rack over the pan and invert pan and rack together. Remove pan and peel off wax paper. Turn brownie right side up by placing another cake rack over it and inverting once again.

Glaze:

Combine semisweet chocolate pieces with butter in small double boiler over medium heat. When chocolate is melted, stir mixture with a wire whisk until smooth.

Remove chocolate from heat and set in refrigerator to cool. Stir occasionally until it is thick enough to spread without running down the sides of the brownie.

Spread the glaze on the brownie with a narrow-blade spatula, and place the brownie in the refrigerator until the glaze is set.

Grandma's persimmon pudding
By Charles A. Sanders

2 cups persimmon pulp
1 cup sugar
2 eggs
2 cups sweet milk
½ cup margarine
2 cups flour

2 tsp. baking powder
½ tsp. baking soda
1 tsp. salt
1 tsp. cinnamon
½ tsp. nutmeg
2 tsp. vanilla

Mix the sugar, pulp and eggs. Add the remaining ingredients and mix well. Bake in slow oven (350°) until done. Simple directions for an exquisite treat.

Fuyugaki persimmon pie
By Alice Brantley Yeager

1 unbaked 9-inch pie shell
½ cup sugar
2 Tbsp. flour
½ tsp. ginger
½ tsp. nutmeg

1½ cups pureed Fuyugaki pulp
(Do not puree skins.)
¼ cup evaporated milk
1 egg, slightly beaten
1/3 cup chopped pecans (optional)

Sift dry ingredients together and combine with persimmon pulp. Add milk and egg. Stir until smooth and pour into unbaked pie shell. Bake at 375° for 45-50 minutes, or until knife inserted in center comes out clean. Optional: Pie may be taken from oven just before completely done, sprinkled with chopped pecans (or other nuts) and returned to oven to finish baking.

Apple and noodle pudding
By Richard Blunt

Ingredients for pudding:
2²/₃ cup whole milk
pinch kosher salt
4 oz. wide egg noodles (broken into 1-inch pieces)
3 large eggs, separated
5 Tbsp. butter or margarine
1/3 cup sugar
1½ tsp. pure vanilla extract

2½ cups freshly sliced pie apples
Ingredients for topping:
2½ Tbsp. all-purpose flour
¼ cup light brown sugar
¼ cup granulated sugar
1 tsp. cinnamon
4 Tbsp. butter or margarine

Preheat oven to 350°. Spray inside of large baking dish with non-stick cooking spray and set aside. Substitute butter, margarine, or shortening if you don't use cooking spray.

To prepare **topping**, combine flour, sugars, and cinnamon. Cut in butter with pastry blender until mixture becomes crumbly, then set topping aside. The flour is to keep topping from collapsing into a puddle on the dessert.

To prepare **pudding**, combine milk and salt in a sauce pan. Bring mixture to a slow simmer over low heat, add broken noodles and cook until just tender. Set pan aside to cool without removing noodles.

While noodles are cooling, separate egg yolks from whites. Cream butter, sugar, and vanilla in large bowl until well-blended. Add egg yolks and beat until mixture is well-blended and has a light texture.

In a separate bowl beat egg whites until stiff.

Gently stir butter, sugar, vanilla, and egg yolk mixture into cooled noodles and milk, then gently fold in beaten egg whites.

Pour this custard mixture into prepared baking dish, and arrange apples on top. Evenly sprinkle topping over apples.

Bake pudding on the middle rack in oven for about 45 minutes or until custard is just set. Serve pudding right from oven or let cool for a few minutes and serve warm.

Ground cherry pie
By Sally Denney

4 cups ground cherries*
¼ cup lemon juice
(or depending on taste
preference, 2 drops
almond extract)

1 cup water
¾ cups sugar
3 Tbsp. cornstarch

Put cherries, flavoring, sugar, and ½ cup water into a saucepan; heat to boiling. Mix ½ cup water with cornstarch and add to hot cherry mixture. Cook until thick. If too thick, add a little more water. Pour into an unbaked pie crust. Adjust top crust. Bake at 375° until crust is baked.

*Ground cherries are similar to tomatoes in their growing habits. Their seeds resemble seeds of cherry tomatoes and can be found in the novelty section of some seed catalogs.

Triple chocolate cheesecake
By Tanya Kelley

Crust:
1½ cups crushed Oreo cookies (about 10 cookies)
¼ cup butter
½ of a 1½-oz. chocolate bar

Filling:
2 eggs
8 oz. softened cream cheese
½ cup sugar
1/8 tsp. salt
1 tsp. vanilla
1½ cups sour cream
3 Tbsp. cocoa powder

Melt butter and chocolate. Stir together until smooth. Mix well with cookie crumbs. Press the mixture on sides and bottom of a 9-inch cake or pie pan. Set aside.

Preheat oven to 375°. Beat all filling ingredients together until smooth. Pour into crust. Bake for 35 minutes. Chill before serving. If desired, drizzle top with melted chocolate or any remaining cookie crumbs. Top with whipped cream.

Raspberry chocolate torte
By Tanya Kelley

Cake:
1 devil's food cake mix
butter for cake
Filling:
2 cups raspberries or pitted
cherries (fresh or frozen)
2 cups sugar
1 cup water

3 cups whipping cream,
whipped
½ cup confectioner's sugar
½ tsp. vanilla
1 1½-oz. milk chocolate bar,
shaved into curls
Maraschino cherries for garnish

Mix cake as directed on box, except replace the oil with the same amount of butter. Bake in 2 greased (not floured) 9-inch round pans according to directions. Let cool.

Mix sugar and water in a saucepan. Bring to a boil and add fruit. Boil for 3 minutes. If using raspberries, you might want to strain the syrup to remove any seeds.

Whip whipping cream on high until stiff. Add sifted confectioner's sugar and vanilla. Mix in.

Cut each cake layer into 2 layers to make 4 layers. Place 1 layer, cut side up, on serving tray. Drizzle ⅓ of syrup mixture on layer. Spread ¼ of the whipped cream on top but not on sides. Place next layer of cake, cut side up, on first layer. Repeat topping with syrup and whipping cream with the next 2 layers. For remaining layer, place cut side down. Top with whipped cream, shaved chocolate, and cherries.

Desserts

Kenneth McKnight's Indian pudding
By Natalie McKnight Haugaard

3 cups milk
½ cup cornmeal
4 Tbsp. butter
1 cup raisins
½ cup brown sugar
½ cup dark molasses

4 eggs, well-beaten
½ tsp. ginger
½ tsp. cinnamon
½ tsp. mace
¼ tsp. salt

Grease a 2-quart baking pan or bowl. Scald milk in the top of a double boiler, and gradually beat in the cornmeal. Cook over hot water until slightly thickened. Remove from stove and add remaining ingredients, beating well after each addition. Pour into baking dish and bake at 300° for about 2 hours. Serve with whipped cream.

Wild blueberry cobbler
By Jackie Clay

2 cups dried wild blueberries
(if using fresh or canned berries, use 4 cups)
½ cup sugar or honey

Topping:
1½ cups flour
1 tsp. salt
¼ cup sugar or honey
2 Tbsp. butter
½ cup milk

Place rehydrated blueberries (or fresh or canned blueberries) in baking dish and sprinkle with sugar or honey.

For the topping, mix all dry ingredients then cut in butter and add as much milk as is needed to make a thick batter. Spoon this on top of the berries and bake for about 1 hour at 350°.

Serve hot with maple syrup, honey, or whipped cream.

Pumpkin pie
By Jackie Clay

1 unbaked pie crust
Filling:
3 eggs
1½ cups mashed pumpkin
½ cup brown sugar
½ cup sugar
½ tsp. ground cloves

¼ tsp. salt
½ tsp. nutmeg
1 tsp. ginger
1 tsp. cinnamon
1 cup milk
2 tsp. melted butter
1 Tbsp. flour

Beat the eggs. Add pumpkin, sugars, salt, and spices. Mix. Add the milk and mix. Add the flour and melted butter. Mix well.

Place in pie crust. Bake for 15 minutes at 400°. Turn down heat to 350° for 45 minutes or until a straw inserted in the center comes out clean.

Rice pudding
By Katherine Dazazel

2 cups cooked rice
1/8 tsp. salt
1 Tbsp. butter, cut up or melted

3 eggs
1 1/3 cups milk
5 Tbsp. sugar
1 tsp. vanilla

Combine everything and mix well. Pour into a greased 9 x 9 inch dish and bake at 325° for 50 minutes or until set.

Rice pudding is good hot or cold. Leftovers are great for breakfast the next morning. If you prefer a sweeter pudding, add a few more Tbsp. of sugar, or sprinkle sugar over the top when it's done. For a richer pudding, use more eggs. For a different taste, substitute a tsp. of cinnamon for the vanilla.

Chocolate pound cake
By Katherine Dazazel

1 cup (2 sticks) butter
8 Tbsp. (½ cup) shortening
3 cups sugar
6 eggs
3 cups cake flour

3 cups cocoa
½ tsp. baking powder
½ tsp. salt
1¼ cups milk
2 tsp. vanilla

Cream the butter and shortening together with the sugar. Add the eggs one at a time, and blend well after each one. Sift all dry ingredients and add alternately with milk. Add vanilla and blend well. The batter will be stiffer than most cake batter. Spoon (it won't pour) into a greased and floured tube pan and smooth the top of the batter so it's even. Bake at 325° for 1 hour and 25 minutes.

Pie crust
By Katherine Dazazel

1 cup all-purpose flour
¼ cup whole wheat flour
½ tsp. salt

6 Tbsp. + 1 tsp. shortening
4-5 Tbsp. cold water

Mix the flours and salt together, then cut in the shortening until the mixture resembles crumbs.
Sprinkle the water over the mixture 1 spoonful at a time, blending it in with a fork, until the dough is just moistened.
Roll out on a lightly-floured surface.
Bake at 450° for about 10 minutes, or until slightly browned. (Weight with beans wrapped in tinfoil if you like.)

Basic apple pie filling
By Jackie Clay

1 double-crust pie pastry
6 cups peeled, sliced tart
  apples
1 cup sugar (may use ½
  brown and ½ granulated)

2 Tbsp. flour
½ tsp. ground cinnamon
pinch salt
2 Tbsp. butter

In medium mixing bowl, combine all ingredients, except for butter. Toss well to combine. Pour filling into unbaked pie shell. Spread filling in the bottom crust. You should have enough filling to heap up in the center; it will cook and become more flat in the baking. Dot in 4 places with butter. Center top crust and seal 2 crusts together. Gently rub margarine over the top crust of pie, then sprinkle a little sugar over it. This makes a crispy, sugary pie crust that people find irresistible. Bake at 350° until the crust is nicely browned, usually about 35 minutes.

Apple crisp
By Alice Brantley Yeager

6-8 medium-sized pie apples
(such as Granny Smith or
  Jonathan)
¾ cup unbleached flour

1 cup brown sugar
½ tsp. nutmeg
½ cup butter or margarine
½ tsp. cinnamon

Wash apples, pat dry with non-fuzzy kitchen towel or paper toweling. Don't peel apples, but core them and remove seeds and seed cavities. Slice in ½-inch slices vertically and place in well-greased medium-sized deep baking dish. Work rest of ingredients together with a pastry blender or fork until crumbly. Pack mixture closely over apples. If apples are dry type apples, you may do well to add a couple Tbsp. of water. Bake in preheated 350-375° oven about 45-50 minutes. Serve warm with dabs of thick whipped cream or enjoy plain. Serves 6 people.

Pecan pie
By Alice Brantley Yeager

3 eggs, beaten
2 Tbsp. melted butter
2 Tbsp. unbleached or all-purpose flour
½ tsp. vanilla flavoring
1/8 tsp. salt

½ cup sugar
1½ cups dark or light corn syrup
1½ cups broken pecan halves
1 unbaked 9-inch pie shell

Combine eggs, butter, flour, vanilla, salt, sugar, and syrup. Mix well. Sprinkle pecans in unbaked pie shell and pour mixture over them. Bake in 375° oven about 45 minutes or until filling is firm and crust is golden brown. (Test firmness by inserting a table knife into the middle of the pie. If it comes out sticky, leave the pie in the oven a few more minutes. If it's clean, pie is done.)

Fresh blueberry pie
By Charles A. Sanders

1 baked 9-inch pie shell
4 cups fresh or frozen blueberries
1 cup sugar
3 Tbsp. cornstarch

¼ tsp. salt
¼ cup water
1 Tbsp. butter or margarine

Line the baked pie shell with 2 cups of blueberries. To make the sauce, cook the remaining berries with sugar, cornstarch, salt, and water over medium heat until thickened. Remove the mixture from heat; add butter and cool. Pour over the berries in the shell. Chill and serve with whipped cream.

Apple whatever
By Richard Blunt

4 large apples (up to as
many as 8 if the apples
are small)
2 cups flour
3 tsp. baking powder
1 Tbsp. sugar
½ tsp. kosher salt (optional)
4 Tbsp. shortening

1 egg, beaten
⅔ cup water
Topping:
¾ cup sugar
2 tsp. cinnamon
½ tsp. nutmeg
whipped cream

Preheat oven to 350°. Pare, core, and slice apples and set aside.
Combine flour, baking powder, sugar, and salt and cut in shortening just as if you were making a pie crust. Stir in egg and water to form a soft dough.

Roll dough to a ½-inch thickness to fit a rectangular cookie sheet. Arrange apples on the surface.

Mix sugar, cinnamon, and nutmeg together and sprinkle evenly over apples.

Bake 30 minutes and serve hot with whipped cream.

Zucchini custard pie
By Sandra L. Toney

1 cup shredded zucchini (if
frozen, thaw completely;
keep the excess liquid)
1 egg
1 tsp. vanilla extract
2½ Tbsp. flour
1 cup sugar

2 Tbsp. butter or margarine
1 cup evaporated milk
1 9-inch unbaked pastry or
pie shell
cinnamon
nutmeg

Preheat oven to 450°.
Mix zucchini (and any excess liquid), egg, vanilla, flour, sugar, butter, and evaporated milk in a blender until thoroughly blended. Pour mixture into unbaked pastry shell. Sprinkle top of pie with cinnamon and nutmeg until it is lightly covered.

Bake pie for 20 minutes at 450°. Lower the oven temperature to 350° and bake for 10 minutes more. Let cool completely.

Choco-zucchini cake
By Sandra L. Toney

3 cups shredded zucchini (if frozen, thaw completely; keep the excess liquid)
4 oz. unsweetened baking chocolate
½ cup vegetable oil
½ cup softened butter or margarine
2 cups sugar

3 beaten eggs
1 Tbsp. vanilla extract
2 cups flour
1/3 cup unsweetened cocoa
2 tsp. baking powder
2 tsp. baking soda
½ tsp. salt
1/3 cup sour cream

Preheat the oven to 350°.

Melt unsweetened baking chocolate and oil in a saucepan over low heat. Set mixture aside.

Cream butter until light and fluffy; add sugar, eggs, and vanilla to it. Beat mixture well. Stir in chocolate and mix ingredients well.

Sift together flour, unsweetened cocoa, baking powder, baking soda, and salt. Stir dry ingredients into batter with the sour cream. Mix zucchini (and any excess liquid from the thawed zucchini) into the batter.

Grease and flour two 9-inch cake pans. Put half of the batter in each pan. Bake cake at 350° for 40 minutes, or until a toothpick placed in the center of the cake comes out clean.

Let the cake cool. Frost the cake with your favorite frosting or whipped topping. Serves 20.

Sourdough applesauce cake
By Charle Bryant O'Dooley

1 cup starter (see page 43
   for recipe)
¼ cup dry skim milk
1 cup white flour
1 cup canned or homemade
   applesauce
½ cup white sugar
½ cup brown sugar
½ cup butter or margarine

1 egg
½ tsp. salt
1 tsp. cinnamon
½ tsp. nutmeg
½ tsp. allspice
½ tsp. cloves
2 tsp. baking soda
½ cup chopped nuts or raisins (optional)

Mix starter, skim milk, flour, and applesauce and set covered in a warm place. Cream together sugars and butter or margarine and add to starter mixture. Add 1 egg beaten well. Mix in salt, cinnamon, nutmeg, allspice, cloves, and baking soda.

Add ½ cup chopped nuts and/or raisins, if desired. Combine all ingredients and beat by hand. Pour into 8-inch square pan. Bake at 350° for 30-35 minutes. Test for doneness, and allow to cool in the pan.

Blue fruit pie (huckleberry version)
By Bonnie Gelle

your favorite 2-crust pastry
3 cups fresh or frozen,
   drained huckleberries
1 cup sugar

4 Tbsp. flour
1 tsp. cinnamon
dash of salt

Prepare your favorite 2-crust pastry recipe. Line pie plate with bottom crust. Fill with mixture of remaining ingredients. Dot with margarine. Cover with top crust. Bake pie at 350° for approximately 1 hour.

Apple dumpling
By Anne Westbrook Dominick

1 pie crust
6 apples, peeled, cored, and
    quartered
cinnamon
sugar

6 Tbsp. butter
milk
½ cup brown sugar (option-
    al)
½ cup butter (optional)

Roll out pie crust and cut into 6 squares big enough to encase the apples. Sprinkle apples with sugar and cinnamon. On each square put an apple's quarters back together, top each with a Tbsp. of butter, and bring up corners of dough to enclose the apple. Seal edges with a little milk and pinch together. Lower into boiling water, cover tightly, and cook 15 minutes. The dumplings can be steamed instead for 30 minutes. Or for variety they can be baked in 350° oven until dough is browned, about 45 minutes. For a rich treat, cream brown sugar and butter and dab on hot dumplings when served.

Huckleberry cake
By Bonnie Gelle

2 cups huckleberries
½ cup water
1 cup sugar

1 Tbsp. cornstarch
1 Tbsp. lemon juice
1 pkg. yellow cake mix

Cook huckleberries in water in small saucepan. Boil 1 minute. Stir in sugar and cornstarch. Continue cooking, stirring constantly, until sauce thickens and looks clear. Set aside to cool.

Prepare yellow cake mix according to directions, except diminish the water by ¼ cup. Pour into a greased and floured 9 x 13 inch pan.

Add lemon juice to cooled sauce and swirl sauce over cake batter (the sauce will sink to the bottom of the pan while the cake bakes).

Bake for the time recommended on the package. Let cool. Cut into pieces and flip over for serving. Good with ice cream or whipped cream or sprinkle powdered sugar on each slice as you serve it.

Polly's Indian pudding
By Joanie Rudolph

3 heaping Tbsp. yellow cornmeal
1 heaping Tbsp. white flour
3 oz. molasses to make a
paste (not runny)
1 qt. whole milk

1 egg, beaten
1 tsp. ginger
1 tsp. cinnamon
1 pint whole milk
¾ cup raisins
1 cup sugar, appoximately

Cook cornmeal, flour, molasses, and 1 qt. of milk on the stove top at a gentle bubble for ½ hour, stirring frequently.

In a second bowl, break egg and beat with a fork. Add 1 tsp. ginger and 1 tsp. cinnamon. Dribble 1 pint whole milk into this bowl, beating as you add the milk.

Combine both mixtures together and stir. Add raisins, stir and add sugar to taste. (About 1 cup sugar should do.) Preheat oven to 400°. Put in oven. In about 12-15 minutes, or when it starts to bubble, reduce temperature to 350°. Cook 1-1½ hours or longer until middle will not shake.

Fudge macaroon pie
By Jean Winfrey

3 squares Bakers unsweet-
ened chocolate
½ cup butter or margarine
3 eggs, slightly beaten
¾ cup sugar
½ cup flour

1 tsp. vanilla
⅔ cup sweetened con-
densed milk
2⅔ cup Bakers Angelflake
coconut

Melt chocolate and butter in saucepan over low heat. Stir in eggs, sugar, flour, and vanilla. Pour into greased 9-inch pie plate. Combine milk and coconut, spoon over chocolate mixture, leaving approximately ½-inch edge.

Bake at 350° for 30 minutes. Cool and serve.

117

Orange honey pudding
By Sharon Freeman

3 Tbsp. cornstarch
½ cup honey
1½ cups water
1 tsp. butter
⅛-¼ tsp. salt

½ cup yogurt
3 Tbsp. frozen orange juice
    concentrate
1 tsp. vanilla

Put cornstarch and a little water in a medium saucepan and mix well. Add the rest of the water, honey, butter, and salt. Bring to a boil, whisking constantly. Boil and whisk for 1 minute. Remove from heat. Whisk in yogurt, orange concentrate, and vanilla until smooth. Pour into 4 dessert cups and chill.

Variations: Experiment with the amount of honey and orange concentrate for the taste you like best. Add a touch of powdered ginger if you like spice. Substitute ⅓ cup cream for the yogurt for a hedonist's delight. Substitute 2 Tbsp. carob or cocoa for the orange concetrate and add a little more yogurt or cream.

Self-crusting apple pie
By Tricia Blunt

5 large apples
1 tsp. cinnamon
1 Tbsp. sugar
1½ sticks margarine (¾ cup)

1 cup flour
1 cup sugar
1 egg
½ cup chopped walnuts

Peel and slice apples and place in large pie plate. Cover top of apples with cinnamon and sugar. Melt margarine and combine with egg, flour, sugar, and walnuts. Spread batter over apples and bake at 350° for 45 minutes.

Chocolate chip cake
By Tricia Blunt

1 cup sour cream
1 yellow cake mix
4 eggs

½ cup oil
1 pkg. vanilla pudding mix
12 oz. chocolate chips

Mix all ingredients. Grease and flour 13 x 9 inch pan. Bake at 350° for 50-60 minutes.

Aunt Mildred's honey cake
By Katherine Myers

1 cup brown sugar
1 cup honey
4 eggs
1 cup strong black coffee
   (cold)
½ cup chopped nuts
1 tsp. vanilla
2 Tbsp. vegetable oil

Sift together:
3½ cups sifted flour
1 tsp. soda
1 tsp. salt
1 tsp. baking powder
1 tsp. ginger
½ tsp. allspice
1 tsp. cinnamon

Beat sugar, honey, and eggs together well. Add sifted dry ingredients alternately with coffee. Add vanilla, then oil, and nuts and beat well. Top may be garnished with almond halves. Bake in greased and floured 9 x 13 inch pan for 1 hour at 350°. Cake is done when toothpick tested in the center comes out clean.

Fifties banana split
By Jo Mason

1 banana
1 scoop chocolate ice cream
1 scoop vanilla ice cream
1 scoop strawberry ice cream
heaping Tbsp. chocolate syrup
heaping Tbsp. strawberry topping
heaping Tbsp. pineapple topping
marshmallow creme
whipped cream (optional)
chopped nuts
1 maraschino cherry

Split banana lengthwise and place in dish. Place ice cream scoops between halves. Put chocolate syrup on chocolate ice cream; strawberry topping on strawberry ice cream; and pineapple topping on vanilla ice cream. Spread generously with marshmallow creme, then whipped cream, if desired. Top with nuts and cherry.

Aunt Jeannette's Hershey bar squares
By Aunt Jeannette Kaner

1 stick margarine, melted
1 cup flour
½ cup brown sugar
½ egg yolk
Hershey bar
chopped nuts

Mix everything but Hershey bar and chopped nuts, flatten evenly on 9 x 13 inch buttered pan. Bake 10 minutes at 350°.
Break up 6 oz. of Hershey bar and scatter over crust. Bake about 1 minute until chocolate spreads evenly. Sprinkle nuts on and cool.

Jams, jellies, & preserves

Fig preserves
By Alice Brantley Yeager

1 lb. small figs (Brown
Turkey, Celeste, etc.)
¾ lb. sugar

juice of ½ lemon (optional)
½ lemon thinly sliced
(optional)

Wash figs. Discard stems and remove any blemishes such as twig damage. (Some recipes state to peel figs, but we only peel large figs such as Texas Everbearing.)
Cut figs in half lengthwise and put in stainless steel or porcelain bowl. (Do not use aluminum.) Mix with sugar, cover and let sit overnight in refrigerator to form juice.
Cook in heavy-bottomed saucepan over low heat until mixture thickens. If using lemon juice and slices, add them to figs when mixture starts to boil. Be sure to stir frequently with wooden spoon to keep figs from sticking. When mixture thickens and desired consistency is reached, spoon immediately into hot, sterilized jars and seal with clean lids and rings that have been standing in hot water. To avoid drafts on hot jars, cover them with a kitchen towel until cooled. When contents have cooled check to see that all lids have popped down. Jars have not sealed if lids are puffed up and are springy to the touch.

Pear honey
By Alice Brantley Yeager

1 qt. of ground Kieffer pears
(peel and core before
grinding)
3 cups sugar

juice of 1 lemon
grated rind of ½ lemon
½ tsp. ground ginger

Boil mixture in stainless steel, porcelain, or graniteware pot stirring frequently until thickened (Do not use aluminum). When desired thickness is achieved, immediately put in hot, sterilized jars and seal. Remember that this is a spread and should not be overcooked to a jelly stage.
A tasty variation is to substitute orange and nutmeg for lemon and ginger.

Easy raspberry jam
By Linda Gabris

6 cups fresh wild raspberries
(the store-bought kind will
do, but honestly, they don't
measure up to the little
wild treasures)

6 cups white sugar
juice of 2 lemons

Combine berries and sugar in a big, heavy-bottomed kettle. Place over heat and stir constantly, bringing to a boil. Boil for 30 minutes, stirring and watching so it doesn't scorch. Add lemon juice. Boil to jellying stage—when a drop of jam sets on a cold plate. Pour into hot, sterilized jars. Seal with paraffin wax. Store in cellar or fridge. Makes about 8 or 9 jelly jars. Recipe can easily be halved or doubled.

Hawaiian poha jam
By Sally Denney

3 lb. poha (ground cherries)
¼ cup water

1 cup sugar per cup cooked
poha
1 Tbsp. lemon juice

Husk and wash fruit. Combine with water and cook slowly for 30 minutes, stirring frequently. Remove from heat and let stand overnight. Measure pulp and juice and combine with an equal quantity of sugar. Return to heat and cook slowly, stirring occasionally for 1 hour. Add lemon juice and continue slow cooking until product reaches jelly stage. Immediately pour into hot sterilized glasses and seal. (I froze my jam.)

Indian pear jelly
By Alice Brantley Yeager

3 lbs. Indian Pear fruit
5½ cups sugar
1 box fruit pectin

Gather at least 3 lbs. of fruit. Wash, remove stems, and drain. Put fruit in graniteware or stainless steel pot (do not use aluminum) and add as much water as necessary to cover fruit. Bring to a boil and then lower heat, cover pan and let fruit simmer 10 minutes. Stir occasionally to keep from sticking.

To separate juice from pulp, strain through a moistened jelly bag or several layers of porous cloth such as cheesecloth. The dripping process may require several hours, so don't be in a hurry to finish. After the dripping has stopped, you may extract a few more drops of liquid by gently squeezing the cloth. Discard pulp. Put juice in clean pot for rest of jelly-making procedure being sure that the pot is of ample size to allow for expansion of a rolling boil.

You should have about 4 cups of juice. (Sometimes, after a very dry season, fruit will not yield as much juice as during a normal season and you will need to add a bit more water.) Stir 1 box commercial fruit pectin into juice and bring to a rolling boil over high heat, stirring constantly. Stir in sugar and bring mixture back to a rolling boil and let boil hard for 1 minute, continuing to stir. Remove from heat, skim off any foam present and pour immediately into hot, sterilized jars and seal. Makes about 3 pints. Serve with hot biscuits on a cold day.

After trying this recipe, if you find that you prefer a bit more tartness, next time add a Tbsp. of lemon juice to strained juice before cooking.

Pumpkin preserves
By Jackie Clay

4 lbs. pumpkin
2 lemons
sugar

½ tsp. each, cloves, cinnamon, nutmeg
pinch salt

Mash the pumpkin and lemon meat in preserving kettle. For every 1 cup pumpkin, add ¾ cup sugar and a pinch of salt. Add the spices. Mix and let stand overnight, refrigerated. In the morning, boil slowly, stirring well. Pour the mixture into sterilized ½-pint jars to within ½ inch of the top. Put on a cap, screw the band firmly tight, and process 5 minutes in a boiling water bath.

Elderberry jelly
By Charles A. Sanders

1 lb. elderberries
½ cup water

1 lb. sugar
juice of 2 lemons

Crush the berries and add the water, heat and simmer. Strain the resulting juice and put back on heat. Add the lemon juice and slowly stir in the sugar. Boil the mixture for 30-45 minutes, stirring to keep it from scorching.

When the jelly sets when tested, remove from heat, pour into jars, and seal.

NOTE: The jelly test is performed as follows: dip a spoon into the jelly mixture. Move the spoon away from the steam and the heat. Tip the spoon on its side. If the jelly clings together and sort of slides off the spoon in one glob, the jelly is ready.

Corn cob jelly
By Charles A. Sanders

12-14 red corn cobs
6 cups sugar
2 pkg. Sure-Jell

Start by gathering a few dozen red corn cobs. Most field corn varieties have red cobs. I'm not sure if the red cobs do anything for the flavor, but they do add the nice red color to the finished jelly.

Take a dozen or so of the cobs and break them into thirds. Put the pieces into a large pot and cover with water. It should take about 9-10 cups of water. Cover the pot and boil for 30 minutes. While the cobs are cooking, get your jars and lids ready. After that time, drain and strain the liquid through a cloth, such as a clean old tee shirt. Take 6 cups of the liquid and put back on the heat. Bring to a boil and add 2 pkg. of Sure-Jell. Next, gradually add 6 cups of sugar. Return the pot to a boil, stirring to prevent sticking or scorching. Boil for 3 minutes. Remove from heat and ladle into the clean and ready jars. Snugly apply the lids, cover the filled jars with a towel and allow them to self-seal. Makes about 5 pints.

Crabapple jelly
By Charles A. Sanders

3 lbs. crabapples (about 10
  cups, cut up)
4 cups water

2 cups sugar
2 Tbsp. lemon juice
1 pkg. Sure-Jell

Add cut-up crabapples and water to a pot and bring to a boil. Simmer, covered, until fruit is soft. Put fruit in a jelly bag or similar cloth bag and allow to drain until you have about 4 cups of juice. Put the juice back on the heat and bring to a boil. Add Sure-Jell and mix well. Slowly stir in sugar. Allow to boil for about 15 minutes, stirring constantly to prevent scorching. Remove mixture from heat and pour into jars. Attach lids and allow to seal. Makes about 3 pints.

Pear honey
By Charles A. Sanders

4 cups pears (peeled, sliced,
  and cored)
½ cup water
4 tsp. sugar

2 tsp. lemon juice
1 cinnamon stick
12 cloves

Mix the pears and water and puree in a food processor or blender. Add the sugar, lemon juice, cinnamon, and cloves. Heat and simmer until thickened as desired. Stir occasionally. Pour the mixture into hot jars and apply the 2-piece lids. Cover the jars with a towel and they should self-seal.

Ginger quince jam
By Jackie Clay

4 lbs. quinces
8 cups sugar

¼ lb. crystallized ginger root
2 lemons

Wash, pare, and core quinces. Chop in fine pieces, cook in moderate amount of boiling water until tender. Add sugar, chopped ginger, and the juice and grated rind of the lemons. Cook until thick, stiring constantly. Pour into sterilized canning jars to within ½ inch of the top. Wipe the rims, put on hot, previously-boiled lids, and screw the rings down firmly. Process in boiling water bath for 10 minutes. Yield: 6 half pints.

Quince preserves
By Jackie Clay

3 cups sugar
2 qts. water

7 cups pared, cored, quartered quinces

When preparing quinces, discard all gritty parts. Combine sugar and water in large kettle. Simmer 5 minutes. Add quinces and cook until transparent and the syrup is almost jellying, about 1 hour. Stir regularly to prevent scorching. Pour hot into hot, sterilized jars, leaving ½ inch of head space. Wipe the rims, put on hot, previously-boiled lids, and screw the rings down firmly. Process in boiling water bath for 10 minutes. Yield: 6 half pints.

Pear preserves
By Alice Brantley Yeager

8 cups pears, thinly sliced
1 or 2 small lemons, sliced
   (seeds removed)
6 cups sugar

Wash, pare, and core pears. Combine all items in a large bowl and chill about 4-5 hours. This will allow juice to form.

Put mixture and juice in a large heavy saucepan (not aluminum) and bring to a boil, stirring frequently. Reduce heat and simmer 50-60 minutes or until pears are translucent and syrup is slightly thickened. Stir often to avoid sticking. If any foam develops on top, remove with a thin metal spoon.

Ladle hot pears and syrup into hot, sterilized jars, leaving about a ½-inch space between preserves and top. Seal with sterilized caps and rings. Set aside in a draft-free place to cool and cover with a kitchen towel. (Never set hot jars on a cold surface.) When they are cool, lids should be sunken and not puffed. If any jars fail to seal, either refrigerate them or reheat the contents and try again.

Blueberry jam
By Charles A. Sanders

4 cups crushed blueberries
2 Tbsp. lemon juice

1 pkg. Sure-Jell pectin or
  equivalent
4 cups sugar

Have jelly jars ready in hot water. Add berries and lemon juice to a saucepan. Add pectin and bring mixture to a full boil over high heat, stirring it constantly. Add sugar and return to a full boil for 1 minute. Keep stirring the whole time. Remove mixture from heat and skim any foam which has formed, if necessary. Take jars from the hot water, 1 at a time and ladle hot jam into the hot jars. Leave about ¼-inch headspace. Wipe the jar rims and threads and apply the lids-fingertip tight. As each jar is filled, place it in the canner of hot water. Once the canner is full, add hot water as needed to cover the lids a couple of inches. Put the lid on the canner and bring to a gentle boil for 10 minutes. (You may need to adjust the time for altitude, adding 5 minutes for every 3,000 feet elevation.) After processing, remove jars and place on a towel to cool. They should each seal themselves shortly. After each jar has sealed and cooled, remove the bands, wipe the jars clean, and store.

Apple butter
By Anne Westbrook Dominick

5 lbs. apples, stems removed
  and quartered
2 cups cider or cider vinegar
brown sugar

2 tsp. cinnamon
½ tsp. allspice
½ tsp. ground cloves
½ tsp. nutmeg

Put apples and cider or cider vinegar in pan and cook slowly until apples are soft. Put apples through food mill or sieve. Measure the pulp and add ½-⅔ cup sugar, depending on taste, for each cup. Add spices and cook over low heat, stirring constantly until the mixture sheets from a spoon or until a small quantity dropped on a plate does not form a liquid rim around the edge. Ladle into hot sterilized jars and seal immediately. Makes about 3 pints.

Western blackberry jam
By Richard Blunt

9 cups mature, barely ripe
  blackberries (13 cups if
  making seedless jam)
4 cups sugar

Sort and wash berries; remove stems and caps. Layer berries in a large stainless steel bowl with sugar, cover and allow to rest in the refrigerator for at least 8 hours.

Transfer berries to sauce pan and bring to a simmer over medium heat and cook until berries are soft, about 20 minutes.

If you are making seedless jam, strain the berry mixture through a fine sieve.

Continue cooking over medium heat until the jell stage is reached.

Ladle hot jam into prepared jars, apply lids, and process in hot water bath canner for 10 minutes.

Blackberry jelly
By Bill Palmroth

6 cups blackberry juice
1½ cups liquid pectin

3 Tbsp. lemon juice
12 cups brown or raw sugar

To obtain juice, wash berries and crush. Place in a jelly bag; squeeze out juice. Mix berry juice, lemon juice, and sugar in a large saucepan. Bring to a boil as quickly as possible and add pectin at once, stirring constantly. Bring to full rolling boil and boil hard exactly ½ minute. Remove from heat; skim and pour into hot sterilized jars. Seal at once.

Quick and easy blueberry jam
By Jan Cook

1 cup tart berries (blueberries, blackberries, rasber-
ries, etc.)

2/3 cup sugar
1 Tbsp. lemon juice
1 whole cinnamon stick

In a pan combine the berries, sugar, lemon juice, and cinnamon
stick. Over a brisk fire, boil fruit mixture, stirring until it reaches
desired thickness. Serve warm or cooled over biscuits, pancakes, or
toast.

Blueberry wine jam
By Jan Cook

1 pkg. (10 oz.) frozen blueberries, unsweetened
4 cups sugar
2 cups berry wine

2 Tbsp. frozen orange juice
concentrate
1 bottle (6 oz.) liquid pectin

Assemble canning jars, lids, and ring bands. Choose jars that are
free of nicks or cracks. Discard rusted or bent ring bands. Always
use new lids. Sterilize jars by placing them in boiling water bath for
15 minutes and keep hot. Scald lids and ring bands. Keep lids in
very hot water until ready to use.

Mash thawed blueberries. Mix with sugar, wine, and orange juice
concentrate. Cook over high heat, stirring to dissolve sugar. Bring to
a boil and let boil very hard for 1 minute, stirring constantly. Remove
from heat and pour in pectin. Stir and skim for 6 minutes.

Pour into hot jars, spoon off any foam, and add more fruit to within
1/8 inch of top. Wipe rims with a clean, damp cloth. Place lids on jars
and screw on ring bands hand tight. Let cool on a towel out of
drafts. Press lids with your finger. If they stay down, they're sealed.

Berry good syrup
By Bill Palmroth

4 cups blackberry juice
2 cups granulated sugar
1-2 cups light corn syrup

1 Tbsp. lemon juice (optional)

To extract juice, mash a small amount of fruit, using a food mill, juicer or food processor, then sieve to remove seeds if desired. (Some people prefer not to mash all the fruit, but leave some whole.)

Place juice, sugar, and corn syrup in a saucepan. Boil for 3-5 minutes. Place in a boiling water bath and process for 10 minutes (from when water returns to a boil) to ensure a seal. The yield is about 3½ pints.

Blueberry syrup
By Charles A. Sanders

2 cups blueberries
½ cup sugar

½ cup water
1 thin slice of lemon

Simmer for about 10-15 minutes. Makes about 2½ cups.

Main dishes

Homemade pizza
By Jackie Clay

3 cups flour
2 Tbsp. olive oil
1 Tbsp. mixed spices (oregano, basil, onion flakes)
1½ cups warm water
1 Tbsp. dry yeast
cornmeal
¾ of 1 pint homemade tomato sauce

½ tsp. oregano
½ tsp. basil
1 Tbsp. brown sugar
toppings such as pepperoni, olives, mushroom, onion, etc.
sundried tomatoes, optional
¾ lb. mozzarella cheese, grated

Mix spices into flour and add olive oil. In a separate bowl, sprinkle yeast onto warm water. Let rest for 5-10 minutes. Add water to flour mixture. The dough should be soft, not sticky. Depending on the humidity of the day you can adjust the flour and water. Put dough in bowl and let rise until double. Add a handful of cornmeal to the dough, working in gently until dough is coated with cornmeal.

Grease pizza pan liberally with olive oil and grease your hands too. Spread out dough on pan. Bake dough by itself in oven at 350° for about 10 minutes. Dough should not get too brown. Take out of oven.

Mix ½ tsp. oregano and ½ tsp. basil with tomato sauce. Spoon sauce over dough. Sprinkle with 1 Tbsp. brown sugar. Layer with desired toppings. I like to add sundried tomatoes. Top with mozzarella cheese. Bake at 350° until cheese is golden brown. Let stand 5 minutes. Makes 1 large pizza.

Main dishes

Tamale pie
By Jackie Clay

½ cup cornmeal
½ cup white flour or freshly
  ground whole wheat flour
¼ cup honey or white sugar
¼ cup shortening
1 egg (equivalent in dry egg
  powder, rehydrated)
1 cup rehydrated dry milk,
  approximately
2 tsp. baking powder

1 tsp. salt
½ cup cooked hamburger
2 cups tomato sauce
½ cup dry chopped onions
¼ cup dry chopped green
  peppers or chili peppers
2 tsp. mild chili powder
¼ cup dry sweet corn or ½
  cup canned corn

Mix first 8 ingredients well, making a medium batter (not runny or not stiff). Then in medium-sized cast iron frying pan or 8 x 8 cake pan, mix the last 6 ingredients well, then top with cornmeal batter. Bake at 350° until top turns golden brown. Serve hot with cold salsa.

Roast beef hash
By Jackie Clay

1 pint (16 oz.) canned roast
  beef (or wild meat)
½ cup rehydrated onion
  flakes

1 qt. (32 oz.) canned potatoes, drained well
oil to fry
favorite seasonings

Grind meat, potatoes, and onion together with hand meat grinder. Heat oil to medium heat in large frying pan. Slide hash into pan, being careful not to spatter. Arrange the hash in a shallow layer, covering the bottom of the frying pan. Allow to cook, turning and stirring with spatula. Add seasonings, finish frying to preference, and serve. Popular condiments include salsa and ketchup. Hash makes a satisfying 1-dish meal. Leftovers are great for breakfast with scrambled eggs.

Charbroiled venison steaks
By Richard Blunt

3 steaks, cut to ¾-inch thickness (about 2 lbs. of meat)
1 large clove garlic
1 Tbsp. Dijon mustard
½ tsp. black pepper, freshly
ground

½ tsp. thyme leaves
¼ cup butter
2 tsp. soy sauce
¼ tsp. savory leaves
3 Tbsp. currant jelly, optional

Place butter in pan over low heat to melt. Squeeze garlic through a garlic press into melting butter and add remaining ingredients. Stir and remove from heat immediately. Do not cook.

Brush steaks with sauce and allow them to sit for ½ hour.

Broil over hot coals until cooked the way you like them, rare or medium.

Option: After brushing some sauce on the steaks, return the remaining sauce to a low heat and add 3 Tbsp. currant jelly. Stir this until the jelly melts. Just before the steaks are removed from the grill, brush this sauce on both sides, serve immediately.

Louisiana gumbo

By Alice Brantley Yeager

1 large dressed frying chicken, including giblets & neck
1½ cups flour for dredging
½ tsp. black pepper
1½ lb. okra, cut crosswise in ¼-inch rounds
2 large tomatoes, chopped
2 medium bell peppers, chopped

1 large onion
1 large garlic clove, minced
3 Tbsp. flour, unbleached
3 qts. hot (not boiling) water
3 large bay leaves
1 lb. fresh shrimp, peeled and deveined
1 pint raw oysters and juice
1 Tbsp. filé
hot rice

Dredge chicken with flour and pepper. In iron skillet fry until brown in enough good grade cooking oil to keep from sticking. Remove from skillet and set aside in large pot equipped with lid. Reserve chicken oil to be used as needed in rest of cooking.

Combine okra, tomatoes, bell pepper, onion, and garlic and fry in just enough chicken oil to prevent sticking. When almost done, put in pot with chicken.

Make a roux (a base for gravy) by combining 5 Tbsp. of reserved chicken oil with 3 Tbsp. flour in a large iron skillet. Stir constantly over medium heat until roux turns dark brown. Be careful not to burn it! Gradually stir water into roux a little at a time. Add pepper and bay leaves and simmer about 5 minutes, stirring when necessary to prevent sticking. Pour over chicken and vegetable mixture, bring to a boil and simmer about 30 minutes.

Add shrimp and oysters to simmering mixture in pot and continue to cook about 15 minutes. Add filé after gumbo has been removed from fire and has ceased to bubble. Do not boil after filé has been added as gumbo will have a tendency to be stringy. Many cooks put a bottle of filé on the table and let guests add their own. (In case you are not familiar with filé, it is made from dried sassafras leaves and is usually available in fish markets or wherever gourmet supplies are sold. A small bottle will last a long time.)

Serve gumbo over hot rice in large flat-type soup bowls. Prepare rice while gumbo is cooking and use either long-cooking unpolished rice or brown rice for good flavor. Be sure to have enough rice ready as folks are almost sure to ask for seconds.

This recipe will serve 6-8.

Española eggs
By Jackie Clay

shortening to fry
1 medium onion, sliced
8 Anaheim, Big Jim, or
  Relleno peppers, green
  roasted
If you want fire for breakfast
  use one chiltipine or habañero, diced

3 eggs
½ cup cheddar cheese, grated
dash salt & black pepper

Sauté the sliced onion, diced hot pepper, and green roasted chili in large frying pan.

When chile is browning on both sides and the onion is transparent, add the eggs, mixed thoroughly, holding the eggs around the peppers. Let eggs cook until you can gently turn over, dividing the batch, as needed to turn over. When all have been turned sprinkle the top with grated cheese and finish cooking.

When done, serve with warm flour tortillas for a great breakfast. I like mine with a dollop of salsa and sour cream.

Quiche Lorraine
By Katherine Dazazel

9-inch piecrust
several thin slices Swiss
  cheese
6 pieces cooked bacon,
  crumbled

1 cup shredded cheddar
  cheese
6 eggs
1¼ cups milk or cream
salt and pepper to taste
1 carrot, shredded

Line bottom of pie crust with Swiss cheese slices. Sprinkle on crumbled bacon and 1/3 of the shredded cheese.

In a bowl, mix milk and eggs together very well and add salt and pepper. Shred carrot over the bowl and mix it in along with another third of the shredded cheese. Pour this mixture carefully into pie dish and top with rest of cheese. Bake at 375° for 40-45 minutes, or until it is set firm.

(The Jiggle Test: Put your finger near the center of the quiche and try to jiggle it. If it doesn't move, it's done.) Let sit 5-10 minutes before serving.

Chilies rellenos

By Jackie Clay

8 large Big Jim, Poblano, or Relleno chilis, green and roasted
1 16-oz. can tomatoes
1 small onion, finely chopped
1 tsp. beef bouillon granules
dash of comino
dash of cinnamon

4 cups shredded cheddar cheese or Monterey jack
8 egg yolks
2 Tbsp. water
¼ cup flour
½ tsp. salt
8 egg whites
shortening for frying

Make tomato sauce from undrained tomatoes, onions, bouillon, comino, and cinnamon, heat thoroughly, then simmer while fixing peppers.

Remove seeds and veins from peppers, slitting each carefully on 1 side only, then stuff each with ½ cup of cheese. Set these aside on a plate.

Slightly beat egg yolks and water. Add flour and salt and beat until thick. Whip egg whites. (If you use the same whip or blades you used to beat the yolks, make sure you first clean them thoroughly because the whites will not get stiff if there is any yolk on them.) Fold whites into yolks.

In large cast iron skillet heat ½-inch of shortening until hot, but not smoking. For each serving, spoon about ⅓-cup of batter into hot fat, spreading it in a circle. Fry 3 or 4 at a time. As the batter begins to set, gently place a stuffed chile on top of each. Cover it with another ⅓-cup of batter. Continue cooking until the underside is browning... not dark. Turn carefully and brown other side. Drain on paper towels and keep warm in 300° oven until all are finished.

Serve with tomato sauce and enjoy the compliments.

Nanny B's benne bake
By Richard Blunt

1 2-lb. frying chicken, cut
into 8 pieces
Undercoating:
1 cup all purpose flour
½ tsp. salt
½ tsp. freshly ground black
pepper
Middlecoating:
¾ cup buttermilk

Overcoating:
12 oz. ground pecans
(ground with the coarse
blade of a meat grinder or
in a food processor)
²/₃ cup white benne (sesame) seeds
½ tsp. cayenne pepper
(ground)
¼ tsp. nutmeg (freshly
ground from whole seed if
possible)
½ tsp. salt

Wash chicken pieces in cold water and dry on paper towels.
Preheat oven to 375°.
Combine undercoat ingredients in brown paper bag and set aside.
Combine overcoat ingredients in a large bowl and mix.
Place middlecoating (buttermilk) in another large bowl.
Oil a roasting or baking pan that is large enough to hold all the
chicken. Place all of the chicken in the bag with the undercoating
and shake until the chicken pieces are evenly coated with the flour
mixture. Remove chicken pieces from bag and shake off any excess
flour.
Place chicken pieces into buttermilk and gently toss to coat each
piece with milk.
Roll each piece of chicken in the overcoating until evenly coated
and place on oiled pan.
Bake on middle shelf of oven until coating is a medium brown and
chicken is cooked through (about 40 minutes).

Main dishes

Barbecued jerked pork roast
By Richard Blunt

Ingredients:
1 4-5 lb. bone-in loin of pork
Paste ingredients:
2 Tbsp. toasted allspice berries
3 tsp. toasted whole black peppercorns
1 cinnamon stick, broken into small pieces and toasted
6 toasted whole cloves
1½ tsp. kosher salt
½ nutmeg berry, grated
2 cups onion, diced medium
4 whole scallions, diced medium
2 cloves fresh garlic, peeled and chopped

1 tsp. malt vinegar
1 tsp. dark brown sugar
5 tsp. fresh thyme leaves
6 fresh habañero or Scotch bonnet chili peppers, stemmed and seeded
2 Tbsp. extra virgin olive oil
a little dry white wine to add moisture and some additional flavor during the pureeing process
Marinade:
½ cup light soy sauce
¼ cup fresh lime juice
1 cup apple juice or fresh apple cider if the season is right

Toast allspice berries, peppercorns, cinnamon stick, and whole cloves over medium heat in a heavy-bottomed pan. Cast iron works best. Be careful, this process can be tricky. For the first minute or two nothing will seem to be happening. Then suddenly the spices will give off a small amount of aromatic smoke and will start browning very rapidly. Stir spices constantly during this process, and remove from heat as soon as cinnamon starts to brown.

Set spices aside to cool, then grind to a fine powder in a spice mill, blender, or a coffee grinder that is reserved for this purpose.

Combine toasted and ground spices with salt and ground nutmeg and set mixture aside.

Combine onion, scallions, garlic, malt vinegar, brown sugar, fresh thyme and prepared chili peppers in a blender or food processor. Add olive oil then add about 2 Tbsp. of wine and process mixture into a coarse paste. Add a little more wine if the mixture seems to be too dry.

Add dry ingredients, and pulse machine a couple of times to mix.

Combine all ingredients for marinade and set aside.

The day before the barbecue, place the pork roast on a cutting board and punch holes, about ½-inch deep and about 1 inch apart, into the roast with a sharp knife. Rub the paste all over roast. Using your fingers push as much of the paste as possible into the holes.

Place the roast in a nonreactive bowl or large plastic bag you can seal, add the marinade, cover and marinate the roast overnight in the refrigerator.

Remove roast from refrigerator and let stand at room temperature for 1 hour. While roast is standing, prepare covered grill for cooking. At the same time put 4 hardwood chunks in warm water to soak.

Fire up about 60 charcoal briquets. When coals are covered with a white ash, divide them into 2 equal piles and push piles to opposite sides of the fire grate, and drop 2 of the soaking hardwood chunks on each pile. Place a disposable aluminum pan, half-filled with water, in the middle of the fire grate. This is your drip pan.

Position roast directly over drip pan, put lid in place, then check to make sure that top and bottom vents are completely open.

Figure on 30 minutes roasting time per lb. of meat. The roast is done when meat thermometer reads 170° at the thickest part of the roast.

Main dishes

Italian meatballs

By Jean Louis L'Heureux

Meatballs:
⅔ cup fresh breadcrumbs
3 Tbsp. milk
1 large egg
1 garlic clove, minced
⅓ cup grated Parmesan
  cheese
¼ tsp. ground black pepper
¼ cup finely chopped onion
2 Tbsp. dried currants
1 lb. sweet Italian sausages,
  casings removed

3 Tbsp. chopped fresh basil
2 Tbsp. pine nuts, toasted
Sauce:
2 Tbsp. extra virgin olive oil
1½ cups chopped onion
2 garlic cloves, minced
4 Tbsp. chopped fresh basil
2 28-oz. cans diced Italian
  tomatoes or regular tomatoes

Meatballs: Preheat oven to 350°. Lightly oil baking sheet. Mix crumbs and milk in mixing bowl and let stand for a few minutes. Mix in Parmesan, onion, basil, egg, garlic, pepper, sausage, pine nuts, and currants. Blend well. Wet hands and form mixture into 1-inch balls. Place on sheet and bake until light brown and cooked through—approximately 30 minutes.

Sauce: Heat oil in heavy pot over medium-low heat. Add onion and sauté for approximately 8 minutes, until golden. Add garlic and sauté 1 minute more. Add the tomatoes with juices and 2 Tbsp. basil and bring to a boil. Reduce heat and simmer until thick, breaking up tomatoes—approximately 1 hour. Mix in 2 Tbsp. basil and season to taste with salt and pepper. Mix sauce with meatballs.

Stuffed sweet peppers
By Alice Brantley Yeager

4 large sweet peppers
2 cups cooked rice
1 cup cooked ground beef
1 medium onion, chopped
1 small clove garlic, minced

1 medium carrot, diced
¼ tsp. dried sweet basil
¼ tsp. dried thyme
1/8 tsp. cayenne pepper
½ tsp. salt (optional)

Select peppers that are blocky in shape and will stand on end without tipping over. Wash the peppers and remove the stems and seeds. Make holes in their tops large enough for easy stuffing. (Any usable pepper pieces may be chopped in with rest of ingredients.)

Combine other items listed and stuff into the peppers. Place in a covered baking dish with a small amount of water and bake in 375° oven for about 45 minutes. Serve topped with your favorite hot gravy or tomato sauce. Serves 4.

Main dishes

Lamb and black bean tamale pie
By Richard Blunt

1½ lb. ground lamb
1 tsp. olive oil
2 cups onion, diced medium
1 large red bell pepper,
    diced medium
3 garlic cloves, diced fine
1 fresh jalapeño pepper,
    diced fine
2½ cups medium salsa
1/8 tsp. ground cumin
¼ tsp. dried oregano
¼ tsp. McCormick spicy
    Montreal steak seasoning
fresh ground black pepper,
    to taste

1 29-oz. can Goya black
    beans, rinsed and drained
1½ cups cornmeal
1½ cups all-purpose flour
3 tsp. baking powder
1 Tbsp. sugar
½ tsp. kosher salt
6 Tbsp. unsalted butter
1½ cups skim milk
2 large fresh eggs, lightly
    beaten
2 cups (8 oz.) shredded
    cheese
2 Tbsp. fresh cilantro,
    chopped

Heat 1 tsp. oil in a heavy-bottomed skillet or Dutch oven and sauté the ground lamb until it loses its pink color and is broken up into pea-sized pieces. Remove lamb and set aside in large bowl.

Over medium heat, sauté onions and red bell pepper until just tender. Add garlic and jalapeño pepper and sauté for 1 minute.

Reduce heat and add salsa and spices. Simmer for 5 minutes and add meat and beans. Gently stir mixture and remove from heat.

Preheat oven to 375°.

In large bowl, combine cornmeal, flour, baking powder, sugar, and salt. Using a pastry blender, 2 knives, or your clean fingers, work unsalted butter into dry ingredients until it forms fine particles.

Gently blend milk with lightly-beaten eggs and 1 cup of shredded cheese. (Save the 2nd cup for later.)

Combine wet ingredients with dry and stir with a wooden spoon until all ingredients are just incorporated.

Coat baking dish with oil or shortening and spread corn bread dough evenly in dish.

Spread tamale mixture evenly over corn bread dough, sprinkle remaining cup of cheese and chopped cilantro on top.

Bake in middle of oven for 30 minutes or until a knife stuck into middle of dough comes out dry.

Jamaican curried lamb
By Richard Blunt

3 lbs. lean lamb, diced in 1-inch cubes
6 Tbsp. peanut oil (use additional oil if needed)
2 Tbsp. peanut oil
3 cups onions, diced medium
1 large red sweet bell pepper, diced medium
3 Tbsp. Jamaican-style curry seasoning
½ tsp. freshly ground allspice
2 jalapeño peppers, diced fine
2 tsp. kosher salt
1 tsp. freshly ground black pepper
1 cup canned coconut milk
1 cup fresh chicken stock or low-salt canned chicken stock
1 bay leaf
2 Tbsp. lime juice
¼ tsp. Angostura bitters
2 Tbsp. dark rum

Preheat oven to 325°.

Pat diced lamb cubes dry with paper towels. (The reason for drying the meat first is that wet red meat will not brown properly.) In a heavy-bottomed skillet heat 2 Tbsp. oil over medium-high heat. Place 6 or 7 of the lamb cubes into hot oil and brown on all sides. When browned, remove lamb and set aside in a bowl. Repeat this process until all of the lamb is browned.

In the same skillet heat the other 2 Tbsp. oil, add onions and red pepper, then sauté over medium heat until onions become soft and translucent but not browned. Add curry seasoning, allspice, and chili peppers and continue to sauté for 1 minute.

Add salt, black pepper, coconut milk, chicken stock, bay leaf, and browned lamb to vegetable mixture in an oven casserole. Loosely cover casserole and place in oven for about 1 hour or until lamb is tender.

Remove cover from casserole, and gently stir in remaining ingredients. Return casserole to oven, uncovered, for an additional 15 minutes.

Main dishes

Chicken and rice
By Alice Brantley Yeager

1 cup uncooked rice (not quick-cooking)
1 tsp. salt
1/8 tsp. ground hot red pepper
1 tsp. dried sweet basil, or fresh leaves from 3 sprigs of sweet basil
1 tsp. dried lemon balm, or fresh leaves from 2 sprigs of lemon balm

1/2 cup celery, chopped
1/4 cup onion, chopped
1 medium-sized fryer, or small hen, cleaned and cut into pieces
1 garlic clove, thinly sliced
additional dried herbs, salt and black pepper (optional)
2 1/2 cups cold water

Place rice in bottom of a large casserole. Add next 6 ingredients. Lay chicken pieces on top of the rice and distribute garlic slices on the chicken or in the rice. Sprinkle a pinch of dried herbs, salt, and pepper over chicken for more flavor. Gently pour water into casserole so as not to disturb seasonings on chicken. Bake, covered, for an hour at 375°, or until rice has absorbed all water and chicken is tender. Serves 4 or 5.

Chicken cacciatore
By Sally Boulding

3 lbs. chicken fryers, cut up
2 Tbsp. oil
2 medium onions, diced
1 clove garlic, crushed
16-oz. can tomatoes
8-oz. can tomato sauce

1 tsp. salt
1/2 tsp. oregano
1/2 tsp. basil
1/2 tsp. celery seed
2 bay leaves
1/4 cup white wine

Brown chicken in oil. Remove. Cook onions in same pot. Add garlic, tomatoes, tomato sauce, salt, and spices. Mix well. Simmer 3 minutes. Return chicken to pot. Spoon sauce over chicken. Cover. Simmer 30 minutes. Add wine. Cook uncovered another 30 minutes. Turn and baste chicken occasionally. Remove bay leaves. Serve with spaghetti or over rice using sauce from the chicken.

Turkey with wild rice stuffing

By Jackie Clay

1 whole wild turkey, cleaned
2 cups cooked wild rice
1 medium onion, chopped
2 medium carrots, grated
chopped giblets or ½ cup
  chopped canned chicken
  breast
1 tsp. dehydrated garlic

1 tsp. coarsely ground pepper
1 tsp. salt
butter for rubbing
1 cup water
2 Tbsp. sweet chili sauce
1 red bell pepper, diced
½ cup sliced water chestnuts
1 cup wild plum jam

In a large mixing bowl, mix wild rice, onion, pepper, carrots, chopped giblets, water chestnuts, and dry spices to make a stuffing. Rub inside of turkey with butter, then stuff with the stuffing mix.

Truss the bird and place in a covered roasting pan with 1 cup of water. Cover and steam until about done.

In a small mixing bowl, mix sweet chili sauce with wild plum jam. With a basting brush, coat the entire turkey. Return to oven, uncovered. Every 20 minutes, bring turkey out and brush with basting sauce. It will develop a beautiful glaze, slightly spicy and sweet.

Grouse fajitas
By Jackie Clay

1 grouse (or other bird)
1 cup Italian dressing
1 Tbsp. cooking oil
1 medium onion, chopped
1 bell pepper, sliced finely
1 seeded jalapeño pepper,
 chopped

6 flour tortillas (gorditas)
1 cup shredded head lettuce
1 tomato, diced
1 cup shredded cheddar
 cheese

Cut grouse into large pieces and marinate in dressing overnight, covered or in plastic bag. The next day place marinated pieces into roasting pan (or pressure cooker if you suspect the bird is old and tough). Cook covered until done and tender. Cool. Remove meat from bones and chop into medium pieces. Heat a frying pan, add cooking oil, and briefly fry meat with chopped onion and both kinds of peppers until vegetables are done but firm.

Immediately heat the tortillas, 1 at a time, on a griddle, then wrap the meat/vegetable mix with some lettuce, tomato, and grated cheese. You can also dress with any of your favorite spicy salad dressings.

Basil chicken
By Kristen Rogers

4 Tbsp. olive oil
3 lbs. chicken, cut up

salt and pepper
¼ cup basil vinegar

Rub the chicken with salt and pepper. Heat olive oil, then brown chicken. Place chicken in a shallow baking dish, pour vinegar over it and bake at 350° for 35-40 minutes, basting 3-4 times with more basil vinegar.

Pheasant and dumplings
By Jackie Clay

1 pheasant (or equivalent
  other bird)
2 Tbsp. butter
2 Tbsp. flour
2 cups broth from cooking
½ pint sliced canned carrots
1 small onion, sliced
½ pint canned mushrooms
½ cup dehydrated peas,
  rehydrated

½ pint canned celery
½ tsp. black pepper
½ tsp. salt
Dumplings:
2 cups flour
1 tsp. salt
2 tsp. baking powder
2 Tbsp. shortening
milk

Cook, cool, and debone pheasant. Chop meat into large pieces. In a deep cast iron frying pan, melt butter, stirring in flour to make roux. Slowly add broth and stir until thickened to medium consistency. Add more broth if necessary. Mix in vegetables and seasonings.

For dumplings, combine flour, salt, and baking powder in a medium mixing bowl. Cut in shortening until it is the size of peas. Mix in enough milk to make a slightly sticky dough. Spoon on top, in individual dumplings.

Cover and bake at 300° for 20 minutes. Do not cheat and peek or your dumplings will not be light and fluffy.

Hoppin' John with fresh asparagus beans
By Alice Brantley Yeager

1 cup uncooked rice (not
   instant)
1 lb. pork sausage broken
   into small pieces
3½ cups water
1 lb. asparagus beans,
   rinsed and snapped

1 medium onion, chopped
1 green bell pepper,
   chopped
⅛ tsp. cayenne pepper
1 tsp. salt
1 tsp. dried sweet basil

Cook rice according to directions on package. (Directions will vary with different types of rice.)

While rice is cooking, sauté sausage to a light brown in a large iron skillet. Drain off most of grease, but leave a bit for flavor. Add the rest of the ingredients and simmer, covered, for 30-40 minutes or until asparagus beans are tender.

Combine sausage mixture with cooked rice and serve hot. A dash of Tabasco (hot) sauce is in order for those who enjoy the Cajun touch.

Served with a salad and drink, this recipe should serve 4-5 people.

Zucchini-turkey burgers
By Sandra L. Toney

1 lb. ground turkey
1 cup natural rolled oats
⅔ cup chopped onion
½ cup shredded zucchini (if
   frozen, thaw completely;
   discard the excess liquid)

¼ cup ketchup
3 Tbsp. Worcestershire
   sauce
1½ tsp. garlic powder
¼ tsp. pepper

Combine all the ingredients in a large bowl. Shape the mixture into 6 patties. Grill (or broil) the burgers until they are cooked.

Algerian honeyed lamb kebabs
By Richard Blunt

meat:
2 lbs. boned lamb leg cut
   into 1-inch cubes
marinade:
3 cloves peeled fresh garlic
2 Tbsp. fresh ginger (peeled
   and chopped)
1 tsp. grated lemon peel
1/3 cup fresh lemon juice (the
   juice from about 3 medium
   lemons)
¼ cup chopped fresh cilantro
   leaves

¼ cup honey
2 Tbsp. anise seeds (toasted
   in a 350° oven and
   crushed)
½ tsp. cayenne pepper
½ tsp. saffron powder
¼ cup finely diced onion
½ cup extra virgin olive oil
¼ cup peanut oil
½ tsp. freshly ground black
   pepper

Finely chop garlic and ginger with food processor or blender.
Finely grate 1 tsp. lemon peel.

Combine garlic, ginger, and lemon peel with remaining ingredients
to complete marinade. Mix well.

Combine diced lamb with marinade in a stainless steel or glass
bowl and marinate overnight in refrigerator.

Preheat grill, broiler, or barbecue. Remove meat-marinade mixture
from refrigerator and bring to room temperature. Skewer meat onto
flat-bladed or twisted skewers and place at least 5 inches from the
heat. Grill meat on 1 side for a few minutes then turn over and baste
with marinade. Continue to cook and coat with marinade until meat
is cooked to your liking. Serve with lemon wedges and fresh mint as
a garnish.

Barbecued spareribs
By Richard Blunt

1 slab of pork ribs, between
   2-3 lbs.
Marinade:
2 cloves fresh garlic, minced
1 tsp. fresh ginger, peeled
   and minced
¼ tsp. five spice powder

2 Tbsp. dry sherry
3 Tbsp. dark soy sauce
2 tsp. plum sauce
1 tsp. red curry paste
   (optional)
⅛ tsp. Tabasco sauce
2 Tbsp. honey

Mix together all marinade ingredients.

Brush meat on both sides with marinade. Combine whole slabs with marinade in large pan. Cover and set in refrigerator to marinate overnight.

Next day: Preheat oven to 375°. Pour 2 cups water into roasting pan.

Remove meat from marinade, place on a rack and set rack into roasting pan. Do not allow ribs to touch the water.

Place pan in oven. After 30 minutes, brush both sides of ribs with marinade and turn over.

After 1 hour remove ribs from oven and turn up to 450°. Pour off water from roasting pan, brush ribs on both sides with remaining marinade and return pan to oven.

In about 10 minutes turn the ribs. After another 20 minutes remove the ribs from the oven. Cut into individual ribs and serve.

Roast leg of venison with lingonberry sauce
By Edith Helmich

1 6-8 lb. leg of venison
1 tsp. salt
½ tsp. ground ginger
½ tsp. ground pepper
½ cup beef stock
½ cup melted butter

Lingonberry sauce:
1 8-10 oz. can of lingonber-
   ries with juice
pan drippings (fat skimmed
   off) plus enough water to
   make 1 cup
6-7 Tbsp. sugar
3 Tbsp. cornstarch, dissolved
   in ½ cup cold water
1 Tbsp. butter

Combine dry seasonings and rub meat. Place roast on rack in a roasting pan and cover with lid or foil. Roast in a 325° oven for approximately 3 hours, or until meat tests tender when pierced with a fork. Baste frequently with butter-and-water mixture while cooking.

Remove roast from pan to serving plate and cover with foil. Save pan drippings and liquid. While the roast sets its juices, make the sauce.

Combine all ingredients in saucepan and bring to boil over medium heat, stirring constantly. Pour a small amount of sauce over the roast before carving, and serve the remaining sauce at the table.

Spaghetti chicken
By Pat Ward

8 chicken legs, separated into thighs and drumsticks
olive oil for frying
garlic powder to taste
1 large (32 oz.) jar spaghetti sauce with mushrooms

2-3 small cans mushroom stems and pieces, drained
salt and pepper to taste
2 lbs. angel hair spaghetti
freshly grated Parmesan cheese

Fry chicken in olive oil until just browned on outside. Drain off all excess fat and sprinkle garlic powder onto chicken pieces. Pour spaghetti sauce over chicken and simmer for ½ hour. Pour mushroom pieces on top.

In a separate pot, cook angel hair spaghetti according to package directions. Drain. Pour spaghetti onto a large platter, arrange chicken on top, then pour sauce over it. Sprinkle a line of freshly grated Parmesan cheese in a row down the middle.

Braised venison pepper steak
By William Shepherd

1½ lbs. venison steak shoulder or round steak
2 Tbsp. cooking oil
1 4-oz. can mushrooms
1 cup water
1 beef bouillon cube
2 Tbsp. soy sauce

1 Tbsp. sugar
¼ tsp. garlic salt
¼ tsp. pepper
1 green pepper, cut in strips
1½ Tbsp. flour
¼ cup water

Venison is naturally lean, so tenderizing is necessary. One of the best methods is marinating with milk, wine, and citrus juices. Overnight marinades tenderize and leave a very distinctive taste that will flatter the venison's flavor.

Marinate meat overnight, remove from refrigerator. Cut into ¼-inch thick strips and brown meat in cooking oil. Add mushrooms, 1 cup water, bouillon cube, soy sauce, sugar, garlic salt, and pepper. Cover and cook 5 minutes. Add green pepper strips, cover and cook an additional 3 minutes. Mix flour and ¼ cup water, add to skillet and stir until thickened. Serve over noodles or rice. Serves 4.

Crown roast of venison
By William Shepherd

1 venison roast, about 4 lbs.
½ tsp. garlic salt
⅛ tsp. pepper
½ lb. bulk pork sausage
20-oz. can apple slices with
   juice
⅓ cup apple cider

10 slices bread, dried and
   cut into ½ inch cubes
2 Tbsp. raisins
¾ tsp. cinnamon
½ tsp. cardamom
¼ tsp. allspice

Mix garlic salt and pepper together, rub mixture into all sides of the roast. Place roast in covered roasting pan. Cook sausage in skillet until brown, drain excess grease. Combine next 8 ingredients with sausage, stirring enough to moisten bread. Pour this mixture over roast; cover with lid. Insert meat thermometer into center of roast. Bake at 325° for 2-3 hours or until meat thermometer reads 135° to 140°. Time will vary. Garnish with cranberry sauce.

Venison pan-fried steak
By William Shepherd

4 steaks, sirloin or rib,
   ¼-inch thick
3 Tbsp. butter or margarine
4 medium onions, sliced thin
4 green peppers, sliced thin

2 Tbsp. Parmesan cheese
1 cup mozzarella cheese,
   grated
½ tsp. garlic
¼ tsp. black pepper

Place butter or margarine in a large heavy skillet, turn heat to medium. Add onions and green peppers, sauté until tender. While onion mixture is cooking, combine remaining ingredients in small bowl. Remove cooked onion mixture from skillet; set aside. Add steaks to skillet. Fry 1 minute on each side, then turn heat to medium low. Spread onion and cheese mixture evenly over steaks. Cover and cook until cheese is melted. Serve hot on fresh bread.

Fried finger steaks
By William Shepherd

1 lb. 1½-inch boneless venison steaks cut from the
round sirloin or backstrap
1 tsp. lemon-pepper seasoning
½ tsp. salt

½ cup buttermilk
1 egg
1 cup all-purpose flour
¾ cup vegetable oil or shortening

Marinate meat overnight in lemon juice. Remove from refrigerator and sprinkle with lemon-pepper seasoning and salt. Cut into strips. Mix buttermilk and egg in small bowl. Dip strips in mixture and dredge in flour. Preheat iron skillet, add vegetable oil or shortening and brown steaks on both sides. Serves 3-4.

Broiled tenderloin
By William Shepherd

2 venison tenderloins, about
1¼ lb. each
1¼ tsp. garlic salt
½ tsp. pepper

2 Tbsp. soy sauce
1 Tbsp. ketchup
1 Tbsp. vegetable oil
¼ tsp. crushed oregano

Mix all ingredients except tenderloins in large container. Add meat, cover and marinate 4 hours in refrigerator. Remove tenderloins from marinade. Briefly sear both sides over hot coals or under broiler. Continue broiling until desired doneness is obtained. Remove from heat, slice thinly and serve while hot. Serves 4-6.

Pan-broiled chops
By William Shepherd

6 venison rib chops
2 Tbsp. bacon fat
3 medium onions, sliced
1½ lbs. fresh mushrooms,
    sliced

⅓ cup all-purpose flour
1 cup beef stock
1 cup milk
½ tsp. salt
¼ tsp. pepper

Lightly brown chops on both sides in bacon fat, using iron skillet over moderately high heat. Transfer chops to shallow pan; retain drippings in skillet. Broil chops at high heat 5 inches below heating element. Turn and broil till medium-rare. In the drippings in skillet, gently cook onions and mushrooms until lightly browned. Blend flour, stock, milk, salt, and pepper. Add to pan. Cook, stirring constantly until thickened and bubbly, about 4 minutes. Serve onion and mushroom sauce over chops while both are hot.

Mexican chicken
By Darlene Campbell

1 large pkg. tortilla chips,
    crushed
2 chickens, de-boned
1 can cream of mushroom
    soup
1 can cream of chicken soup

1 cup chicken broth
1 can Ro*Tel tomatoes
1 lb. cheddar cheese, thinly
    sliced
1 onion, chopped

Boil and de-bone the chicken. Combine soups, Ro*Tel tomatoes and broth. Place chopped onion in a pan and follow with layers of chicken, ½ the cheese, ⅔ pkg. tortilla chips, soup mixture, remaining cheese; top with tortilla chips. Bake in 300° oven for 25 minutes.

Main dishes

Scrapple
By Richard Blunt

1¼ lb. good quality sausage
  meat
1 lb. ground smoked ham
  (ground cooked veal,
  chicken, or turkey can be
  used in place of smoked
  ham)
1⅓ cups yellow cornmeal
4⅔ cups rich soup stock
  (beef or chicken)

1 tsp. salt (more or less
  according to taste)
freshly ground black pepper
  to taste
2 Tbsp. finely chopped onion
⅛ tsp. dried red pepper
  flakes
3 medium eggs

Break sausage meat into small pieces and sauté in a large frying pan, over medium heat, until it loses its pink color. Continue to break it up as it cooks. Remove pan from heat and add ham, salt, black pepper, onion, and red pepper flakes.

Pour stock into a sauce pan and place over medium heat. Slowly sprinkle cornmeal into stock as it heats, stirring all the while with a wire whisk. Continue stirring until mixture thickens and there are no lumps. Then cook 5 more minutes while stirring constantly. Cover saucepan and place in a larger pan of simmering water and continue to cook this way for another 40 minutes. During the last 5 minutes, remove cover and stir cornmeal with a wooden spoon until it holds its shape on the spoon.

Combine cooked cornmeal with meat mixture in large pan over low heat and continue stirring with wooden spoon until thoroughly mixed. Remove pan from heat and allow to cool. Lightly beat eggs and add them to mixture, 1 at a time, stirring them in with the spoon.

Grease a loaf pan and a piece of aluminum foil large enough to cover it. Pack scrapple into pan. Bang pan on counter to remove air pockets. Cover with aluminum foil. Place pan in pre-heated 350° oven and bake for about 1 hour. When done, scrapple will be firm and slightly swelled. Allow to cool, then place in refrigerator until cold.

When cold, remove scrapple from loaf pan and slice off pieces that are about ¾ inch thick. Coat each slice with cornmeal or flour and sauté them in a frying pan with oil, margarine, or butter until both sides are browned.

Schoolhouse chicken pie
By Darlene Campbell

2 Tbsp. margarine
1 cup sliced mushrooms
1 clove garlic, minced
2 Tbsp. cornstarch
1½ cups milk
2½ cups cooked chicken, cut into bite-sized pieces

2 cups peas, canned or frozen
1 whole pimento, chopped
½ tsp. dried thyme leaves
1 tsp. salt
¼ tsp. pepper
1 recipe for double-crust pastry

Melt margarine in a skillet. Add mushrooms and garlic. Sauté over medium heat until lightly browned. In a saucepan stir together cornstarch and milk until smooth. Mix in mushrooms, garlic, and pan drippings. Bring to a boil over medium heat, stirring constantly; boil 1 minute. Stir in next 6 ingredients. Pour into pastry-lined 9-inch pie pan. Cover pie with pastry; seal and flute the edge.

Cut slits in top and bake in 375° oven for 35 minutes or until crust is golden.

Down-home chicken dumplings
By Richard Blunt

Dumplings:
1¾ cups all-purpose flour
¾ tsp. salt
1½ tsp. baking powder
3½ Tbsp. margarine or butter
3 medium eggs (slightly
  beaten)
Chicken and sauce:
1 2-lb. frying chicken cut into
  8 pieces
½ tsp. salt
¼ tsp. freshly ground black
  pepper

¼ tsp. mustard powder
¼ tsp. garlic powder
¼ tsp. thyme leaves
⅛ tsp. rubbed sage
¼ tsp. basil leaves
¼ cup vegetable oil (to fry
  chicken)
1 small onion, diced medium
1 stalk celery, diced fine
4 Tbsp. margarine or butter
¼ cup flour
4½ cups chicken stock

Mix flour, salt, and baking powder together.

Cut margarine or butter into flour mixture until mixture becomes crumbly. Do this in the way that you would when making pie crust.

Add eggs. Mix to form a stiff dough and allow dough to rest for 20 minutes.

On a well-floured counter, roll dough to about a ¼-inch thickness. Cut dough into strips about ¾-inch wide by 2 inches long. Set aside in refrigerator until ready for use.

Mix salt and spices together. Sprinkle mixture onto chicken and rub each piece to coat completely. Set chicken aside for 30 minutes.

In large fry pan, heat vegetable oil and fry chicken pieces until evenly browned on each side. If necessary, fry only a couple of pieces at a time, adding more oil as required. Set chicken aside on paper towels when done.

After frying chicken, remove all oil from pan and return pan to stove on a medium heat. Melt margarine and add onion and celery and sauté until lightly browned. Add flour and mix with sautéed vegetables and margarine. Cook mixture for 5 minutes, stirring all the while to prevent burning. While still stirring constantly to prevent lumps, add chicken stock to flour and vegetable mixture to form a sauce. Allow to simmer for a few minutes until it thickens then remove from heat.

Place chicken pieces in a 3-qt. casserole. Heat sauce to a simmer again and pour over chicken pieces,
Arrange dumplings in the casserole so that they do not lay on top of one another. If you have too many, freeze the excess for later use. Cover casserole and place in oven and bake for about 1 hour or until chicken is very tender and dumplings are cooked. Serve this with your favorite rice or noodles dish.

$59-an-hour pizza
By Jo Mason

1 loaf frozen bread dough
3 Tbsp. extra-virgin olive oil
1 6-oz. can tomato paste
1 can water
½ tsp. garlic powder
1 tsp. sugar
¼ tsp. black pepper
½ tsp. dried oregano
¼ tsp. fennel seeds
¼ tsp. basil
dash of salt
1 lb. grated mozzarella
   cheese

½ lb. hamburger, cooked and
   drained
4 oz. sliced pepperoni
1 8-oz. can mushrooms,
   drained
1 small can pitted ripe olives
½ medium onion, chopped
½ medium bell pepper,
   chopped
1 small can anchovies
   (optional)
Parmesan cheese, optional
dried hot peppers, optional

(Note: For a thicker crust, use only 1 loaf for 1 pizza. You can add more or less of the suggested amounts of the last 7 ingredients, or omit any of those items.)
Grease loaf with vegetable oil before thawing. Grease 2 pizza pans. To prepare sauce: combine olive oil, tomato paste, water, sugar, salt, and spices in small saucepan. Stir and let simmer over low heat for 15 minutes.
Preheat oven to 400°.
(All ingredients should be ready before doing this step because once the dough has been patted out, it should not be allowed to rise.) Cut loaf in half. Place 1 half in each pan. By stretching and patting, spread dough over each pan. Spread on sauce. Sprinkle on cheese and other ingredients. Bake 14-20 minutes (oven times will vary) until cheese is melted and crust is lightly browned. Serve with Parmesan cheese and dried hot peppers. Makes two 12-inch pizzas.

Chicken fajitas
By Jo Mason

3-4 skinned boned chicken
   breasts
¼ cup salad oil
¼ cup vinegar
juice from 1 lime
1 tsp. sugar
¼ tsp. ground cumin
2 cloves minced garlic

flour tortillas
½ cup shredded cheese
2 bell peppers, sliced and
   sautéed
1 onion, sliced and sautéed
salsa
guacamole

Cut chicken breasts into long thin strips. Combine the next 6 ingredients (the marinade), and marinate chicken in it (in glass bowl in refrigerator) for a few hours. Cook on foil-lined grill over hot coals for about 15 minutes, turning once. (Chicken is done when no pink shows after piercing with fork). Heat tortillas until soft. Place everything on the table and allow each person to fill his tortilla.

Sweet and sour pork
By Jo Mason

Pork:
½ lb. lean pork, cut in 1-inch
   cubes
½ cup flour
¼ cup cornstarch
½ tsp. baking powder
dash salt
1 egg, beaten
¼ cup water
vegetable oil

Sauce:
¾ cup sugar
¾ cup water
2-4 Tbsp. soy sauce (to
   taste)
½ cup ketchup
½ cup cider vinegar
½ bell pepper, chopped
1 small can chunk pineap-
   ple, drained
cornstarch/water mixture

For pork: Combine flour, cornstarch, baking powder, salt, egg, and water to form a smooth batter. Heat oil to about 375°. Dip pork in batter and add one at a time to hot oil. Fry until golden brown.

For sauce: Combine sugar, water, soy sauce, and ketchup in a saucepan and bring to a boil. Add vinegar and peppers. Stir cornstarch mixture into sauce a little at a time and cook and stir until thickened. Add pineapple.

Down-home sauerkraut
By Tom Barth

2 lb. sauerkraut (put it in a colander and rinse under running water for less sour flavor)
2-3 slices of chopped bacon
1 onion, chopped
2-3 cloves garlic, minced
2 bay leaves
1 tsp. caraway seeds
1 oz. gin
¾ cup dry white wine
¾ cup chicken stock
1 lb. ham, diced ¾ inch
1 lb. polish sausage, diced ¾ inch
salt and pepper

Sauté bacon in a heavy pot until just browned. Add the onion and garlic and cook until translucent.

Add the sauerkraut, bay leaves, caraway seeds, gin, wine, and chicken stock and bring to a boil. Add ham and sausage, reduce heat to a simmer and cover. Cook for approximately 1 hour.

If there is too much liquid, turn up heat and reduce a little.

Watch carefully, and stir frequently to avoid sticking. Add salt and pepper to taste.

Lasagna
By Jan Cook

sauce:
1 lb. Italian sausage
2 cloves minced garlic
1 Tbsp. whole basil
1½ tsp. salt
2 cups canned tomatoes
2 6-oz. cans tomato paste

noodles and cheese:
10 oz. lasagna noodles
3 cups ricotta cheese
½ cup Parmesan cheese
2 Tbsp. parsley flakes
2 beaten eggs
1 tsp. salt
½ tsp. pepper
1 lb. mozzarella cheese,
   thinly sliced

Brown meat. Drain off excess fat. Add garlic, basil, salt, tomatoes, and tomato paste. Simmer uncovered for 30 minutes, stirring occasionally.

Cook lasagna noodles in boiling salted water until tender. Drain and rinse in cold water.

Combine remaining ingredients except mozzarella.

Place half the noodles in a 13 x 9 x 2 baking pan; top with half the ricotta cheese mixture, half the meat mixture, and half the mozzarella cheese. Repeat layers.

Bake at 375° for about 30 minutes. Let stand 15 minutes before cutting. Makes 10-12 servings.

Fancy backwoods chicken
By Rodney Merrill

Italian sauce:
15 oz. tomato sauce
6 oz. tomato paste
1 Tbsp. parsley
1 Tbsp. garlic
1 Tbsp. basil
1 Tbsp. Italian seasoning

Chicken:
2 chicken breasts
3 oz. ham
2 oz. Swiss cheese
1 cup Italian sauce
Parmesan cheese

For the sauce: Mix ingredients well with a wire whip. Cover and let cure in refrigerator at least an hour. Tastes best if cured overnight.

For the chicken: Remove and discard chicken skins. Boil chicken until bones can be removed easily (about 30 minutes). Meanwhile, cut ham and cheese into strips (julienne). Italian sauce can be commercial marinara sauce or leftover spaghetti sauce. Or use basic Italian sauce above. When chicken is cooked, begin heating Italian sauce while you remove the bones from chicken. If chicken is cooked enough, bones will just slide out. Place chicken in ovenproof dish and cover with heated Italian sauce. Lightly place half of ham slices on each sauced chicken breast. Cover with sauce again; then top each with half of Swiss slices. Sprinkle with Parmesan.

Place in the broiler section of the oven until Swiss melts. If you don't have a broiler, you can use a conventional oven, toaster oven, or microwave oven.

Serving suggestion: Serve with any green vegetable and either a baked potato or cooked noodles lightly sautéed in olive oil, then sprinkled with basil and pepper.

Main dishes

Texas hash
By Kate Merrill

1 lb. ground meat (beef or
   turkey)
1 onion, diced
3 Tbsp. chili powder
2 tsp. garlic powder

1 tsp. cumin
1½ cups brown rice
1 27-oz. can stewed toma-
   toes
water

Brown meat in a large Dutch oven. Add onion, chili powder, cumin, and garlic powder and cook until onion is soft. Add brown rice and can of stewed tomatoes (drained, but save the liquid). To the tomato liquid, add enough water to make 3 cups and add that to the pot. Bring entire mixture to a boil and reduce heat to very low and cook for 45 minutes to 1 hour WITH THE LID ON. Do not stir until finished. Feeds 4.

Serving suggestion: Corn bread and salsa and a nice fresh salad makes this a complete meal.

Bar-B-Que meatballs
By Sarah Blake

3 lbs. ground beef
1½ cups milk
1 cup oatmeal
1 cup cracker crumbs
2 eggs
2/3 cup chopped onion
2 tsp. salt
½ tsp. pepper
2 tsp. chili powder

sauce:
2 cups ketchup
1 cup brown sugar
½ tsp. liquid smoke
½ tsp. garlic powder
1/3 cup chopped onion

Using hands, thoroughly mix first 9 ingredients. Shape into walnut-sized balls and place in 9 x 13 pan. Pour sauce over balls and bake at 350° for 1 hour. Yield 80 meatballs. This recipe is a great stretcher when served over rice, and will serve 8 people, or 6 hungry backwoodsmen.

Our favorites

These are the favorite recipes of
Backwoods Home Magazine employees.
They range from appetizers to main dishes.

Thai fried rice
By John Silveira

6-8 oz. thinly sliced chicken
(shrimp can be used *)
2½ oz. cooking oil
1 egg
4 cups cooked rice
2-4 oz. chicken stock
2 Tbsp. fish sauce

1 Tbsp. seasoning sauce
1½ tsp. sugar
4 oz. sliced onions
3 oz. peas and carrots
1 whole sliced tomato
4 oz. pineapple chunks
2 cloves crushed garlic

Heat oil in a frying pan over medium heat until hot. (Use medium heat so you don't dry out the rice.) Add chicken* and cook until almost done. Move chicken to the side of the wok and add a little oil and break an egg into the pan, add rice, and mix. Add a little bit of chicken stock, fish sauce, seasoning sauce, and sugar. (Add the liquids around the side of the wok.) Cook for a minute then add the vegetables and pineapple. Cook a few more minutes until the vegetables are done, then add some crushed garlic and remove from heat.

*If shrimp has been used, don't add it until just before the vegetables are added.

Meaghan's bean dip
By Meaghan Silveira

2 15-oz. cans pinto beans
with jalapeños
8 oz. cheese (mixture of jack
and cheddar)
8 green onions including the
"chives," chopped
1/3 can black olives, sliced

5 oz. salsa ranchera
cilantro to taste, chopped
(about ½ cup or so)
salt to taste
garlic powder to taste
freshly ground black pepper
to taste

Pour beans with all the liquid in a bowl and mash them up. Put mashed beans in a pan over low heat. As beans heat up, add the cheese and let it melt into the beans while stirring to prevent scorching. Stir in remaining ingredients and serve with tortilla chips.

Our favorites

Moone baking biscuits
By Ilene Duffy

¼ lb. butter
5 Tbsp. sugar
2 eggs
1 cup sour cream
2 cups flour

3 tsp. baking powder
3 Tbsp. moone (poppy)
   seeds
salt

Moone means poppy seed in Yiddish. These are quick, easy biscuits. They are yummy with butter and jam.

Cream together butter and sugar. Add eggs and sour cream and mix. Combine dry ingredients, then add to butter mixture. Blend together. Bake at 425° for 10-15 minutes.

Salmon loaf
By Ilene Duffy

1 large can of salmon,
   drained
1 egg
1 generous Tbsp. of ketchup
1 tsp. soy sauce

½ tsp. Worcestershire sauce
a few good shakes of Mrs.
   Dash seasoning
breadcrumbs

Mix all the ingredients in a bowl. Spoon into lightly-greased loaf pan. Bake at 350° covered for about 20 minutes. Uncover and sprinkle on the breadcrumbs. Bake uncovered for another 5-10 minutes.

Kugel (noodle casserole)
By Ilene Duffy

8 oz. wide egg noodles
2 eggs
1 can cream of celery soup
1 cup cottage cheese

½ cup sour cream
about ½ cup milk
1/3 of a cube of butter, melted

Cook noodles according to pkg. directions. While noodles are cooking, lightly beat the eggs in a large bowl. Add the soup, cottage cheese, sour cream, and milk. Mix. Melt the butter. Use some of the butter to grease the bottom of a 9 x 13 inch pan. Add the remainder to the mixture. Drain the noodles. Add to the egg and milk mixture. Spread into baking pan. Bake at 350° for about 1 hour.

Quiche
By Ilene Duffy

1 unbaked pie shell
4 eggs
1 cup milk
1 cup sour cream
salt and pepper
chili powder

about 8 oz. salami, cut and
 fried
1 cup cheese, grated (jack
 cheese works best)
1/3 cup of each, (sliced)
 onion, green pepper,
 mushrooms

Prepare the pie shell. Set aside. Fry salami and drain. In bowl, beat eggs slightly, then add milk and sour cream. Add a few shakes of salt, pepper, and chili powder. Sprinkle salami on bottom of pie shell, then the cheese and vegetables. Pour in egg mixture. Bake in preheated 425° oven for 15 minutes. Turn down to 300° and bake for 30 minutes more or until knife comes out clean. Cool for 10 minutes before serving.

Broccoli casserole
By John Silveira

2 pkg. frozen chopped broccoli
1 chopped onion
1 can cream of mushroom
soup

1 cup shredded cheddar
cheese
¾ cup Helman's mayonnaise
2 eggs, beaten
bread crumbs

Cook broccoli until tender (not mushy). Drain and press out water. Mix everything but the bread crumbs together and pour into a buttered casserole dish. Sprinkle bread crumbs on top and bake at 350° for 45-60 minutes (until a knife comes out clean).

Fay's baked broilers
By Muriel Sutherland

broilers, split, ½ to each person
rice, cooked, ¾ cup to each
person
butter or margarine

salt
paprika
pepper
onion or garlic salt

Grease an oblong dish or roaster if you're having a party. Lay the cooked rice, seasoned, in a mound in the center. Lay the split broilers over the rice, skin side up. Dot with butter or margarine, and bake in a slow oven at 325° until broilers are done, 30-45 minutes. Turn once during the baking and add a little more butter or margarine to the underside of the broilers.

Old-fashioned applesauce cake
By Muriel Sutherland

2 cups sifted all-purpose
   flour
½ tsp. salt
1 tsp. soda
1 tsp. cinnamon
½ tsp. cloves
½ tsp. nutmeg

½ cup shortening
1 cup sugar
2 eggs, unbeaten
1 cup thick, cold applesauce
¾ cup raisins or chopped
   dates
½ cup broken walnut meats

Have shortening at room temperature. Assemble all ingredients and utensils needed. Grease a deep 8 or 9-inch square baking pan, sprinkle with flour, shaking out excess. Break nut meats in pieces. Sift flour once before measuring. Preheat oven to 350°.

In a bowl sift together flour, salt, soda, cinnamon, cloves, and nutmeg. Set aside.

Put the shortening, sugar, and eggs in a large bowl and beat at medium to high speed with an electric mixer for 1½ minutes, scraping bowl while beating.

Add the applesauce, raisins or chopped dates, walnuts, and sifted flour mixture. Beat at low speed for 1½ minutes, scraping bowl while beating.

Pour batter into prepared pan and bake at 350° for about 45-50 minutes. Cool. Ice with your favorite icing. I use Penuche icing out of the Betty Crocker Cookbook, 1950 edition.

Aunt Ona's strawberry delight
By Edwina Gower

1 angelfood cake
1 large + 1 small box of
   vanilla pudding mix

1 8-oz. CoolWhip
1½ pkg. (box) strawberry
   glaze

Slice angelfood cake in thin slices. Mix pudding according to box directions, add the CoolWhip and set aside. Mix strawberry glaze according to directions, putting in 1 extra cup of water. Put a layer of thin sliced cake in a 9 x 13 inch pan, then a layer of pudding, and a layer of strawberry glaze syrup. Continue layers and refrigerate.

Aunt Ona's Butternut pound cake
By Edwina Gower

3 cups sugar
¼ cup Crisco
2 sticks margarine
5 large eggs

3¼ cups flour
1 cup milk
¼ tsp. salt
2 Tbsp. butternut flavoring

Cream together Crisco, sugar, and salt. Add eggs 1 at a time, beating after each. Add flour and milk alternately, blend well. Fold in flavoring by hand.

Bake in greased and floured tube pan 1½ hrs at 325°. Do not preheat oven, put cake into cold oven then turn it on. Do not open oven door while baking.

Aunt Ona's Mandarin orange cake
By Edwina Gower

1 butter cake mix (or yellow)
1 can mandarin oranges
4 eggs
½ cup oil
filling:
1 large box instant vanilla
    pudding mix

1 large can crushed pineapple and juice
1 medium (8 oz.) CoolWhip

In a large bowl mix together cake mix, mandarin oranges, eggs, and oil. Beat by hand 4 minutes. Pour batter into three 9-inch round layer pans that have been greased and floured. Bake at 350° for 20 minutes. Cool.

Mix together the pudding mix, pineapple and juice, and the CoolWhip. Spread on cake and between layers. Refrigerate cake until ready to serve.

Minestrone-hamburger soup
By Nathele Graham

1 lb. hamburger
1 cup diced onion
1 cup cubed potatoes
1 cup sliced carrots
½ cup diced celery
1 cup shredded cabbage
¼ cup rice

4 tsp. salt
1/8 tsp. pepper
¼ tsp. basil
½ tsp. thyme
1 small bay leaf
1½ qts. water
1 large can of tomatoes

Cook hamburger and onion in a large kettle until meat is slightly brown. Add water, potatoes, carrots, celery, cabbage, and tomatoes. Bring to a boil. Sprinkle rice into kettle. Add remaining ingredients. Cover and simmer for 1 hour. Serve with Parmesan cheese or shredded cheddar cheese on top.

Beer bread
By Nathele Graham

3 cups self-rising flour
3 Tbsp. sugar
1 10-oz. can beer (room
   temperature)
butter

Mix flour and sugar together. Add beer and mix. Put in a well-greased loaf pan and bake 1 hour at 350°. When done, melt butter on top. Serve warm with lots of butter. Goes well with Minestrone soup.

Baked chili relleno casserole
By Nathele Graham

1 8-oz. can whole green chilies
½ lb. jack cheese
4 eggs, separated
4 Tbsp. melted butter

Sauce:
1 8-oz. can tomato sauce
¼ cup chopped onion
¼ tsp. garlic powder
¼ tsp. ground cumin
¼ tsp. oregano leaves

Drain and split chilies. Remove seeds. Cut cheese into strips and stuff into chilies. Beat egg whites until stiff, moist peaks form. DON'T WASH BEATERS and beat yolks until lemon colored. Fold into whites. Brush bottom and sides of a shallow baking dish with butter. Spoon in half of the egg mixture. Arrange chilies on top. Spoon in the remaining egg mixture and drizzle with butter. Bake at 350° for 25-30 minutes or until brown and puffy.

Sauce: Combine all ingredients in a saucepan. Heat and simmer 10 minutes.

Pour over casserole before serving. Makes about 4 servings.

Marinated chicken
By Nathele Graham

¼ cup vinegar
1 clove garlic, minced
6 skinless chicken breasts

½ cup soy sauce
dash of pepper

Mix vinegar, soy sauce, garlic, and pepper. Rinse chicken and put in a kettle. Pour vinegar mixture over chicken and let stand for 30-45 minutes. Turn occasionally to be sure all of the chicken gets marinated.

Place kettle on the stove. Bring to a boil and reduce heat. Simmer for 45 minutes or until chicken is tender. This is very good served with rice. The cooked marinade can be spooned over the rice.

Italian dressing noodles
By Nathele Graham

1 8-oz. pkg. egg noodles
1 envelope powdered Italian
   salad dressing mix
½ cup heavy cream

¼ cup butter, melted
¼ cup Parmesan cheese
1 cup fresh or frozen peas,
   cooked

Cook the noodles as directed on the package. Combine the dressing mix, butter, cream, and cheese. Drain the noodles and put in serving dish. Add dressing mixture and toss until well-blended. Add peas.

Layered casserole
By Nathele Graham

1 cup uncooked rice
1 can whole-kernel corn,
   drained
2 cups tomato sauce
¾ cup water
½ cup finely chopped onion
½ cup chopped green pepper

1 can green beans, drained
¾ cup diced chicken
   (cooked) or cooked ground
   beef
4 slices bacon, cut into small
   pieces
salt and pepper to taste

Pour rice and corn into the bottom of a large casserole. Mix tomato sauce and water. Pour ½ of mixture over corn and rice. Sprinkle with salt and pepper. Add the onion, green pepper, green beans, and meat. Sprinkle with salt and pepper. Pour the remaining tomato sauce over the top. Cover tightly.

Bake at 350° for 1 hour. Remove the lid and continue to bake for an additional ½ hour. Serves 4 or 5.

Simple peanut butter cookies
By Nathele Graham

1 cup peanut butter
1 cup sugar

1 egg
1 tsp. vanilla

Cream peanut butter and sugar. Mix in egg and vanilla. Drop small teaspoonfuls onto cookie sheet and press with a fork dipped in sugar. Bake at 350° for 7 minutes. Check cookies. They will be soft, but harden as they cool (if cooked too long they will get HARD). Makes about 12.

Joe's pasta salad
By Lisa Nourse

1 pkg. pasta (your choice, I like spiral shaped, it holds the dressing better)
1½ cups Italian salad dressing

1 small red onion, sliced
1 green bell pepper, sliced
1 can black olives, sliced
3 Tbsp. Johnny's salad elegance

Cook pasta according to package. directions. Drain and rinse with cold water. Add all other ingredients and toss to coat pasta completely. Refrigerate for a few hours and toss again before serving.

Creamy white bean soup with kale
By Lisa Nourse

8 oz. Kielbasa, thinly sliced
(or if you like things spicier
you can use hot Italian
sausage)
1 Tbsp. olive oil
4 cloves garlic, minced

½ small onion, diced
2 14.5-oz. cans chicken
broth
2 19-oz. cans cannelini
beans, rinsed and drained
4 cups chopped kale

Brown sausage in a large saucepan over medium-high heat about 4 minutes. Remove cooked sausage from the pan and drain in a colander. Set aside.

Add oil to pan and cook garlic and onions 30 seconds. Add broth and bring to a boil. Reduce heat, add beans and simmer 5 minutes.

Remove 1 cup of soup including beans and puree in blender until the mixture is smooth. Stir bean puree, cooked sausage, and chopped kale into soup and simmer until kale is just tender, about 5 to 7 minutes. Makes about 4 servings.

Duane's shrimp dip
By Lisa Nourse

1 can cream of mushroom
soup
1 block cream cheese
1 cup mayonnaise
1½ cups celery, chopped
fine

1 cup green onions, chopped
fine
½ lb. (or more) small salad
shrimp

Warm soup and cream cheese over medium heat until they melt together and become creamy. Remove from heat, add mayonnaise and stir. Add celery, green onions, and shrimp. Refrigerate for at least a few hours but overnight is best. This dip is just as good without the shrimp if you are serving someone who has an allergy to shellfish.

Jim's dirty rice
By Lisa Nourse

1 tsp. salt
½ tsp. black pepper
1 tsp. dry mustard
½ tsp. thyme
1¼ tsp. paprika
1 tsp. ground cumin
½ tsp. oregano
2 Tbsp. vegetable oil
2 bay leaves
1½ lb. ground pork

1 medium onion, chopped
1 medium bell pepper,
  chopped
3 cloves minced garlic
2 Tbsp. minced fresh parsley
1 Tbsp. butter
2 cups chicken broth
2 cups long grain white rice
2 green onions

Place 2 cups of washed rice and 2 cups of chicken broth in a large saucepan with enough water to fill 1 inch above the rice. Bring to a rolling boil, stir once when a boil is reached, scraping the bottom of the pan well. Boil until the water is below the top of the rice, then cover and set over LOW heat until water is all absorbed. While the rice is cooking combine dry spices, mix and set aside. In a large skillet warm oil and bay leaves, then add ground pork and brown well. Drain excess grease. Add reserved seasonings, onions, bell pepper, garlic, and parsley. Continue cooking until vegetables are soft, about 5 minutes. Fluff rice with a fork when it is done, add vegetable and pork mixture and green onions and heat through. Serves 8.

Baked yams
By Annie Tuttle

1 29-oz. can yams
about ½ cup brown sugar

1 stick butter, melted
small marshmallows

Empty yams into a glass baking dish (a pie plate is ideal.) Sprinkle liberally with brown sugar. Pour melted butter over. Sprinkle a couple handfuls of mini marshmallows on top. Bake at 350° for 30-40 minutes. When done, yams should be tender and marshmallows melted.

Chinese noodles
By Lisa Nourse

8 oz. thin spaghetti or soma noodles
1 Tbsp. vegetable oil
2 medium zucchini, cut in ¼ inch thick, 1 inch long strips
2 cloves garlic, minced
2 medium carrots, shredded
5 scallions, trimmed and cut into 1-inch pieces
2 cups cooked pork, beef, or chicken cut into narrow 1-inch strips

2 cups bean sprouts, rinsed
2 cups green cabbage, shredded
½-1 Tbsp. sesame oil
Sauce:
½ cup chicken broth
¼ cup oyster sauce
¼ cup soy sauce
½ Tbsp. cornstarch
½ Tbsp. sugar
¼ tsp. pepper

Have all ingredients cut and ready to go before you start cooking. Whisk sauce ingredients in a bowl until blended, set aside. Cook pasta according to pkg. directions. Drain, rinse with cold water, set aside.

Heat a large skillet or wok over high heat until hot, but not smoking. Add oil and tilt to coat pan. Add zucchini and garlic and stir fry for 1 minute. Add carrots, scallions, cabbage, and meat and stir fry for 1 minute longer. Stir sauce again, then add it and cook, stirring occasionally, 2 minutes or until thickened. Add pasta and bean sprouts and cook long enough to heat through. Remove from heat, pour sesame oil over the top and toss to mix oil in.

Cranberry sauce
By Evelyn Leach

1 can whole cranberry sauce
¼ cup honey
¼ cup light soy sauce

2 cloves minced garlic
1 Tbsp. freshly ground ginger
dash pepper

Bring to boil and simmer for approximately 10 minutes until reduced. Cover pan with foil sealed tight. Good sauce to use over baked salmon.

185 *Our favorites*

Southwestern corn chowder
By Ilene Duffy

1-2 Tbsp. vegetable oil
½ cup onion, chopped
1 large potato, peeled and
diced
½ cup water
1 can cream style corn

1 can cream of mushroom
soup
5-6 mushrooms, sliced
2 cups milk
1 tsp. salt (scant)
1 can (4 oz.) chopped green
chili

In a large pot or Dutch oven, fry onion in oil until tender. Add chopped potato and stir for about 1 minute. Add water. Cover pot, turn down heat, and simmer until potatoes are just tender. Stir in corn, soup, mushrooms, milk, and salt. Heat thoroughly, but do not boil, lower heat, add chili and continue to heat and stir a few minutes. Serves 6. To make a bigger pot of soup, I add more onions and potatoes, a little more water, and a few more mushrooms. A bit more milk can be added as well.

Sour cream date dreams
By Ilene Duffy

¼ cup butter
¾ cup brown sugar
½ tsp. vanilla
1 egg
1¼ cups flour
½ tsp. soda
¼ tsp. baking powder

¼ tsp. salt
¼ tsp. cinnamon
1/8 tsp. nutmeg
½ cup sour cream
2/3 cup dates, chopped
walnut halves

Mix together butter, sugar, and vanilla. Add egg. Mix well. Sift together dry ingredients. Add to butter mixture alternating with sour cream. Mix in dates. Drop by spoonfuls onto cookie sheet. Top with a walnut half. Bake at 400° for 8-10 minutes. I often double this recipe.

Cloud biscuits
By Ilene Duffy

2 cups flour
4 tsp. baking powder
1 Tbsp. sugar
½ tsp. salt

½ cup butter
1 egg beaten slightly into ⅔ cup milk

Mix dry ingredients. With pastry fork, cut in butter until pea sized. Stir in milk and egg mixture until dough follows fork around. Turn out on well-floured pastry cloth. Knead about 10-20 times. Pour a small amount of oil in 1 muffin cup. Cut dough into 12 pieces. Roll each piece gently in hands to make a ball. Dip dough ball in oil and coat with hands. Bake at 450° 10-14 minutes. Dough can be made ahead and chilled.

Chicken enchiladas
By Ilene Duffy

1 whole chicken, boiled and picked from the bone
4 stalks celery, chopped
1 onion, chopped
½ bell pepper, chopped
3 green onions, chopped
1 green or yellow zucchini, chopped (optional)
10-15 mushrooms, sliced

1 large can enchilada sauce
2 cans cream of chicken soup, not diluted
1 4-oz. can tomato sauce (more if you like saucy enchiladas)
1 lb. jack cheese
1 dozen + flour tortillas

Boil chicken and pick off all meat, dice into chunks, and set aside. In a pan, fry onion, celery, bell pepper, green onions, zucchini, and mushrooms. Add chicken to this with 1 can of soup and ½ can of enchilada sauce. In a separate pan mix and heat gently the remaining soup, enchilada sauce, and tomato sauce. Slightly fry tortillas. Fill tortillas with chicken mixture and cheese. Place rolled enchiladas in baking dish. Cover with remaining sauce and cheese. Bake at 325° for ½ hour or until warm.

Egg thingies
By John Silveira

For each egg:
1 Tbsp. or so of olive oil
1 green onion, diced
1 Tbsp. diced red bell pepper
1 medium mushroom, diced
2 garlic cloves, minced
2 strips of pickled nopalitos, diced
1/8 tsp. Italian seasoning

salt and fresh ground black pepper to taste
1/4 cup diced ham
1/2 piece of pre-sliced Swiss cheese
Korean medium hot sauce, to taste
corn tortilla
cilantro, chopped, to taste

Heat olive oil in a skillet. Sauté green onion, bell pepper, mushroom, garlic, nopalitos, Italian seasoning, salt, and black pepper until onions and bell pepper start to get tender. Add diced ham. Continue sautéing until ham is cooked.

Beat egg. Bunch up the sautéed veggies and ham in the corner of the skillet. Pour beaten egg over them and form an omelet. As the omelet sets up, place the piece of cheese on top and fold the omelet over it.

The problem here is that the egg on the bottom now wants to burn before the egg in the middle cooks and the cheese melts. Before it begins to burn, I put a corn tortilla on a microwave safe plate, take the omelet out of the skillet, place it on the tortilla, place the plate in the microwave, and nuke it on high for 30 seconds.

Take it out, put some Korean medium hot sauce and fresh chopped cilantro on the omelet, and roll up the tortilla.

Baked macaroni and cheese to kill for
By John Silveira

2½ cups uncooked elbow
macaroni
3/8 cup butter
½ cup flour
1¾ cups milk
½ cup sour cream
½ cup grated Parmesan
cheese
½ tsp. salt
1 tsp. pepper, freshly ground

1 tsp. dry mustard, freshly
ground, if possible
1½ cups (8 oz.) diced sharp
cheddar cheese, divided
4 oz. mozzarella cheese, cut
into strips
1 cup ricotta cheese
1 15-oz. can whole toma-
toes, drained and cut into
quarters or sixths
¾ cup diced ham

Preheat oven to 350°.

Cook macaroni in salted boiling water according to package directions. Drain and rinse with cold water. Pour into a 3-quart baking
dish.

In a saucepan, melt butter and stir in flour. Cook and stir for 1 minute. Gradually stir in milk. Add sour cream, Parmesan cheese, salt,
pepper, and mustard. Cook over medium-low heat, stirring constantly, until sauce bubbles and thickens. Stir in half of cheddar cheese
until melted.

Toss macaroni with remaining cheddar cheese, the mozzarella
cheese, ricotta cheese, tomatoes, and ham. Pour sauce over this
macaroni mixture and mix thoroughly.

Bake, uncovered, for about 50 minutes. Then cook an additional 5
minutes under the broiler to bake the top. Yield: 6 servings.

(Don't add any more than ¾ cup of ham as it starts to take over
the recipe. A 15-oz. can of whole tomatoes isn't many tomatoes.
So, if you decide to use the same size can of diced tomatoes, use
only ½ or 2/3 of the can because they want to take over the recipe
too and it ceases to be about macaroni and cheese.)

Chicken with galanga in coconut milk soup
By John Silveira

6 oz. thinly sliced chicken
10 oz. coconut milk (stir before using)
10 oz. chicken stock
½ cup thinly sliced young galanga (cut across)
1 lemon grass stem cut into 1½-inch lengths and pounded
2 smooshed chilies (fry in oil)

4 Kaffir lime leaves
1½ Tbsp. fish sauce
1½ tsp. sugar
1 Tbsp. lime juice (or lemon juice)
chili pepper flakes (to taste)
3 oz. sliced mushrooms
cilantro leaves, coarsely chopped (to taste)
1½ Tbsp. shrimp paste

Heat coconut milk with chicken stock over a medium heat and bring to a boil. Add galanga, lemon grass, smooshed chilies, lime leaves and continue to boil. Add chicken (separate the slices of chicken in the broth but do not stir until the chicken is cooked), fish sauce, sugar, lime juice, shrimp paste, and chili pepper flakes (to taste). Cook for a few minutes until the meat is done. Add sliced mushrooms and remove from heat. Sprinkle with cilantro. I serve this with rice.

Egg, ham, & cheese sandwich
By Dave Duffy

1 egg
1⅓ medium slices of pepper jack cheese
1 slice of ham

2 pieces of bread
butter (for buttering toast)
Tu'o'ng ó't Sriracha hot chili sauce

Fry egg over low heat in oil or butter. Lightly toast the bread. After whites of egg are no longer runny, flip egg. On the other side of the pan, heat ham with the cheese on top to melt. Lift egg with spatula, then place 1 piece of buttered toast on pan. Put egg on toast and cover the egg, ham, and cheese with the other piece of toast. Turn heat to medium and toast bread until lightly browned. Flip sandwich. The trick is to keep the egg to desired doneness (runny yolk). Put hot sauce inside sandwich.

Cod with sauce
By John Silveira

1 medium onion, chopped
1 medium green pepper, chopped
1 stalk celery, chopped
3+ Tbsp. cooking oil
½ tsp. Italian seasoning
1 tsp. curry powder
½ tsp. pepper flakes (optional)
freshly ground black pepper to taste (I start with about ½ tsp. and go from there)

2 Tbsp. Korean medium hot sauce
2 15-oz. can of diced tomatoes with liquid
1 15-oz. can tomato sauce
3 Tbsp. hot salsa
1½ lbs. cod fillets, diced into about ¾-inch cubes
2 Tbsp. lemon juice
4 cups boiled rice

After chopping the onion, pepper, and celery, set half of each aside. Fry one half of the onion, green pepper, and celery in the oil until the onion is browned. Next, add the Italian seasoning, curry powder, and black pepper and fry for about 3 more minutes. Then add the Korean hot sauce, tomatoes and liquid, salsa, and the rest of the vegetables. Simmer until the vegetables are done. Add the fish and cook until the fish is done. (The fish cooks up fast.) Add the lemon juice and cook one more minute. Serve over the rice.

Lemon and garlic chicken
By Annie Tuttle

1 chicken, cut up with skin on
1-2 heads of garlic
2 lemons

2-4 Tbsp. olive oil
¼ cup white cooking wine

Separate but do not peel the garlic cloves. Cut the lemons into 8 pieces each. Put the chicken, garlic, and lemon in a baking dish and pour the oil and wine over. Mush everything around to coat. Cover with aluminum foil and bake in a 300° oven for 2 hours, then remove the cover and turn up the oven to 400° for an additional 30-40 minutes. The lemons will caramelize slightly, and can be eaten skin and all. Mush the garlic with the back of your fork to squeeze out the baked garlic and use it like a sauce on the chicken.

Eggs baked into ham and potato hash
By Meaghan Silveira

4 Tbsp. butter
1 large onion, chopped
12 oz. cooked ham, diced
1 lb. cooked potatoes, diced
1 cup grated cheddar
  cheese
2 Tbsp. ketchup
2 Tbsp. Worcestershire
  sauce

6 eggs
few drops of Tabasco sauce
salt and freshly ground pepper to taste
chopped fresh parsley to
  garnish

Preheat oven to 325°. Melt half of the butter in a frying pan. Cook onion until soft, stirring occasionally, then place it in a bowl and stir in ham, potatoes, cheese, ketchup, and Worcestershire sauce.

Season the mixture with some salt and pepper and spread it in a buttered baking dish in a layer about 1 inch deep. Bake this for about 10 minutes.

Make 6 "wells" in the hash. Break each egg, in turn, into a bowl or saucer and pour one egg into each of the wells.

Melt the remaining butter and season it with Tabasco sauce. Dribble the seasoned butter over the eggs and hash. Bake for 15 to 20 minutes or until the eggs are set. Garnish with the parsley and serve.

Salsa
By John Silveira

1 15-oz. can tomato sauce
1 4-oz. can diced green chil-
  es (Ortega)
1 7-oz. can salsa verde
  (Ortega)
5 chopped green onions
1 large tomato, diced
¼ tsp. sugar

1 or 2 Tbsp. salsa ranchera
  (hot) (La Victoria)
chopped cilantro to taste
  (start with about 3/8 cup)
¼ tsp. ground cumin
3 cloves garlic, minced

Mix all ingredients and serve with tortilla chips.

Kale soup
By John Silveira

6 cans Swanson vegetable stock
2 cans Campbell's chicken stock (dilute)
2 lbs. linguica, sliced into ½-inch pieces
1 large red onion, chopped
1 green pepper, chopped
2 stalks celery, chopped
4 medium red potatoes, unpeeled, and cut into 1-1½ cubes
¼ cup parsley, chopped
1½-2 lbs. kale, stems and all, cut into manageable bite-sized pieces. Use the real curly type of kale, not the decorative type (one bunch of kale is about ½ lb.)

2 15-oz. cans kidney beans, drained
2 15-oz. cans diced tomatoes, with the liquid
2 bay leaves
1 tsp. Italian seasoning
1 tsp. red pepper flakes
freshly ground black pepper, to taste (I start out with about ½ tsp.)
8 cloves garlic, minced
12 oz. uncooked elbow macaroni

Add all ingredients except garlic and macaroni to the stock and bring to a boil. Turn heat down to a slow boil until potatoes and kale stems are tender, about 25-30 minutes. Add garlic and macaroni and cook until macaroni is tender. This is one of those soups that, if it's possible, should be made a day ahead and, when it's done, put into the refrigerator overnight and served reheated the next day, as all of the flavors will have married by then.

Our favorites

Mac's lamb curry bake
By O.E. MacDougal

1 lb. lamb, cut into ¾-inch
   cubes
4+ Tbsp. butter
1 large onion, chopped
2 stalks of celery, chopped
1 medium red bell pepper
   (with seeds and pulp
   removed), diced
1 medium green bell pepper
   (with seeds and pulp
   removed), diced
1 large portobello mush-
   room, diced

1½ inches of ginger root,
   peeled, then "shaved" with
   the vegetable peeler
3 Tbsp. curry powder
cayenne pepper to taste
   (optional)
2½ cups beef consummé
1 14½-oz. can diced toma-
   toes with liquid
1 14½-oz. can coconut milk
4 cloves garlic, minced
2 tsp. salt
2 cups converted (or par-
   boiled) rice

In a skillet, brown lamb in butter. Once browned, remove lamb and set it aside. Add ½ the onion, ½ the celery, ½ the peppers (both red and green), ½ the mushroom, and all of the ginger shavings. Sauté until vegetables are browned. If you need more butter, add another Tbsp. or so. When vegetables are browned, add curry powder and cayenne pepper and fry for about 2 minutes.

Add about half of the stock to the skillet, stir to deglaze the pan. Pour mixture into an ungreased baking pan. Pour rest of stock into skillet to catch the rest of the seasoning and vegetables left in the skillet and pour that into the baking pan. Add browned lamb, tomatoes and their liquid, and coconut milk. Add remaining vegetables, minced garlic, and rice. Mix well in the baking pan.

Preheat oven to 350°. Cover baking pan with aluminum foil and bake for about 30 minutes. Uncover and bake another 20 minutes or until rice is cooked, liquid is reduced, and top is lightly browned.

This is good just the way it is, but it's even better when served with a suitable sauce such as creole sauce.

You can substitute chicken for lamb in this recipe. In that case you should also substitute chicken stock for the lamb or beef stock.

Mole
By John Silveira

2 Tbsp. butter
½ onion, chopped
1 celery stalk, chopped
6-8 mushrooms, sliced

1 jar mole
3 cups chicken stock
2½ lbs. chicken

Melt butter in large pot. Add onion, celery, and mushrooms and cook until celery is soft.

Add mole and melt down. Add chicken stock and cook until mole dissolves into the chicken stock. Add chicken and cook until done.

Serve over rice.

Sausage/corn bread casserole
By Meaghan Silveira

½ pound sausage (I use Jimmy Dean)
½ medium onion, chopped
½ medium green pepper, chopped
½ tsp. Italian seasoning
1 tsp. red pepper flakes (optional)

¾ cup broccoli florets (optional)
½ cup sharp cheddar cheese, shredded
1 package Jiffy or other cornbread mix
1 egg
1/3 to ½ cup milk

Brown sausage, then add onion, green pepper, Italian seasoning, red pepper flakes, and broccoli and cook until onions are not quite translucent.

Grease a 9-inch cake pan and put sausage, onion, and green pepper mixture in the bottom, then shredded cheese on top of that. Then mix up the cornbread mix, egg, and milk and pour that on top of the cheese.

Bake at 450° for about 15 minutes.

Our favorites

Spaghetti with garlic and oil
By John Silveira

½ cup plus 1 Tbsp. extra virgin olive oil
2 tsp. very finely chopped garlic (Can be increased if you like. I add a lot more.)
2 tsp. salt
1 lb. spaghetti, spaghettini, or angel hair
freshly ground pepper, 6-8 twists of the mill

2 Tbsp. chopped parsley
freshly grated Parmesan cheese (Freshly ground Parmesan is really a lot better than the pre-grated stuff.)
mushroom, chopped (optional)
pine nuts (optional)

Boil spaghetti water. Add spaghetti. If it's a 10 minute spaghetti, while the spaghetti cooks, add the garlic and salt to ½ cup oil and sauté in a very small saucepan over a low heat. Keep the heat very low. The garlic shouldn't even start to bubble until it's been cooking about 5 minutes. Stir the oil frequently. When the spaghetti is done, pour the garlic and oil sauce over the spaghetti, toss rapidly, add the pepper, chopped parsley, and the Tbsp. uncooked olive oil. If you're making enough to save some for leftovers, remove the garlic before pouring the oil on the spaghetti as, otherwise, the garlic gets mushy in the oil. If using the thin, 5-minute type spaghetti, start the sauce 5 minutes before you put the spaghetti in the water. I think the real thin spaghetti tastes better but the regular spaghetti makes for better leftovers. Serve with grated Parmesan cheese. Serves 4 ordinary people, or 2 people who like it as much as I do.

If you can, avoid cooking this in stainless steel or with stainless steel utensils. It may just be my imagination, but I think it flattens the taste somehow.

Mushrooms can be added. If you add a lot of mushrooms, increase the oil by about ¼ cup and cook them with the garlic.

Try onions. If you add onions, make it a tablespoon or two minced real fine.

A really good way to make this spaghetti is with pine nuts. Add one Tbsp. with the garlic and cook them in the oil. Add another Tbsp. when you're done cooking the garlic so you have some cooked and some raw.

Italian wedding soup
By John Silveira

Broth:
2½ quarts of chicken stock
1 stalk celery, thinly sliced
1 large carrot, thinly sliced
3 Tbsp. fresh parsley
3 shallots, thinly sliced
2 large mushrooms, without
the stems, thinly sliced
freshly ground black pepper,
to taste

Meatballs:
½ lb. extra lean ground beef
1 egg, beaten
½ cup seasoned bread
crumbs
3/8 cup Parmesan cheese,
grated
2 cloves of garlic, pressed
freshly ground black pepper,
to taste

3 oz. egg pastina

Combine all of the ingredients for the broth and let simmer until vegetables are tender.

While the stock simmers, combine all of the ingredients for the meatballs. Form meatballs into balls slightly smaller than marbles (because they're going to puff up).

When the broth is done, keep it simmering and drop the meatballs, still raw, into the broth. You almost have to put them in 1 or 2 at a time to keep them from breaking up. As they cook, the meatballs will float to the top. As they continue to cook, they'll sink again.

About 5 minutes before you are ready to serve the soup, add the pastina.

Our favorites

Marinated shrimp
By John Silveira

24 medium shrimp
1 bay leaf
1 Tbsp. fresh lemon juice
1½ cups water
12 peppercorns
Marinade:
¼ cup finely chopped onions
¼ cup finely chopped parsley
4 tsp. olive oil

1 Tbsp. chopped dill weed
1 Tbsp. Dijon mustard
2 tsp. cider vinegar
½ tsp. salt
¾ tsp. Tabasco sauce
¼ tsp. paprika
3 garlic cloves
¼ tsp. black pepper
¼ tsp. cayenne pepper
3 Tbsp. chopped cilantro

Bring water, lemon juice, pepper corns, and bay leaf to a boil. Add shrimp and boil 4 minutes. Drain, shell, and devein shrimp. Combine marinade ingredients and stir in shrimp. Chill 2-3 hours and serve.

Skillet Spanish rice
By John Silveira

1 lb. lean ground beef
8 oz. sweet Italian sausage
2 small red or green bell peppers, seeded and chopped
1 medium onion, chopped
1 rib celery, chopped
1½ cups hot water

1¼ cups uncooked converted-style rice
1 8-oz. can tomato sauce
1 tsp. chili powder
1 tsp. Worcestershire sauce
½ tsp. each seasoned salt, ground cumin, and black pepper

Crumble beef and sausage into large skillet. Add vegetables; stir over medium heat until meat is no longer pink. Drain fat; stir in remaining ingredients. Bring to a boil. Reduce heat, cover and simmer 20 minutes until rice is tender.

Yum Neeyah (beef salad)
By John Silveira

8 oz. beef, grilled med. rare and sliced thin (Charn, the man who taught the cooking class, used tri-tip)
4-5 crushed garlic cloves
2 tsp. rice powder (rice powder can be made by browning white rice in an unoiled skillet and grinding the browned rice with a blender or a mortar and pestle)
chili pepper flakes (to taste)

3 Tbsp. fish sauce
3 Tbsp. lime juice (or lemon juice)
2-2½ tsp. sugar
4 oz. sliced red onions
2 oz. thinly sliced carrots
5-6 slices of cucumber
2 stems fresh mint leaves or fresh sweet basil leaves
lettuce leaves
cilantro leaves (to taste)

Mix garlic, rice powder, chili pepper flakes, fish sauce, lime juice, and sugar and toss with the meat, onions, carrots, and cucumber. Add mint leaves or sweet basil leaves, then place on a lettuce bed and garnish with cilantro.

Beef & cheese
By John Silveira

2 lbs. stew beef
1 lb. sharp cheddar cheese, cut in ½-inch cubes
2 jars green chili salsa
2 cans beef stock concentrate

2 cans water
mushrooms
can of diced green chilis

Boil beef, salsa, green chilis, beef broth, and water. Simmer until the beef is tender (about 2 hours). Just before serving, add the cheese and let it melt. Serve over rice.

Our favorites

Pie crust
By Evelyn Leach

1 cup whole wheat flour
¼ cup margarine, softened

¼ cup sesame seeds
2 Tbsp. water

Mix all together and pat into 9" pie plate. Bake at 350° for 10 minutes before filling.

Fat-free pie crust
By Evelyn Leach

1 cup Grape Nuts cereal
¼ cup apple juice concentrate
¼ tsp. vanilla (optional)

Preheat oven to 350°. Mix ingredients together. Let stand for 3 minutes. Pat into a 9" pie pan and bake for 10 minutes. Cool before filling.

100% whole-wheat raisin-nut bread
By Evelyn Leach

3 cups whole-wheat flour
¼ cup toasted wheat germ
2 tsp. baking powder
1¼ tsp. baking soda
1½ cups buttermilk or rice milk

½ cup honey
¼ cup salad oil or apple-sauce
½ cup each raisins and chopped walnuts

In a 6-8 cup bowl, stir together flour, wheat germ, baking powder, soda, and salt. In a separate bowl, combine the buttermilk, honey and oil. Pour all at once into the flour mixture, stirring just until all ingredients are combined. Add raisins and nuts, being careful not to overmix the batter.

Pour batter into a Pam-sprayed loaf pan. Bake in a 325° oven about 1 hour or until a wooden pick inserted in the center comes out clean. The loaf top should be slightly pebbled and evenly browned. Let cool in pan for 10 minutes, then turn out on a rack. Makes 1 loaf.

Our favorites

Macaroni with meat gravy
By Oliver Del Signore

Meatballs

1 lb. ground beef
2 eggs
½ cup bread crumbs
¼ cup grated romano
  cheese
1 Tbsp. dried parsley
1 tsp. garlic powder
½ tsp. salt
½ tsp. black pepper

Meat Gravy

2 28-oz cans crushed tomatoes
2 28-oz cans tomato puree
2 cups water
1 4-oz can mushrooms, with
  liquid
4 carrots, peeled and cross-
  cut into thirds or quarters
4 cloves garlic, peeled and
  minced (or more, to taste)

1 large onion, chopped
¼ cup extra virgin olive oil
2-3 Tbsp. Italian seasoning,
  to taste
1 tsp. salt
1 tsp. black pepper
¼-½ tsp cayenne pepper
  (optional, to taste)
meatballs, uncooked from
  above
1 lb. Italian sausage
1 stick (about 8 oz.) pepperoni, cross-cut into 1-½
  inch pieces
1 lb. chicken pieces (any)
[Note: almost any meat can
  go into the gravy. Different
  combinations will result in
  different flavored gravies.]
Your favorite pasta/macaroni

Place meatball ingredients in a mixing bowl. Using freshly washed hands, plunge in and squish it all around until well mixed. Roll into 1½" to 2" diameter balls. Set aside.

To make the gravy, pour the olive oil into a large heavy bottom stainless-steel pot over medium-high heat. When hot, add the onion and garlic and saute until onion is translucent. Add the crushed tomatoes, puree, water, carrots, mushrooms with liquid, seasoning, salt, and peppers and mix well. Heat, stirring frequently, until gravy just starts to boil. Add meat in any order. Stir in carefully so as not to break meatballs.

Continue heating and stirring until gravy just starts to bubble again. Immediately reduce heat and simmer, partially covered, for 3 hours or more until all meat is cooked and gravy reaches desired consistency. Stir frequently, scraping the bottom of the pan to pre-vent sticking and burning. If gravy starts to get too thick too soon, add a little water. After two hours, taste and adjust seasonings.

When gravy is done, cover and leave in pot until ready to serve or cover and refrigerate if preparing a day ahead of time.

If gravy was prepared a day ahead, heat on low until gravy and meat are hot.

Cook your favorite macaroni according to package directions or until firm to the bite.

While macaroni is cooking, use a slotted spoon to remove meat from saucepan to a serving platter. (If you added chicken, be sure you find and discard any small bones from pieces that may have fallen apart.)

When macaroni is done, drain, place in serving bowl, add several ladles of gravy and mix to prevent sticking. Serve with additional gravy on the side, grated Romano or Parmesan cheese, the meat, a nice Italian bread, and a good Chianti wine.

Mangia di gusto. (Eat heartily)

(Ask an Italian cook for a recipe, and the instructions you get will probably sound something like this: "Take about a pound of this, add a little of that, a handful of this, a shake or two of that, and a pinch of the other." It is for that reason that Italian family cooking is always an adventure in good eating. Ask 20 Italian cooks to use the exact same ingredients to make a dish and you'll end up with 20 different results.

With that in mind, feel free to make the above recipes your own by altering the ingredients to suit your own taste.

And in case you were wondering, while young folk have adapted to terms like "pasta" and "tomato sauce," we older folk know that "tomato sauce" is what comes in those little cans while "gravy" is what mom made at home. And we stubbornly cling, like a nice thick gravy, to "macaroni.")

Butter tarts
By Evelyn Leach

pastry for a double-crust pie
1 egg
1 cup brown sugar
1 cup raisins or currants

¼ tsp. vanilla
1 Tbsp. butter
½ cup chopped nuts (optional)

Line muffin tins with pie dough. Mix all other ingredients in saucepan. Cook over medium heat until bubbly. Fill muffin tins ½ full with above mixture. Bake at 325° for 20 minutes, or until brown. Makes 12.

40-clove chicken
By Evelyn Leach

1 frying chicken, cut up
40 cloves fresh garlic, whole
½ cup white wine
¼ cup olive oil

1 chopped onion
a few shakes of dried oregano

Place chicken in a baking pan. Sprinkle all the ingredients over the top. Cover with foil and bake at 375° for 40 minutes. Remove the foil and bake an additional 15 minutes.

Salmon patties
By Ilene Duffy

2 lbs. salmon fillet
juice of ½ lemon
orange juice
½ medium onion, diced fine
½ cup mayonnaise

¼ cup bread crumbs
1½ tsp. curry powder
1 egg
freshly ground pepper
oil for frying

Wash salmon fillet and place on baking dish. Pour lemon juice and a little orange juice to cover the fish. Cover with foil and bake at 350° for about ½ hour or when fish flakes easily. Let cool slightly so you can chunk up the fish into a large mixing bowl, making sure to discard any bones and skin. Add remaining ingredients except the oil.

Heat oil in large fry pan. Wash hands. Mix salmon with remaining ingredients except oil until blended. Form into patties. Add a little water if you think the salmon won't hold the shape of the patties. Fry on both sides until browned. My family loves these with a side dish of hot, buttered noodles with Parmesan cheese.

Mary Wilkins' sugar cookies
By Ilene Duffy

½ cup shortening
1 stick of butter, softened
2 cups sugar
2 eggs
1 tsp. vanilla
1 cup sour milk (1 cup of
  milk mixed with a small
  dollop of sour cream)

1 tsp. baking powder
1 tsp. soda
1 tsp. salt
approx. 4 cups flour
cinnamon sugar (for sprinkling)

Cream shortening, butter, and sugar. Add eggs and vanilla. In another bowl sift flour, baking powder, and salt. In a small bowl, mix the milk with a dollop of sour cream and mix in the baking soda. Add about ⅓ of the flour to the creamed butter and about ⅓ of the milk mixture. Blend well. Continue until all the flour and milk mixtures are incorporated. Drop by spoonfuls onto cookie sheet. Sprinkle cinnamon sugar on top and bake at 350° for about 15 minutes. This is a family favorite from my dad's youth in Michigan.

Our favorites

Mama Peluso's pizza recipe
By Don and Nancy Childers

½ cup grated Parmesan
   cheese
1 lb. mozzarella cheese
2 lbs. jack cheese
1 pkg. pepperoni
1 pkg. hot roll mix
1 small can tomato paste

1 small can tomato sauce
1/8 tsp. pepper
1/8 tsp. salt
1 tsp. garlic salt
½ tsp. oregano
1 onion, chopped

Grate mozzarella and jack cheeses, mix together, put aside. Chop onion and saute in olive oil.

Add tomato paste and sauce, pepper, salt, garlic salt, and oregano. Stir well.

Prepare dough. Cover dough lightly with olive oil and spread sauce mixture over pizza dough.

Sprinkle Parmesan cheese over sauce, then add mozzarella and jack cheeses, then pepperoni.

Preheat oven to 450°. Bake for 15-20 minutes (some ovens may vary)

Don and Nancy's enchiladas
By Don and Nancy Childers

1 large can black olives
   (sliced or whole)
2 dozen corn tortillas
2 lbs. cheddar cheese, grated
2 onions, chopped
2 lbs. hamburger

1 tsp. salt
1 tsp. garlic salt
¼ tsp. pepper
1 pkg. Lawry's enchilada
   sauce mix
1 large can tomato sauce

Brown hamburger. Add salt, pepper, and 1 chopped onion. Fry tortillas until soft enough to roll. Fill each one with hamburger and a little cheese. Roll and place side by side in rectangular baking dish or pan.

Cover rolled tortillas with sauce, olives, and cheese.

Top with additional chopped onion if desired or place in side dish.

Bake in oven at 350° for 30 minutes until crispy on top.

Jack Fazio's corn bread
By Ilene Duffy

1½ cups flour
1½ cups cornmeal
1 Tbsp. baking powder
½ tsp. nutmeg
½ tsp. cinnamon
¼ tsp. salt

¾ cup sugar or honey
2 eggs
½ cup melted shortening or
  vegetable oil
1 cup milk

Mix flour, cornmeal, baking powder, sugar, nutmeg, cinnamon, and salt thoroughly. (If using honey, mix it with the wet ingredients.) In a separate bowl mix eggs, oil, and milk. Add dry ingredients to the wet and mix until just blended. Lightly grease a 9 x 13 pan. Spread batter in pan and bake at 400° for about 25-30 minutes. I check it after about 20 minutes to make sure it isn't getting too done as it's a hot oven.

(Jack was a friend of ours at the lake where we lived before coming to Gold Beach. Sadly he passed away a few years ago. He was a heck of a carpenter, a fabulous bread maker, and a really nice guy. We think of him when I make his delicious corn bread.)

Fruit smoothies
By Dave Duffy

1 banana
2 heaping Tbsp. yogurt
½ orange, broken into wedges
½ apple, sliced into chunks

4 big frozen strawberries (or
  6 if they're small)
OR handful of frozen blueberries (instead of the
  strawberries)
3-4 ice cubes

Blend all ingredients in blender or Vita-Mix until smooth. Other fruits can be substituted for the orange and apple, but the banana is an essential ingredient because it gives it the necessary texture for the smoothie to be "smooth."

Our favorites

Pasta, rice, & beans

Old-fashioned baked beans
By Jackie Clay

2 cups dry navy beans
¼ cup ham or bacon
½ cup dehydrated chopped
  onions
8 Tbsp. molasses

4 Tbsp. honey
1 Tbsp. dry mustard
3 Tbsp. vinegar
½ cup tomato sauce
¼ cup ketchup

Sort beans, soak overnight in enough water to cover. In the morning, drain beans, discarding water. Place beans in 6-quart or larger heavy pot with 12 cups water and simmer, covered just long enough for beans to get tender (older beans require longer cooking). Drain and discard water. In a 3-quart or larger casserole, mix beans with other ingredients and bake at 350° for 1½-2 hours, adding water if necessary to keep beans from drying out. Serve hot with fresh whole wheat bread for a comforting, hearty meal.

Baked barbeque beans
By Jackie Clay

2 cups dried beans
1 tsp. baking soda
¼ lb. chopped ham or other
  smoked meat
1 cup barbecue sauce

½ tsp. salt
dash black pepper
I Tbsp. molasses
1 medium onion, chopped

Soak beans overnight, adding a little baking soda to the water. In the morning, cook them gently until skins begin to break. Drain off water, saving 1 cup. Empty beans into a baking dish, bury meat and onions in them and pour cup of water saved over them. Sprinkle with salt and pepper, and drizzle molasses and half the barbecue sauce over the beans. Cover and bake in a slow oven (about 300°) for 4-5 hours (or until tender) adding a little water, as needed, to keep them from drying out. When beans are done, add the rest of the barbecue sauce to the top of the beans and return to oven until your mouth waters.

Homemade noodles in chicken broth

By Jackie Clay

1½ cups flour (either freshly
   ground whole wheat
   or white)

¼ tsp. salt
2 eggs, reconstituted or
   fresh

Place flour in mound on board, making a nest or well in center of mound. Pour eggs into nest. Beat eggs with fork, gradually bringing flour into the mix. Work dough into a ball with hands, picking up only as much flour as it takes to make a stiff but workable ball. Knead dough for about 5 minutes. It should not stick to the board. If it seems too moist, add a little more flour; if too dry, dampen your hands and knead longer.

Divide the ball into quarters. Cover 3 and reserve 1 to work with immediately. Lightly sprinkle board with flour and roll out dough, pulling it into a uniform thickness oval. Make it as thin as workable and let rest in a warm, dry place. Repeat with other 3 quarters.

When all dough is dry, but not stiff and brittle, roll like a jelly roll, cutting into desired thickness with a sharp knife. You can then either fluff out to separate and then carefully hang to dry or lay it flat to air dry for an hour.

Pour a qt. of chicken broth (or use dry chicken granules to make a broth) into a large pot. Add diced, canned, or freeze-dried chicken meat, if desired, as well as onion, carrots, and spices as desired. Bring to a medium boil, then carefully add noodles, simmering just long enough to make them tender. The flour on the noodles provides natural thickening. You'll get raves for this simple, yet satisfying meal.

No-fail boiled rice
By Richard Blunt

1 cup long grain white rice
½ tsp. kosher salt
1¾ cups cold water

Place the rice, salt, and water in a heavy-bottomed sauce pan and cover tightly. Bring the mixture to a boil over medium heat.
When steam starts escaping from the cover, turn the heat to very low. Do not remove the cover.
Cook the rice for exactly 20 minutes on low heat, then remove the pan from the burner. Do not remove the cover.
Let the rice stand, undisturbed, for another 20 minutes. Remove the cover and lightly fluff the rice with a fork.

Fajita rice
By Richard Blunt

3 Tbsp. virgin olive oil
2 medium yellow onions,
  diced medium
2 cloves fresh garlic, minced
1½ cups long grain parboiled
  (converted) rice
1 pkg. fajita seasoning
  (Ortega, Taco Bell, Old El
  Paso, Chi-Chi's etc.)

3 cups chicken stock
1 14-oz. can of pinto beans,
  drained
1/3 cup canned or bottled
  roasted peppers, diced
  medium

Heat olive oil in Dutch oven over medium heat. Add diced onions and cook until lightly browned.
Add garlic and cook for 1 minute, stirring constantly, then stir in rice.
Stir fajita seasoning into chicken stock and add this mixture to the pot. Increase heat to medium high. Bring mixture to a boil, then add drained pinto beans and diced roasted peppers.
When mixture again returns to a boil, put the lid on the pot, adjust heat to low, and cook mixture for 20 minutes or until all of the liquid is absorbed. Remove pot from heat and serve as soon as possible.

Baked aromatic rice
By Richard Blunt

2 cups long grain Basmati
  rice
cold water to rinse and soak
  the rice
1 tsp. kosher salt
4 qts. water

4 Tbsp. unsalted butter
1 Tbsp. virgin olive oil
kosher salt, to taste
freshly ground black pepper,
  to taste

Preheat oven to 350°.

Place rice in a large bowl and fill bowl with cold water. Rub rice between your fingers to remove the surface starch from grains. Carefully change water and repeat rinsing until the water is clear. Drain off and discard water.

Place rice in a smaller bowl with 1 qt. of fresh cold water. Let rice soak in this water for at least 30 minutes. Drain and discard water.

Combine salt with 4 qts. of water and bring to a boil over medium-high heat. Add rice and stir mixture to ensure that rice does not stick to bottom of pot.

Cook rice until grains are cooked ¾ of the way through. (When you remove a grain from the pot and bite into it, it should be fully cooked on the outside and slightly crunchy on the inside.) This should take about 10 minutes.

Immediately drain rice and rinse with warm water.

In small, heavy-bottomed sauce pan, over low heat, melt butter with olive oil. Season mixture to taste, with salt and freshly ground black pepper. The more black pepper you add, the more flavor this rice will have.

Place rice in non-stick baking pan and evenly drizzle melted butter and olive oil on top of rice. Cover pan tightly with aluminum foil and bake in oven for 15-20 minutes.

Remove from oven and let rest for 5 minutes before serving.

Spiced red beans
By Richard Blunt

1 cup dried red kidney beans
5 cups cold water to soak
beans
3 cardamom pods
1 cinnamon stick, 2 inches
long
2 bay leaves
3 Tbsp. peanut oil
1 large onion, thinly sliced
3 cloves fresh garlic,
chopped fine

1 Tbsp. fresh ginger root,
peeled and chopped fine
½ tsp. ground turmeric
1 tsp. garam masala
¼-½ tsp. powdered cayenne
pepper
4 fresh plum tomatoes,
peeled, seeded, and
chopped
1 cup low salt chicken stock,
fresh or canned
½ tsp. kosher salt

Pick over beans to remove any foreign matter or damaged and discolored beans. Soak beans in 5 cups cold water for 12 hours or overnight.

Drain soaked beans, discard soaking water, then rinse beans under cold running water. Put beans and 5 cups fresh water in a pot that will hold everything with room to spare. Bring beans to a boil over medium-high heat, reduce heat and let beans cook at slow simmer for 1 hour or until they become tender. Drain beans and set aside.

Heat a heavy-bottomed skillet over medium heat for 1 minute, then add the cardamom, cinnamon stick, and bay leaf. Roast spices for 1 minute, being careful not to let them burn.

Add oil. When spices start to sizzle, add onion and cook until onion starts to brown. Add garlic and ginger and continue cooking mixture until onions turn a medium brown. Add turmeric, garam masala, and cayenne pepper, and cook for another minute, stirring constantly to prevent burning.

Add chopped tomatoes, chicken stock, salt, and beans. Adjust heat to lowest possible point, cover skillet, and slowly simmer mixture for about 10 minutes. Let beans rest after cooking for 10 minutes before serving.

Spider rice casserole
By Richard Blunt

Special Equipment: 1 5-qt. or larger cast iron Dutch oven

Ingredients:

6 skinless chicken thighs
½ tsp. kosher salt
¼ tsp. freshly ground black pepper
3 Tbsp. peanut oil or other light vegetable oil
1 cup diced yellow onion
2 cloves fresh garlic, minced
1 Tbsp. fresh ginger, minced
4 whole cloves
4 whole green cardamom pods
1 3-inch stick cinnamon
¼ tsp. whole cumin seeds
1⅓ cups long grain brown rice
1 10-oz. can diced tomatoes with chili peppers (Ro-Tel brand is best)
1 cup canned low fat chicken stock
¾ cup your favorite ale or beer, room temperature and flat
kosher salt to taste
½ tsp. freshly ground black pepper

Garnish:

2 Tbsp. fresh cilantro, chopped
¼ cup toasted sliced almonds

Combine salt and pepper and rub mixture onto washed chicken.

Heat oil in Dutch oven over medium heat, then add chicken in a single layer and fry until chicken is browned on both sides and cooked about 2/3 of the way through. Remove chicken from pan and set aside.

Add onions to pan and cook over medium heat until lightly browned. Add garlic, ginger, whole cloves, cardamom seed, stick cinnamon, and cumin seed. Cook mixture while stirring constantly for about 2 minutes.

Add brown rice and stir mixture for 1 minute.

Add tomatoes, chicken stock, beer, salt and pepper to taste, increase heat to medium high, and bring mixture to a boil. Return chicken to pot and put cover in place. When mixture begins to boil again, reduce heat to low and cook casserole for exactly 1 hour.

Remove pot from heat and let casserole rest, with cover in place, for 15 minutes.

Before serving, sprinkle the chopped cilantro and toasted almonds evenly over the casserole.

The reason whole spices are used in this recipe is that under cooking conditions the flavors are slowly released into the casserole. You can try to find them and pick them out before serving the meal, but I just let people do it themselves from their own plates.)

Beans for Sarah
By Richard Blunt

1¼ cups dried pinto beans
water to soak beans
3 Tbsp. extra virgin olive oil
12 oz. green cabbage (diced small)
2 cloves minced garlic
1½ cups low salt chicken stock (fresh or canned)
1 cup apple cider
1 large onion (diced medium)
1 large carrot (peeled and diced medium)
1 stalk celery (diced medium)

1 bay leaf
3 whole cloves
4 oz. piece lean salt pork (optional, for additional flavor)
1 cup peeled, seeded, and diced fresh plum tomatoes
1 cinnamon stick (broken in half)
¼ cup apple brandy (optional)
3 Granny Smith apples (peeled, cored, and diced medium)

Soak beans for 4 hours in water. Drain and discard water.

In heavy-bottomed pan heat olive oil and sauté cabbage and garlic until cabbage is tender.

In large heavy-bottomed pot, combine beans, chicken stock, apple cider, onion, carrot, celery, bay leaf, and cloves. Bring to a boil over high heat and remove from heat immediately.

Transfer bean mixture to a bean pot or earthenware casserole, add salt pork, cabbage mixture, tomato, cinnamon stick, and apple brandy.

Cover casserole, place in a 325° oven for 1 hour, then add apples and bake until beans are tender, about 1½ hours. Total cooking time 2-2½ hours.

Vermont baked beans
By Richard Blunt

1 cup dried white beans
1 cup dried kidney beans
water to soak beans
water to simmer beans
1 tsp. whole cumin seed
½ tsp. whole coriander seed
1 stick cinnamon
6 whole black peppercorns
4 whole cloves
2 dried bay leaves
½ lb. smoke-cured slab
  bacon, diced (If you don't
  eat pork, omit the bacon. It
  will change the flavor of
  the dish somewhat but the
  casserole will still be delicious.)

1 Tbsp. olive oil
1 medium onion, diced
1 carrot, peeled and diced
3 fresh garlic cloves,
  chopped fine
1 Tbsp. marinated fresh ginger, chopped fine
½ cup beer or ale
1 cup chicken stock
1 10-oz. can diced tomatoes
  with chili peppers
½ cup pure maple syrup
zest from one orange
¼ cup fresh cilantro,
  chopped

Soak beans overnight in cold water. Use enough water to cover by at least 2 inches. Change water and add fresh water at least once during soaking process.

Discard soaking water, rinse beans in cold water, and set them in a pot over medium heat. When water starts to boil, reduce heat to a point where beans are just simmering. Simmer for 45 minutes, or until they begin to soften. Test them for tenderness by biting into 1 or 2 beans from pot. Drain beans, discard cooking water and set beans in an 8-10 cup casserole or bean pot.

In a heavy-bottomed skillet, roast each of the spices over low heat until they begin to brown and add them to beans. Add bay leaves without roasting them.

Add diced bacon to same skillet and sauté over low heat until it begins to brown and about half of the fat has been rendered out. Remove rendered bacon from fat and add to casserole.

Add olive oil to same pan, increase heat to medium, and add onion and carrot. Sauté mixture until onion becomes opaque, add garlic and ginger. Continue to sauté mixture for about 30 seconds then add mixture to casserole.

Preheat oven to 250°. Combine beer or ale with chicken stock, diced tomatoes and maple syrup. Add mixture to casserole. Put lid on casserole and place in oven. Slow cook beans for 5-6 hours or until beans are very tender without being mushy. If beans become dry during this time, rehydrate them by adding a little chicken stock.

During last hour of cooking remove cover from casserole or bean pot.

While beans are cooking, remove zest (the colored part of the skin) from orange with a hand grater and mix with chopped cilantro. **Caution:** Don't remove any of the white under flesh from the orange. This flesh is usually very bitter and will ruin the delicate flavor of the casserole. Sprinkle this mixture on top of the casserole just before serving.

Oriental chicken-fried rice
By Jackie Clay

2 cups cooked white rice, cooled
½ cup finely diced onions (you may substitute rehydrated dry)
¼ cup rehydrated freeze-dried or air-dried green peas
1 cup rehydrated shredded carrots (or fresh)

¼ cup oil or shortening
1 Tbsp. peanut butter
½ cup chopped cooked chicken
2 Tbsp. soy sauce
2 eggs, equivalent in dehydrated egg powder
spices to taste, including garlic, turmeric, hot pepper

In a large, heavy frying pan, heat oil. Add rice, onions, chicken, and carrots. Stir frequently with spatula until rice begins to lightly brown. Add peanut butter (no, it doesn't taste "weird"), soy sauce, peas, and spices. Continue stirring while flavors mix. As rice mixture appears to be done, quickly add beaten egg mixture and continue stirring with spatula until egg is cooked. Serve at once with soy sauce, sweet and sour sauce, or hot mustard sauce.

Hoppin' John
By Richard Blunt

6 oz. lean salt pork cubed
1 medium onion, diced medium
2 cloves minced garlic
1 cup long grain Texmati brown rice
2½ cups water
½ tsp. kosher salt
½ tsp. freshly ground black pepper

1 bay leaf (fresh if you can find it, but dried bay works well also)
¼ tsp. red pepper flakes or cayenne pepper
4 cups fresh or frozen black-eyed peas (I grow my own and freeze what I don't eat during the season. High quality frozen varieties are also available in most markets.)

Place salt pork in heavy skillet (cast iron works best), and fry over medium heat until lightly browned. Add onions and garlic and sauté until onion is translucent.

Add rice and stir to coat grains with fat. Add water, salt, black pepper, bay leaf, and red pepper; bring water to a boil, reduce heat to very low, cover skillet and cook rice on low heat for 10 minutes. Remove cover and add black-eyed peas. Do not stir.

Cover skillet again and cook slowly for 30 minutes. Remove skillet from heat and let stand undisturbed for another 10 minutes. Remove cover and gently fluff rice with a fork to incorporate the black-eyed peas. Serve at once.

Sourdough noodles
By Charles Bryant O'Dooley

1 egg, well-beaten
½ cup starter (see page 43 for recipe)

1 cup flour
1 tsp. salt

Mix together well. Add enough extra flour to make a stiff dough. Knead 8-10 minutes. Roll out to ⅛-inch thickness on well-floured board. Sprinkle flour evenly over the top of dough. Fold and cut ½-inch wide slices. Spread out and let dry overnight or 8 hours. Use immediately or freeze. Cook the same as regular noodles.

Black beans and rice
By Tom Barth

1 lb. black beans, rinsed and sorted
2 Tbsp. margarine
2 onions, coarsely chopped
3-4 bay leaves
3 garlic cloves, minced
½ lb. diced turkey ham

2 10¾-oz. cans chicken stock
1 Tbsp. chili powder (or to taste)
½ tsp. cayenne pepper (or to taste)
2-3 cups cooked long grain brown rice

Cover beans with cold water and boil 3 minutes, remove from heat, and let stand for 1 hour.

Drain beans. Heat margarine in a large heavy pot over medium heat. Add onion and bay leaves and cook until onions are soft. Add garlic and turkey ham and cook for 2-3 minutes more. Add chicken stock, black beans, chili powder and cayenne. Add water to cover mixture if necessary. Cover and simmer beans until tender but not mushy, approximately 2 hours. Stir occasionally.

When beans are cooked stir in brown rice and adjust seasonings and liquid, if necessary. Mixture should be very moist but not soupy. Serve with a green salad and warm tortillas or French bread.

Note: to prepare a nice light brown rice make sure you are using long grain brown rice. Use a ratio of slightly more than 1 part water to 1 part rice (e.g.; 1⅛ cup of water to 1 cup of rice) Put rice and water in a heavy saucepan, bring to a boil, reduce heat to a very low simmer and cover with a tight-fitting lid. Cook rice for exactly 31 minutes. Do not remove lid during cooking! After removing rice from heat let set about 10 minutes. Remove cover and fluff rice with a fork.

Blunt family chili
By Richard Blunt

6 Tbsp. peanut oil
3 lb. lean ground beef chuck, chili grind
1½ lbs. lean pork, cut into thin strips about 1-inch long by ½-inch wide
2 medium yellow onions, diced
6 garlic cloves, diced fine
4 Tbsp. chili seasoning
1 16-oz. jar chunky salsa, medium or hot
1 14-oz. can low-fat beef stock
1 12-oz. bottle brown ale, precooked to boil off the alcohol
1 28-oz. can crushed tomato in puree
1 oz. bittersweet chocolate
salt and pepper to taste

Heat 2 Tbsp. oil in heavy-bottomed skillet or Dutch oven. Add ground beef and sauté over medium-high heat until meat loses its pink color and starts to brown. Remove cooked beef and hold in bowl or other container.

Heat 2 Tbsp. oil in same pot and sauté pork over medium-high heat until it loses its pink color and is browned to suit your taste. Add cooked pork to beef.

Heat remaining 2 Tbsp. oil and sauté onions over medium heat until translucent and are starting to brown. If you have the patience to bring your onions to an even light brown color, it will add a pleasant light sweetness to your chili.

When onions are done add garlic and continue to cook mixture for about 30 seconds.

Add chili seasoning and continue to cook mixture for another 30 seconds.

Add salsa, beef stock, pre-cooked ale, and crushed tomato to pot and heat mixture to slow, even simmer. Gently stir in meat and return stew to same slow, even simmer. Cook chili for 1½-2 hours.

Add the chocolate during the last ½ hour of cooking. Salt and pepper to taste.

If at any time during the cooking the chili seems too dry for your taste, add more liquid of your choice.

Tricia's chicken chili
By Richard Blunt

8 oz. dried, red kidney or
  pinto beans
cold water to soak the beans
2 Tbsp. peanut oil or other
  light oil
2 lbs. boneless, skinless
  chicken breasts diced in
  ½-inch pieces
1 medium onion, diced medium

1 large red bell pepper,
  diced medium
2 cloves fresh garlic, minced
2 tsp. chili seasoning
1 tsp. McCormick Grill Mates
  Montreal Chicken seasoning
½ cup chicken broth
1 10-oz. can diced tomatoes
  with chilies
1 tsp. dried marjoram

Soak beans for 6-8 hours in enough cold water to cover beans by 2 inches.

Drain beans and discard soaking water. Rinse beans in cold running water. In a pot, cover the beans with enough fresh water to cover by 2 inches. Over medium heat, simmer beans until tender and fully cooked. Drain beans immediately and set aside.

Heat oil in a Dutch oven or other heavy-bottomed pot over medium heat. Add chicken and sauté until it loses its pink color. Add onion, bell pepper, and garlic to chicken and continue to cook mixture until chicken is fully cooked.

Gently stir in chili seasoning and chicken seasoning. Continue cooking mixture for another 60 seconds.

Stir in chicken broth, diced tomatoes, and marjoram and slowly simmer chili, uncovered, for 20 minutes.

Gently fold in beans and simmer chili for another 2-3 minutes, just long enough to heat beans.

Serve immediately over rice or with your favorite warm-from-the-oven corn bread.

Rice and beans
By Richard Blunt

½ cup dried kidney beans
water to wash and soak the
beans
1½ cups Basmati rice
water to wash and soak the
rice
2 cups canned coconut milk
2 Tbsp. peanut oil
½ cup onion, diced fine
1 garlic clove, chopped fine
2 whole scallions, diced
medium

¼ tsp. dried leaf thyme
1¼ cups canned vegetable
stock
¼ tsp. kosher salt
½ Tbsp. granulated sugar
1 Tbsp. dark Jamaican rum
2 Tbsp. fresh coriander
leaves—also called cilan-
tro, chopped (note: fresh
mint is a nice substitute for
coriander leaves if you
can't find them)

Put beans in a heavy-bottomed saucepot with about 1 qt. of water. Boil beans for 2 minutes then set aside for 1 hour.

Add 2 qts. of cold water to rice and gently rub rice between fingers to remove excess starch. Repeat this process with fresh water until the water remains clear. Soak rice in 1 qt. of cold water for at least 30 minutes.

Drain and rinse beans with fresh cold water. Combine beans with coconut milk and cook beans in the coconut milk over medium heat until tender but not mushy.

Drain rice and set aside.

Heat oil in a 2-quart heavy-bottomed saucepot over medium heat. Add onion and sauté until onion becomes translucent. Add rice and continue to sauté mixture for 2 minutes, while stirring gently with wooden spoon.

Add garlic and scallion and continue sautéing mixture for 1 minute. Add thyme, vegetable stock, salt, granulated sugar, rum, and beans along with coconut milk.

Bring mixture to boil over medium high heat, reduce heat to low and stir gently with a wooden spoon to prevent rice from sticking to bottom of pot.

Place a lid loosely on pot and cook rice mixture for 15 minutes. Remove pot from heat, place lid tightly on pot and allow rice to rest, undisturbed, for another 15 minutes.

Transfer rice and beans to a serving platter and sprinkle chopped coriander on top. Serve immediately.

Easy, flat homemade manicotti
By Jean Winfrey

Pasta:
6 eggs
1¼ cups flour
1¼ cups water

Filling:
1 lb. ricotta cheese
1 egg
¼ cup Parmesan cheese
fresh parsley
½ tsp. salt

For pasta: Beat eggs. Add flour and water. Drop by spoonfuls on greased griddle. Pick up with a spatula and lay on smooth surface to fill.

For filling: Mix all ingredients together, fill manicotti and bake at 350° until cheese melts.

No chili powder chili
By Jan Cook

1 lb. ground beef
1 medium onion, chopped
2 Tbsp. margarine
2 15-oz. cans pinto beans
   with jalapeños
1 28-oz. can tomatoes
1 6-oz. can tomato paste

1 4-oz. can mild diced chili
   peppers
2 Tbsp. sugar
1 bay leaf
1 tsp. marjoram
½ tsp. garlic powder

Cook ground beef and drain. Sauté onion in margarine. Add beef, onion, and remaining ingredients in large pot and simmer for 1 hour.

Fried rice
By Richard Blunt

3 cups cold cooked rice
¼ cup chopped ham, cooked pork, lamb, shrimp, or beef
¼ cup slivered blanched almonds, toasted
1 egg (scrambled ahead of time)
Vegetable mixture:
4 chopped water chestnuts
¼ cup chopped fresh mushrooms (choose your favorite type)
4 chopped scallions
¼ cup fresh or frozen peas

½ cup fresh Mung bean sprouts
1½ tsp. fresh lemon grass, chopped fine, or ½ tsp. ground dried lemon grass (optional)
2 Tbsp. peanut oil
Sauce:
1 Tbsp. dark soy sauce
2 tsp. oyster sauce
1 Tbsp. dry sherry
2 Tbsp. chicken or beef broth (fresh or canned)

Chop ham, cooked pork, chicken, lamb or beef, place in bowl, and set aside.

Heat oven to 325°. Toss almonds in 1 Tbsp. of oil until coated, then spread evenly on a baking sheet and roast until golden brown. This takes about 15 minutes. Shake pan a couple of times to ensure even roasting. Remove from oven and combine with scrambled egg and set aside.

Chop water chestnuts, fresh mushrooms, and scallions and combine in a bowl with peas, bean sprouts, and lemon grass. Set mixture aside.

Combine and mix ingredients for sauce.

In wok or sauté pan, heat 2 Tbsp. of peanut oil over high heat. Do not allow the oil to get so hot that it smokes. (As soon as the oil starts to smoke, it starts to become saturated.)

When oil is hot, add vegetable mixture and stir fry for about 30 seconds. Now add meat, eggs, and almonds. Stir fry for another 30 seconds.

Place rice on top of mixture, cover and allow to cook for 1 minute. Remove cover, add sauce and stir entire mixture thoroughly and heat to serving temperature for about 3 more minutes. Remove from heat and enjoy.

Chuckwagon beans
By Lucy Shober

1 16-oz. pkg. dry pinto beans
9 cups water
2 large onions, peeled and
  chopped
2 tsp. salt
½ tsp. oregano

½ tsp. garlic powder or 2
  cloves of sliced garlic
¼ tsp. pepper
1 Tbsp. brown sugar or
  molasses (add this last,
  and put in a little more if
  you like)

Wash beans and heat along with 6 cups of water until they boil for 5 minutes, then turn the stove off. Let them sit for 1 hour. Add 3 more cups of water and boil it all again. Now add everything else, stir it up, and cook it for about an hour.

Rice cakes
By Lucy Shober

1 egg
2 cups cooked rice
2 spring onions, chopped

Mix ingredients, shape into cakes and fry in an oiled skillet.

North woods baked beans

By Richard Blunt

2 cups white pea beans
(regular, not quick)
½ cup diced onion
2 cloves fresh garlic,
chopped
3 Tbsp. maple syrup
3 Tbsp. chili sauce
2 Tbsp. dark unsulphured
molasses
2 Tbsp. dijon mustard
1 Tbsp. dark brown sugar

½ cup favorite beer or ale
¼ cup good beef or chicken
stock
1 bay leaf
1 tsp. salt
½ tsp. cider vinegar
1 tsp. curry powder
4 oz. piece salt pork (scored
almost down to the skin
but leave skin attached)

Cover beans with water and discard any beans that float to the surface. Drain beans and cover with cold water again. Put them in the refrigerator and let them soak for at least 8-9 hours (or overnight).

After beans have soaked, drain off what water remains and cover beans again with fresh water. Place beans over medium heat and bring to a boil. Reduce heat and simmer beans for another 30 minutes to soften them. Drain again but save about 2 cups of bean stock for later use in recipe.

Place salt pork in some boiling water and simmer for 10-15 minutes. Remove salt pork from boiling water and place in bottom of a 2-3 qt. greased oven casserole. Next, add the well-drained beans to the casserole, covering the salt pork.

Combine and mix all of the flavoring agents in a small bowl, and add this mixture to beans and stir in.

Cover casserole and place in a pre-heated 250° oven and bake for 7-9 hours, when the beans will be tender and have absorbed the flavoring liqueur. Check casserole every couple of hours. If beans seem to be prematurely drying, add a little of the reserved bean water to restore consistency.

During the last ½ hour of baking, remove cover from casserole. This allows mixture to thicken a little bit while still retaining some moisture.

Dragon's breath chili
By Rodney Merrill

1/3 lb. kidney beans
1/3 lb. pinto beans
1/3 lb. navy beans
6 cups water
2 medium onions, chopped
1 garlic clove, minced
1 lb. lean ground beef (or
  lean ground turkey)
1 lb. pork or turkey sausage

1 can tomatoes (28 oz. or 1
  qt. home-canned)
1 Tbsp. chili powder
1 tsp. cumin
1 tsp. paprika
1 tsp. salt
½ tsp. crushed red pepper
½ tsp. cayenne pepper

Sort beans to remove any sand or pebbles, then wash and drain. Cover beans with 6 cups of water. Bring to a boil for about 15 minutes. Cover and let stand for about 1 hour.

(When cooking ground meats, stir gently to avoid smashing and compacting.)

Cook sausage on medium heat. Remove sausage with a slotted spoon and add to beans. Sauté onion and minced garlic in sausage fat until slightly golden. Add ground meat (beef or turkey) and cook on medium-high heat until meat is browned. Add to beans.

Break up tomatoes into bite-sized pieces and add to beans. (Hint: Press tomatoes against the inside of can (or jar) with sharp knife, or hold each tomato over pot and crush it between fingers). Add spices.

Simmer, uncovered, for about 1½ hours. Taste-testing is the only sure way to know when chili is done. Beans should be slightly soft all the way through (no "gritty" texture in the middle) and should leave the taste-tester thinking only of water. Serves 5-6.

Pasta, rice, & beans

Chicken chili
By Arthur Vernon II

5 Tbsp. vegetable oil
3 large onions, chopped (about 6 cups)
3 fresh or canned jalapeño peppers, seeded, finely chopped
3 Tbsp. minced garlic (about 9 medium cloves)
2 Tbsp. chili powder
1 Tbsp. ground cumin
2 tsp. dried coriander
1 tsp. ground cinnamon
4 cups chicken broth
2 12-oz. beer cans
2 16-oz. cans crushed tomatoes
3 15-oz. cans pinto or kidney beans, drained
8 cups cubed cooked chicken or turkey
1 oz. unsweetened chocolate, grated
2 Tbsp. fresh lime juice
2 tsp. salt
3 medium yellow or red bell peppers, seeded, cut into ½ inch pieces
Sour cream, salsa, grated sharp cheddar cheese, and chopped scallions or red onion for garnish (optional)

Heat 3 Tbsp. oil in Dutch oven or large saucepan over medium heat. Add onion and sauté until softened, 5 minutes. Add jalapeño peppers, sauté 1 minute. Add garlic, chili powder, cumin, coriander, and cinnamon. Cook 1-2 minutes stirring to coat thoroughly. Stir in broth, beer, and tomatoes. Cook 1 hour stirring occasionally. Add beans and cook uncovered 30 minutes. Add chicken, chocolate, lime juice, and salt to Dutch oven stirring until chocolate is melted. Taste and adjust seasonings. Meanwhile, heat remaining 2 Tbsp. oil in medium skillet over medium heat. Add bell pepper and sauté only until crisp-tender, 3-5 minutes. Serve chili hot with sautéed bell peppers, sour cream, salsa, grated cheddar cheese, and scallions or red onions, if desired. Serves 12.

Howard's chili pinwheels
By Richard Blunt

2 lbs. lean ground beef (80-85% lean is best, regular grind—don't use the chili grind for this)
8 oz. onion, diced fine
3 oz. celery, diced fine
3 cloves garlic, diced fine
2 Tbsp. chili seasoning
1½ cups tomato sauce
1 Tbsp. masa harina or fine cornmeal

salt and black pepper to taste
biscuit dough (recipe follows)
Biscuit dough:
3 cups all-purpose flour
1½ Tbsp. double-acting baking powder
¾ tsp. kosher salt
6 Tbsp. butter, margarine, or shortening
1⅛ cups buttermilk

In large heavy-bottomed skillet or Dutch oven, sauté ground beef over medium heat until it loses its red color. Drain off fat. Add onions and celery and continue to cook until beef is completely cooked. Add minced garlic and chili seasoning and continue to cook mixture for 1 minute, stirring constantly.

Heat tomato sauce in small heavy-bottomed pot, stir in cornmeal, and cook mixture over low heat for 1 minute.

Add tomato sauce mixture to beef mixture in large skillet or Dutch oven. Simmer mixture for 5 minutes over low heat. Transfer mixture to a large, shallow casserole dish, cover and refrigerate overnight. The next day prepare the biscuit dough.

Sift flour, baking powder, and salt together in a mixing bowl. Cut shortening into flour until mixture becomes grainy. Add milk and stir into flour mixture just enough to make grains stick together and form a soft dough. Turn dough onto a floured surface and knead lightly for about 30 seconds.

On a floured board, roll dough into rectangle approximately 12 x 25 x ¼-inches. Place chilled chili mixture into center of dough and spread evenly to about ½ inch from edges. Moisten edges of dough with a little milk. Roll up dough from the longer (25") side. Seal edges when roll is complete. Pat roll lightly with floured hands to shape evenly.

Lightly coat 2 cookie sheets with vegetable shortening.

Using a very sharp knife, slice roll into disks about 1-inch thick.

Space disks evenly on cookie sheets and bake in preheated 425° oven for 25 minutes or until pinwheels turn a golden brown. Serve immediately with your favorite sauce.

Poor man's pierogi with red beans
By Richard Blunt

Ingredients for noodles:
12 oz. (dry) medium egg
noodles
4 oz. unsalted butter
1½ lbs. green cabbage
(diced medium)
1 large white onion (diced
medium)
4 cloves minced garlic
1 Tbsp. freshly ground black
pepper
¼ tsp. ground nutmeg
6 dried juniper berries
(crushed)
1 oz. warm gin
½ cup fresh beef stock
**Ingredients for red beans
and sausage:**
½ lb. dry red kidney beans
water to soak the beans
3 large ham hocks
2 cups water

1 cup light fresh beef stock
1 cup of your favorite beer or
ale
1 cup celery (diced medium)
1½ cups onion (diced medium)
1 cup red bell pepper (diced
medium)
2 bay leaves
8 oz. smoked chourico sausage (cut into ½-inch pieces)
2 tsp. dried cilantro
2 cloves minced garlic
1 tsp. chopped fresh mint
1 tsp. dried oregano leaves
1 tsp. ground coriander
½ tsp. cumin powder
½ tsp. cayenne pepper
½ tsp. black pepper
2 fresh tomatoes (peeled,
seeded, and chopped)

Noodles: Cook noodles in lightly salted boiling water until just tender, drain and cool under running water. Set aside.

Melt butter in large frying pan over medium heat and add cabbage, onion, garlic, black pepper, and nutmeg. Sauté until cabbage
is tender and translucent.

Combine juniper berries with warm gin in a flame-proof bowl.
Ignite gin with a match and allow flame to burn out. Combine this
with beef stock and add to cabbage mixture.

Reduce heat and cook cabbage mixture for about 30 minutes, or
until cabbage is very tender. Stir every few minutes to prevent burning.

Combine cabbage with noodles in a large casserole, cover and
refrigerate until beans and sausage are ready.

Beans and sausage: Soak beans for at least 4 hours in cold
water 2 inches above beans. Drain and discard soak water.

Place ham hocks, water, beef stock, ale, celery, onion, red pepper, and bay leaves in a large heavy-bottomed pot, cover, bring to a boil, reduce the heat and simmer until meat is fork tender.

Remove ham hocks and set aside. Add beans to stock, bring to a boil, cover, reduce heat and cook beans over low heat until just tender.

Remove meat from ham hocks and combine with sausage. Stir meats into beans along with remaining ingredients. Transfer mixture to a large earthenware casserole, cover and place into a preheated 300° oven. Bake until beans are very tender and sauce has thickened. This should take from 1½-2 hours. Check casserole occasionally, and if beans become dry add more beef stock as needed.

During last ½ hour that the beans are cooking, place noodle mixture in oven to heat.

Serve red beans and sausage over noodles.

Wild rice and vegetables
By Aunt Gert Kenner

1 cup wild rice
1 cup chicken broth
3 cups water
½ cup celery, chopped

½ cup onion, chopped
5-6 mushrooms, chopped
sliced almonds
2 Tbsp. margarine or butter

Rinse rice 3 or 4 times. In pot, cook rice, chicken broth, and water covered about 55 minutes. In fry pan, sauté celery, onion, mushrooms, and almonds in butter or margarine. When rice is tender mix vegetables with the rice.

Salads

Sweet potato salad
By Richard Blunt

1 cup grated raw sweet potato or yam
2 cups diced apple
¼ cup celeriac (diced)

½ cup broken walnuts
¼ cup seedless raisins
¼ cup dried apricot diced
your favorite lettuce

Combine grated sweet potato, apple and celeriac. Add walnuts, raisins, and diced apricots and toss gently to mix.

Chop lettuce and arrange it on a platter with the sweet potato salad on top of the lettuce.

Below is one of my favorite dressings for this salad.

Walnut vinaigrette
By Richard Blunt

¼ cup extra virgin olive oil
½ cup walnut oil
¼ cup of your favorite her-
bed vinegar

1 Tbsp. apple brandy
kosher salt and freshly
ground black pepper to
taste

Whisk the oils, vinegar, and brandy together and season to taste with salt and pepper. Refrigerate for 1 hour before using.

Celery seed dressing
By Alice Brantley Yeager

½ cup sugar
1 tsp. dry mustard
1 tsp. salt
1 tsp. paprika
¼ tsp. freshly ground black
pepper

¼ medium onion, grated
⅓ cup table vinegar
1 cup salad oil
1 Tbsp. celery seed
1 drop red food coloring

Add a little vinegar to the dry ingredients and then slowly add oil a little at a time, beating well after each addition. Add the remainder of the vinegar and celery seed. Add a drop of red food coloring to make a pink color—more if your artistic bent wants a darker color. Keep the salad dressing in a sealed jar in the refrigerator. It will keep for several days.

Sweet pepper salad
By Alice Brantley Yeager

4 medium sweet peppers,
blocky, cubanelle, or blunt
type
4 medium tomatoes, sliced
2 cups cooked chicken,
chopped
1 small red sweet pepper,
chopped

1 small stalk celery, chopped
1 small onion, minced
¼ cup mayonnaise
¼ tsp. dried sweet basil
¼ tsp. dried dill weed
salt and pepper to taste

Wash peppers and remove stems and seeds. Cut each pepper into 4 or 5 lengthwise pieces. On 4 salad plates, arrange the pepper pieces to extend out from the center in a sunburst pattern. Place slices of tomato between the outer edges of the pepper pieces. Thoroughly mix the rest of ingredients. Divide into 4 portions and place a mound in the middle of each plate. Garnish with chopped green onions, parsley, black olives—whatever suits your fancy. Serve with crackers, chips, iced drinks, etc. Serve with crackers or chips. Serves 4.

Two beans and wild asparagus salad
By Jackie Clay

½ cup cut wax beans
½ cup canned red kidney
  beans or other red bean
½ cup cut asparagus spears

4 Tbsp. vegetable oil
4 Tbsp. vinegar
2 Tbsp. sugar or honey

Cook the vegetables until tender. Drain well. Make dressing by mixing the oil, vinegar, and sugar. You may also add a bit of French dressing if you wish. Toss vegetables with dressing and place, covered, in refrigerator to marinate well. Serve chilled.

Tomato and coriander salad
By Habeeb Salloum

5 medium-sized tomatoes,
  quartered, then thinly
  sliced
¾ cup chopped fresh coriander leaves
1 tsp. salt

½ tsp. pepper
⅛ tsp. cayenne pepper
3 Tbsp. lemon juice
3 Tbsp. olive oil

Place tomatoes and coriander leaves in a salad bowl, then gently toss and set aside.

In a small bowl, thoroughly mix remaining ingredients. Pour over tomatoes and coriander, then toss just before serving. Serves about 6.

Herb salad
By Habeeb Salloum

1 small bunch dandelion
  greens, thoroughly washed
  and chopped
1 cup finely chopped
  stemmed parsley
1 cup finely chopped fresh
  coriander leaves
2 medium tomatoes, diced
  into ½-inch cubes

1 large clove garlic, crushed
4 Tbsp. olive oil
4 Tbsp. lemon juice
1 tsp. salt
½ tsp. pepper
¼ tsp. cumin
about 10 pitted black olives,
  sliced in half

Combine dandelion greens, parsley, coriander leaves, and tomatoes in a salad bowl, then set aside.

In a small bowl, thoroughly mix remaining ingredients, except olives, then pour over salad bowl contents. Toss, then decorate with olives and serve. Serves about 8.

Eggplant salad
By Habeeb Salloum

1 large eggplant (about 2
  lbs.)
oil for frying
4 cloves garlic, crushed
1 small hot pepper, very
  finely chopped

4 Tbsp. lemon juice
2 Tbsp. olive oil
1 tsp. salt
½ tsp. pepper
1 small piece of tomato
sprigs of parsley

Peel, then dice eggplant into about ¾-inch cubes. Place in a strainer in a sink, then place heavy weight over top of eggplant cubes. Allow to stand for an hour in order to drain.

Heat oil in a frying pan to about an inch deep, then fry eggplant cubes until they begin to brown. Remove with slotted spoon, then drain on paper towels.

In the meantime, combine remaining ingredients, except tomato and parsley, then set aside.

Place eggplant cubes on a serving platter, then decorate with the tomato and parsley and serve. Serves about 8.

Apple ham salad
By Anne Westbrook Dominick

4 McIntosh or Liberty apples,
  cored and diced (not
  peeled)
1 Tbsp. lemon juice
2 cups diced cooked ham

²/₃ cup sliced celery
½ cup crumbled blue cheese
¼ cup vegetable oil
2 Tbsp. vinegar

In a bowl mix the first 5 ingredients. Thoroughly mix oil and vinegar and add to apple ham mix. Serves 4.

Waldorf salad
By Anne Westbrook Dominick

2 cups apples, cored and
  diced (not peeled)
1 Tbsp. lemon juice
1 Tbsp. sugar
salt to taste

1 cup sliced celery
½ cup diced walnuts
½ cup raisins
½ cup mayonnaise

In a bowl, mix the apples and the lemon juice. Add all the remaining ingredients. Serves 4.

Apple slaw
By Anne Westbrook Dominick

4 cups shredded cabbage
2 large apples, cored and
  diced (not peeled)
1 small onion, minced

2 Tbsp. lemon juice
½ cup yogurt or sour cream
¼ cup mayonnaise
1 Tbsp. sugar

In a bowl combine the first 4 ingredients. Mix the last 3 ingredients until well mixed and add to the salad. Serves 6.

3-bean salad
By Jo Mason

1 can red kidney beans
1 can green beans
1 can yellow wax beans
¼ cup minced bell pepper

½ cup minced onion
½ cup salad oil
½ cup cider vinegar
¾ cup sugar

Drain beans (using colander). Put in glass container. Add onion and peppers. Combine remaining ingredients and pour over beans. Refrigerate several hours before serving.

Jo's Kentucky-fried cole slaw
By Jo Mason

½ medium-sized head cab-
  bage
1 small carrot
½ bell pepper
½ cup mayonnaise

¼ cup vinegar
¼ cup sugar
½ tsp. dry mustard
dash of salt
dash of black pepper

Shred cabbage finely. Grate carrot and pepper finely. Place vegetables in large bowl. Put mayonnaise in small bowl. Stir in sugar,
then gradually add vinegar while stirring. Add remaining ingredients
to small bowl. Mix well. Stir dressing into vegetables. Cover and chill
several hours before serving.

Tofu salad dressing
By Arline Tobola

1 cup tofu
2-4 Tbsp. oil
1 tsp. salt

4 Tbsp. lemon juice
2 Tbsp. sugar
⅛ tsp. garlic powder

Blend ingredients in blender until smooth. Use for salad dressing
or in place of mayonnaise.

Jan's potato and egg salad
By Jan Cook

10 cups peeled and sliced
cooked potatoes
1 dozen hard-cooked eggs,
peeled, quartered and
sliced
4 tsp. sugar
4 tsp. flavored vinegar (use
your own choice on flavor,
such as tarragon, wine,
balsamic, rice, etc.)
2 cups finely chopped
onions
3 cups mayonnaise
salt, pepper, and celery seed
to taste

Place peeled and sliced potatoes in a large bowl and sprinkle with sugar and vinegar. Let set for a few minutes to allow the vinegar to soak into potatoes. Add chopped onions and mayonnaise. Toss. Add salt, pepper, and celery seed to taste. Fold in hard-cooked eggs. Chill for several hours before serving. Makes 16 servings.

Broccoli/tomato salad
By Bonnie Maruquin

2 stalks broccoli (at least),
chopped into small bite-
sized pieces. Use both
stalks and flowers. Trim
away some of the outer,
stringy part of the stalk.
4 medium tomatoes,
chopped into small bite-
sized pieces.
2 scallions, chopped
1 lb. imitation crab, broken
into small pieces
1 cup mayonnaise, thinned
down with a little milk
scant ½ tsp. sugar
scant tsp. vinegar

Mix sugar and vinegar with the mayonnaise. Add more of either, to taste.
Mix dressing with salad ingredients.

Nameless salad
By Rodney Merrill

2 cups lettuce, coarsely diced
3 stalks green onion, ¼-inch slices
1 medium tart green apple, ¼-inch cubes
1 medium sweet red apple, ¼-inch cubes

1 small grapefruit, segments cut into thirds
2 small or 1 large ripe banana, ¼-inch slices
2 cups miniature marshmallows
1 cup raw unsalted trail mix

Combine ingredients in a large bowl. Toss to mix thoroughly. Stir in Nameless salad dressing (below) 15-20 minutes before serving. Lightly toss until salad is evenly coated.

Nameless salad dressing
By Rodney Merrill

1/3 cup plain nonfat yogurt
1/3 cup extra-lowfat sour cream
¼ cup nonfat Italian dressing

¼ cup lowfat mayonnaise
¼ cup mild-flavored honey (orange or avocado)

Combine all ingredients in any order. Blend lightly with a wire whip just until dressing is uniform and smooth. Beating will make the dressing too thin.

Sauces & marinades

Old-fashioned hot dog pepper relish
By Richard Blunt

3 cups seeded and coarsely chopped bell peppers (use a mixture of yellow, green, and red)
4 cups coarsely chopped white onions (about 5 medium onions)
1 cup finely chopped green cabbage
Boiling water to cover
½ cup 5% white vinegar
½ cup water
1½ cups 5% cider vinegar
1 tsp. peeled, minced fresh ginger
4 cloves minced fresh garlic
4 seeded jalapeño peppers, minced (the hottest you can find)
1½ cups sugar
1 Tbsp. kosher salt
2 Tbsp. mustard seeds
2 Tbsp. celery seeds
1 tsp. whole allspice
1 tsp. dried chilli pepper flakes

Place chopped bell peppers, onions, and cabbage in large stainless steel or heat-resistant glass bowl and add enough hot water to cover. Let mixture stand for 15 minutes then drain and return to bowl.

Combine ½ cup white vinegar with ½ cup water. Heat mixture to boiling and pour over drained vegetables. Let mixture stand for 15 minutes and drain again.

Place drained vegetables in stainless steel pot, large enough to hold all of the ingredients, then add remaining ingredients and bring mixture to boil over medium-high heat. Cook for 30 seconds, then remove mixture from heat.

Pour mixture into clean, hot, 1-pint canning jars and process in a boiling water bath for 5 minutes to seal the jars. Let relish mellow for 1 month in a cool dark place before serving.

Once opened, store tightly closed jar in refrigerator.

Pickled chili peppers
By Richard Blunt

Brine:
2 lbs. (1 gallon) fresh, ripe, chili peppers
1 gallon water
2 cups of sea or kosher salt
Marinade:
1 cup water
5 cups white vinegar (5% acidity)
2 Tbsp. sugar
1 tsp. dried thyme
10 whole allspice
1 tsp. whole coriander seeds
12 black peppercorns
12 white peppercorns
1 tsp. whole mustard seeds
2 juniper berries
6 whole cloves
Herb Oil Garnish:
4 dried bay leaves
12 whole, unpeeled, garlic cloves, parboiled for 2 minutes
2 carrots, par boiled for 2 minutes and sliced into 1/8-inch coins
6 peeled shallots
12 Tbsp. virgin olive oil

Wash the peppers, trim the stems to a stub and prick each pepper twice with a fork on opposite sides.

Bring the water to a boil, immediately remove it from the heat, and dissolve the salt in it to make a brine. Let it cool.

Combine the washed peppers and the cooled brine in a glass, plastic, stainless steel, or other non reactive container. Place a china plate on top of the peppers to hold them down in the brine. Use 2 if necessary. Soak the peppers in the brine for a minimum of 12 hours.

Combine all the marinade ingredients in a heavy bottom stainless steel sauce pan. Bring this mixture to a boil, then reduce the heat to low and simmer, uncovered, for 10 minutes.

Wash and sterilize 8-12 pint-size canning jars and lids. In each sanitized, hot jar place ¼ of a dried bay leaf, 1 garlic clove, several carrot slices, ½ of a shallot and 1 tablespoon of olive oil, then pack the peppers into the jars. Pour marinading liquid into each jar leaving at least ½-inch of head space from the top of the liquid to the rim.

Use a boiling water bath method to seal the jars and process the peppers for 5 minutes. Store the jars in a cool, dark place for 3-4 weeks before using.

Refrigerate unused portions after you've opened a jar.

Nana V's fire sauce
By Richard Blunt

1 pint homemade pickled chili peppers (See previous recipe.)
1 12 oz. bottle chili sauce
½ cup pickling marinade strained from the chili peppers
½ cup Lairds Applejack or brandy

1 Tbsp. Worcestershire sauce
¼ tsp. freshly ground black pepper
¼ tsp. ground coriander
⅛ tsp. liquid smoke
⅛ tsp. ground cumin

Strain peppers, saving pickling liquid, garlic clove, shallot, and carrot slices. Discard spices.

Remove stems and seeds from each of the peppers, and process peppers, garlic clove, shallot and carrot slices into a paste, using a food processor or blender.

Combine chili pepper paste, chili sauce, pickling liquid, applejack and Worcestershire sauce in a stainless steel saucepan. Simmer mixture over low heat for 5 minutes. Stir in black pepper and coriander and simmer for another minute.

Remove sauce from heat and stir in liquid smoke and cumin.

Let sauce cool in refrigerator.

You may prefer a thinner sauce, so before bottling, adjust the thickness of the sauce to suit your preference by adding a little more pickling liquid or applejack. Store in refrigerator in a sanitized pint canning jar or other sanitized container of your choice.

Mystery salsa
By Richard Blunt

1 28-oz. can name brand whole plum tomatoes (avoid bargain brands)
½ cup red onions
⅓ cup red bell pepper, finely diced
2-3 home pickled jalapeño or cherry peppers, finely diced

2 Tbsp. Lairds Applejack or brandy
¼ cup fresh cilantro, washed, drained and finely chopped
½ tsp. malt vinegar
kosher salt to taste
fresh lime juice to taste

Strain tomatoes over a bowl and save juice. Gently remove as many of the seeds from each tomato as possible without mashing the flesh. With a very sharp knife, dice drained tomatoes into medium chunks.

Pour juice into a heavy-bottomed, stainless steel saucepan and simmer over low heat until reduced by half. Combine reduced tomato juice with diced tomatoes in a stainless steel or glass bowl.

Combine red onion, bell pepper, pickled peppers, applejack, cilantro, and malt vinegar. Add mixture to tomatoes, and let salsa mellow at room temperature for a couple of hours.

After mellowing period, taste salsa and add salt and lime juice to suit your taste. This salsa is best when served the day it is made, but it will hold in the refrigerator for a couple of days with only a slight loss of flavor.

Raspberry ketchup
By Richard Blunt

1½ cups fresh or frozen
   raspberries
1-3 home pickled chili peppers (let your taste be the
   judge) or substitute ⅛ tsp.
   cayenne pepper
⅓ cup fresh or canned
   tomato puree
⅓ cup wine vinegar

¼ cup medium or dry sherry
⅔ cup firmly packed light
   brown sugar
¼ tsp. ground clove
¼ tsp. ground ginger
½ tsp. freshly ground nutmeg
¼ tsp. kosher salt
1 Tbsp. butter or margarine

If you are using fresh raspberries, carefully pick them over and use only firm unblemished berries. If you are using home-pickled chili peppers, (see page 250) remove seeds and stems.

In stainless steel heavy-bottomed sauce pan, combine raspberries and pickled chili peppers with tomato puree, wine vinegar, and sherry. If you are substituting cayenne pepper for the peppers, do not add it at this time. Simmer mixture over low heat for 60 seconds.

Over a bowl put the mixture through a food mill or press the mixture through stainless steel strainer and discard pulp.

Return strained mixture to stainless steel saucepan along with sugar, ground clove, ground ginger, ground nutmeg, salt, butter, and, if you are substituting it for the pickled peppers, cayenne pepper. Return pan to stove and simmer for about 10 minutes over low heat until desired consistency is reached. If sauce appears to be too thick adjust the consistency with a little more vinegar mixed half-and-half with water.

Transfer sauce to a sanitized pint canning jar, and place in the refrigerator to cool. This sauce is at its best when warmed over low heat to just below the simmering point.

Homemade salsa
By Jackie Clay

4 medium tomatoes
½ cup onion, finely chopped
¼ cup celery, finely chopped
¼ cup bell pepper, finely
   chopped
¼ cup olive oil

3 Tbsp. fresh jalapeño or
   Tam Jalapeño pepper,
   finely chopped
2 Tbsp. vinegar or juice from
   one small lime
1 tsp. fresh cilantro, finely
   chopped
1 tsp. salt

Peel tomatoes by plunging them into boiling water for 30 seconds, then dipping into ice cold water. Cut out the stem and core, then slip off the peel. Add the other ingredients, cover and refrigerate overnight. Stir before serving.

Stir-fried nopalitos with chilies
By Jackie Clay

1 cup sliced nopalitos
1 cup sliced mushrooms
1 cup sliced roasted chilies
½ cup sliced onion

3 chopped firm ripe toma-
   toes, chopped
2 Tbsp. oil or shortening

Stir fry the nopalitos, mushrooms, roasted chilies (seeded, mild, thick-meated), and sliced onion. When tender, add the chopped tomatoes and cook just until the tomatoes are no longer hot.

Serve as you would a salsa, dipped up with crispy fried corn tortillas and sour cream and grated cheddar cheese.

Highland malt mustard
By Richard Blunt

½ cup brown mustard seeds
½ cup yellow mustard seeds
4 Tbsp. water
½ cup honey
⅔ cup cider vinegar
1 Tbsp. freshly ground nutmeg
1 Tbsp. kosher salt

⅔ cup single malt Scotch whiskey (Use Scotch for a full body and smoky flavor. For a lighter flavor substitute Irish or Canadian whiskey. For alcohol-free, substitute fresh apple cider.)

Grind brown and yellow mustard seed together to a desired consistency in a blender. Some people like a coarse mustard and some like it smooth.

Mix processed seeds with water in a glass or stainless steel bowl and let mixture stand covered for 1 hour.

Combine mustard mixture, honey, vinegar, nutmeg, salt, and whiskey (or cider) in blender or food processor. Process until mixture forms desired consistency. Add more honey if mixture looks dry.

Transfer mixture to glass or stainless steel bowl, cover and let stand for 24 hours.

Pour into sterilized 4-oz. jelly jars and process in a boiling water bath for 10 minutes. Store in a cool dark place for 3 weeks. Refrigerate after opening.

This will yield about 10 4-oz. jars (about 2 ½ cups).

Apple barbeque sauce
By Richard Blunt

6 Tbsp. vegetable oil
2 cups onions, chopped fine
1 cup celery, chopped fine
3 Tbsp. fresh ginger,
   chopped fine
4 cloves fresh garlic,
   chopped fine
1 lb. McIntosh or Granny
   Smith apples, peeled,
   cored, and chopped
2 tsp. chili powder
2 Tbsp. dried mustard
   (Coleman's is best)
2 tsp. dried thyme
½ tsp. dried oregano
⅓ cup cider vinegar
¼ cup molasses

4 cups homemade beef
   stock (You can substitute
   commercial beef stock, but
   the consistency of the final
   product isn't as good
   because commercial beef
   stock has no collagen.)
1½ cups chili sauce
⅓ cup tomato paste
1 tsp. kosher salt
2 tsp. freshly ground black
   pepper
½ cup Worcestershire sauce
1 cup hard cider
⅓ cup Calvados
2 bay leaves

Heat 6 Tbsp. oil over medium-high heat in a large, heavy-bottomed fry pan. Add onions, celery, ginger, garlic, and apples. Sauté mixture until vegetables become tender and apples become soft and start to break up. Remove pan from heat and set aside, allowing mixture to cool.

Combine remaining ingredients in large sauce pot and bring mixture to a slow simmer over medium heat. Continue simmering until the volume of the sauce is reduced about ¼.

While sauce is simmering, puree apple and vegetable mixture in a food processor or blender. Add this puree to reduced sauce. Return sauce to slow simmer and continue cooking until sauce is thick, but can still be poured. If it seems to be too thick, thin it with a little hard cider.

Mustard marinade
By Richard Blunt

¼ tsp. salt
½ tsp. freshly grated white
  pepper
1½ tsp. Dijon mustard
½ tsp. dried thyme leaves

½ tsp. freshly grated nutmeg
⅛ tsp. allspice
½ tsp. ground ginger
1 clove finely minced garlic
1 tsp. vegetable oil

In a bowl, combine and mix all of the marinade ingredients. Rub this marinade on fish and set aside for 30 minutes to 1 hour.

Pesto
By Richard Blunt

2 cups fresh basil leaves,
  loosely packed
2 cloves fresh garlic
½ tsp. kosher salt
1½ oz. pine nuts

2 Tbsp. grated Romano
  cheese
1 Tbsp. grated Parmesan
  cheese
4 Tbsp. unsalted butter
¾ cup virgin olive oil

In a blender place ½ the olive oil along with other ingredients, except butter and cheeses, and blend for about 45 seconds until a paste is formed that is still thin enough to run off a spoon.

Scrape mixture into another bowl and blend in butter and cheeses with a wooden spoon. Adjust consistency as desired.

Sauces & marinades

Tomato and basil sauce
By Richard Blunt

1 clove of garlic
1 small onion
4 fresh basil leaves or 2
  dried leaves
4 Tbsp. virgin olive oil
12 fresh plum tomatoes,
  peeled and seeded, or 3
  cups of canned tomatoes
  without the juice

1 tsp. kosher salt
freshly ground pepper to
  taste
1 lb. of your favorite pasta to
  serve 4-6 of your favorite
  people
freshly grated Parmesan
  cheese as a topping

Chop onion, garlic, and basil finely.

Sauté them in olive oil until onions and garlic are light gold in color.

Chop tomatoes finely and carefully add them to olive oil. I suggest you remove oil from heat to prevent spattering.

Cook over a low heat until natural juices have boiled down and sauce has thickened. This should take about 20 minutes to ½ hour.

Add the salt and freshly ground black pepper to taste and cook for a few minutes more.

Cook pasta, get your friends to the table and excite those taste buds!

Tomato and meat sauce
By Richard Blunt

1 small onion
1 small carrot
1 stalk of celery
¼ cup virgin olive oil
3 chicken necks with the skin removed
½ lb. lean ground beef
½ lb. lean ground pork
¼ cup dry red wine
½ cup dark ale

4 cups peeled and seeded plum tomatoes (fresh or canned)
1½ Tbsp. tomato paste
1 tsp. or more kosher salt to suit your taste
freshly ground black pepper to taste
freshly grated Parmesan cheese for a topping

Chop onion, carrots, and celery until very fine. Sauté in olive oil until onion and garlic are light golden color. Add chicken necks and ground meats and sauté until lightly browned. Work meats with a wooden spoon to break up all the lumps. When meats are browned add ale and wine and cook to allow alcohol to evaporate.

Add salt, tomatoes, and tomato paste and enough freshly ground pepper to suit your taste.

Bring to boil, reduce heat and slowly simmer for about 2 hours. Continue to check the consistency. If sauce seems too thick before it is done, add a little water. If you see any fat rising to the surface, remove immediately. The less fat the better the sauce will be.

To serve 4-6 people, cook 1¼ lbs. of your favorite pasta.

All-purpose chilli pepper sauce
By Richard Blunt

¼ cup olive oil
1 cup chopped onion
4 cloves minced fresh garlic
2-inch piece fresh ginger,
    peeled and minced
¼ cup your favorite vinegar
4 cups ketchup
¼ cup molasses
1 cup mild commercial chilli
    sauce
¼ cup Worcestershire sauce
½ cup your favorite "strong"
    ale

2 tsp. coarse Dijon style
    mustard
1 Tbsp. liquid smoke
2 tsp. medium or hot curry
    powder
½ tsp. ground coriander
    seed
½ tsp. cumin seed
1 Tbsp. finely minced hot
    pickled peppers (optional)
½ tsp. freshly ground black
    pepper
1 tsp. cayenne pepper (more
    or less according to taste)

Heat olive oil in heavy-bottomed sauce pan and add onions. Sauté onions over medium heat until translucent, then add garlic and ginger and continue to sauté for 2-3 minutes. Combine all other ingredients in a separate container and stir. Add to the sautéed vegetables, cover pan, and simmer over low heat for about 45 minutes. Stir frequently to prevent burning. Adjust thickness with more ale (or fresh apple cider for a real taste treat) to thin if necessary.

Hot chili sauce
By Jo Mason

3 Tbsp. bacon drippings
3 cloves minced garlic
3 Tbsp. flour

6 Tbsp. chili powder
3½ cups water
1 beef bouillon cube

In a large saucepan, melt bacon drippings over low heat. Add garlic, flour, and chili powder. (Be careful at this point as chili burns easily.) Stir in water and bouillon cube. Simmer 10 minutes.

Ballpark mustard
By Richard Blunt

¾ cup yellow mustard seeds
¼ cup brown mustard seeds
4 Tbsp. water
½ cup honey
2/3 cup cider vinegar
2/3 cup flat dark ale or beer
¼ tsp. chilli pepper flakes
1 Tbsp. horseradish
1 Tbsp. freshly ground nutmeg
1 Tbsp. kosher salt

Grind mustard seeds to desired consistency in blender.

Mix processed seeds with water in a glass or stainless steel bowl and let mixture stand covered for 1 hour.

Combine mustard mixture, honey, vinegar, flat ale, chilli pepper flakes, horseradish, nutmeg, and salt in blender or food processor. Process until mixture forms a consistency you like. Add more honey if mixture looks dry.

Transfer mixture to glass or stainless steel bowl, cover and let stand for 24 hours.

Pour into sterilized 4-oz. jelly jars and process in boiling water bath for 10 minutes. Store in cool dark place for 3 weeks. Refrigerate after opening.

This will yield about 2½ cups.

Corn and nopalito salsa
By Jackie Clay

1½ cups cooked sweet corn
½ cup chopped nopalitos
2 Tbsp. chopped sweet red
pepper
¼ cup cooked black beans
2 Tbsp. brown sugar
½ tsp. salt
pinch black pepper
pinch turmeric
3 Tbsp. vinegar
1 seeded, chopped jalepeño
(optional)

Combine all ingredients in a saucepan and mix well. Heat thoroughly. Cool and refrigerate. Serve cold. We love it on tacos and chalupas with a bit of sour cream. Remember, the nopalito is a vegetable, and can be used in any pickle recipe for mixed vegetables, sweet or sour.

Seafood

Fried tuna patties
By Jackie Clay

2 cans light tuna, drained
1 cup crushed dried bread
  crumbs
¼ cup dehydrated onion
  flakes

3 eggs or rehydrated equivalent
½ tsp. lemon pepper
flour to coat patties
oil to fry

Mix drained tuna, bread crumbs, egg, onion flakes, and lemon pepper. Divide into golf ball-sized portions, pat into patties, dip both sides in flour. Heat oil to medium heat and gently place patties into frying pan. After one side is done, turn and finish cooking. This is a quick and easy alternative to "fish sticks."

Hearty breakfast fillets
By Richard Blunt

½ cup flour
kosher salt and freshly
  ground black pepper to
  taste
1 egg

½ cup milk
1 cup cornflake crumbs
1 lb. fish fillets (small thin fillets preferred)
½ cup peanut oil

Equipment: 7-inch well-seasoned cast iron skillet or an equivalently sized skillet with a nonstick surface.

Combine and blend flour with salt and pepper in a shallow bowl.

In separate bowl, combine and blend egg with milk.

Place the cornflake crumbs in a third bowl.

Coat fillets with flour, then shake off any excess flour. Dip fillets in egg mixture, making sure that fillets have no dry spots.

Coat fillets with cornflake crumbs. Inspect fillets to ensure that each is completely coated with crumbs. If necessary redip the bare spot in the egg mixture, then back into the crumbs.

Heat oil over medium flame. Fry each fillet until golden brown on each side. Corn flake crumbs brown quickly, and the thin fillets cook equally as fast, so the whole process will only take a couple of minutes.

Seafood

Masala jheenga
By Richard Blunt

1½ tsp. white poppy seeds
2 lbs. medium-sized raw
  shrimp (about 30-35
  shrimp per lb.)
½ tsp. turmeric
2½ cups cold water
¼ cup regular or lowfat milk
¼ cup cottage cheese
3 Tbsp. peanut oil
2 cups onion, chopped finely

3 cloves fresh garlic, minced
2 tsp. garam masala
1 tsp. paprika
4 fresh plum tomatoes,
  peeled, seeded, and
  chopped
¼-½ tsp. cayenne pepper
1 tsp. kosher salt
2 Tbsp. fresh cilantro leaves,
  chopped

In small fry pan, dry roast poppy seeds over medium heat until brown. Let cool for a few minutes then grind to a powder in a spice mill or blender.

Peel and devein shrimp, then wash in cold running water. Put in a colander and let drain for 15 minutes.

Put shrimp, turmeric, and cold water in a pot to poach over a medium flame. Watch shrimp carefully because they will cook completely before the water boils. Drain shrimp and save poaching water.

Process milk and cottage cheese in a blender until thoroughly blended together with creamy consistency.

Heat oil in Dutch oven (or other heavy-bottomed skillet with a non-stick surface) over medium heat. Fry onions, stirring constantly, until medium brown (about 10 minutes). Add garlic and cook for another minute.

Reduce heat to low, and stir ground poppy seeds, garam masala, and paprika into onion mixture, and cook about 15 seconds.

Add chopped tomato, cayenne pepper, salt, and 1½ cups of the reserved poaching liquid. Increase heat to medium high and boil mixture uncovered for 15 minutes, or until sauce becomes thick and pulpy. Be sure to stir sauce every few minutes to prevent sticking.

Reduce heat and add cottage cheese and milk puree. Cook mixture over low heat for another 2 minutes, stirring constantly. Gently stir in shrimp, cover, and slowly simmer mixture until shrimps are heated through. Turn off heat and let mixture rest for 1 hour before serving.

At serving time slowly heat mixture. Sprinkle cilantro leaves on top as you bring the dish to the table.

Sauté Meunière Amandine
By Richard Blunt

6 Tbsp. blanched, slivered almonds
4 8-oz. skin-on fish fillets, steaks, or pan-dressed fish
½ cup milk

½ cup Wondra flour (I like the grainy texture with this process)
6 Tbsp. butter or margarine
¼ cup fresh lemon juice
¼ cup fresh, sliced mushrooms

Equipment: 7-inch well-seasoned cast iron skillet or an equivalently-sized skillet with a nonstick surface.

Dry roast almonds over medium-low heat until light golden brown, then remove from pan and set aside.

Dip fish fillets or steaks in milk, then dredge in flour. Shake off any surplus flour.

Melt butter or margarine over medium-low heat, then sauté mushrooms lightly. Remove mushrooms and combine with almonds.

Place fish in pan. If you are using fillets, have the skin side up. Sauté fish, slowly, over low heat until brown on one side, then flip fish over to brown on other side. Remove fish to a warm platter and set aside.

Add lemon juice, almonds, and mushrooms to butter in pan, raise heat to medium flame. Stir mushrooms and almonds until heated, then pour this sauce over the fish and serve immediately.

Broiled fish fillet with piri piri sauce
By Richard Blunt

1 lb. fish fillets
1½ cups white wine
⅓ cup fresh lemon juice
2 Tbsp. mixed pickling spice, crushed
½ tsp. cumin seeds, crushed
3 cloves chopped garlic

6 Tbsp. butter or margarine, melted
½ tsp. paprika
enough piri piri to coat the fish after cooking (See recipe below.)

Cut fillets into serving-sized portions, place in a single layer in baking dish.

Combine wine, lemon juice, pickling spice, cumin seeds, and garlic and pour over fish. Marinate fish in refrigerator for 20 minutes.

Remove fish from marinade, brush off spices and place on a well-greased broiler pan. Blend paprika with melted butter or margarine, and brush onto fish.

Preheat broiler and broil fish at a distance from heat to ensure even cooking. Broil fish until cooked on 1 side. Turn fillets over, brush with butter and paprika mixture, return fillets to broiler to finish cooking.

Heat piri piri sauce, (recipe follows) spread on fish, serve immediately.

Piri piri sauce
By Richard Blunt

⅓ cup extra virgin olive oil
1 medium onion, chopped fine
4 garlic cloves, chopped fine

1 12-oz. jar pickled hot jalapeño peppers, drained and chopped fine
1 4-oz. jar pimentos, chopped fine
1 12-oz. bottle chili sauce

Heat olive oil in 7-inch cast iron skillet over medium heat. Add chopped onions and sauté until translucent.

Add chopped garlic and cook for 2 minutes, then add drained and chopped jalapeño peppers, chopped pimento peppers, and chili sauce. Reduce heat to low and simmer for 5 minutes.

Let sauce cool, then transfer to an airtight container and place in refrigerator. It will keep for up to 2 weeks under refrigeration.

Basic fish stock
By Richard Blunt

1 small bouquet garni (½ tsp. dried basil, ½ tsp. dried thyme, 1 sprig fresh rosemary)
4 lbs. fresh fish heads, and bones

1 small onion, chopped
1 small carrot, chopped
8 cups water

Make the bouquet garni by tying basil, thyme, and rosemary in a small piece of cheese cloth.

Remove gills from fish heads if they haven't been removed already. Discard gills and all skin and wash fish under cold running water.

In a stockpot combine all ingredients except the bouquet garni. Bring mixture to boil and reduce heat. Let stock simmer, uncovered, at the lowest possible heat for 15 minutes. Add the bouquet garni and continue to simmer stock for 15 minutes.

Strain stock though dampened cheese cloth that is 4 layers thick.

Return stock to pot and simmer uncovered until is reduced by half. Do not boil the stock. Boiling will make it muddy.

Cool stock in refrigerator. Freeze or refrigerate in plastic containers. Makes 2 cups of concentrated stock.

Boiled crawfish
By James Robertson

1 sack of live crawfish (35-40 lbs.)
2 26-oz. boxes of salt
5 medium onions, halved
½ 4-oz. bottle cayenne pepper
7 lemons, halved
3 pods garlic, halved
4 oz. liquid crab boil or 2 boxes crab boil mix
10 gallons cold water

Always wash the crawfish and pick out the dead ones before cooking. Place water and seasonings in a 30-gallon pot. Cover and bring to a full boil. Lower heat and add crawfish. Some cooks add potatoes and corn to the pot during boiling. Return to a full boil and continue boiling for 5-8 minutes. Turn off heat and soak covered for 10-15 minutes. Remove from water promptly to prevent overcooking and heap onto paper-covered table. Peel and enjoy. Serves 5-6.

Crawfish fettucine
By James Robertson

½ cup butter
1 lb. crawfish tails
1 tsp. soy sauce
1 medium onion, chopped
2 cloves garlic, chopped
salt and pepper
6 oz. fettucine noodles, cooked and drained
2 Tbsp. butter, melted
½ cup Parmesan cheese

Melt butter in a saucepan. Stir in crawfish, soy sauce, onion, garlic, salt, and pepper. Sauté until onions and garlic are wilted. Toss fettucine with 2 Tbsp. butter and Parmesan cheese until nicely coated. To serve, mound warm noodles on a plate and spoon the crawfish mixture over it. Serves 4.

Cajun-style shrimp
By Tom Barth

2 lb. large shrimp, unpeeled,
slit down the back and
deveined
2 Tbsp. unsalted butter
5 Tbsp. olive oil
1 Tbsp. Worcestershire
sauce

2 Tbsp. chili sauce
1 Tbsp. fresh lemon juice
3-4 garlic cloves, minced
¾ tsp. cayenne pepper
¾ tsp. liquid smoke
½ tsp. dried oregano
¼ tsp. Tabasco sauce

Spread shrimp in a shallow baking pan. Combine the remaining ingredients in a small saucepan and simmer approximately 10 minutes. Pour sauce over shrimp and mix well. Cover and refrigerate a minimum of 3 hours, stirring every ½ hour.

Place shrimp in a 300° oven and bake, turning frequently, until they just turn pink. DO NOT OVERBAKE. Large shrimp will be done in about 15-20 minutes.

Jay's gourmet tuna burgers
By Jay Ansama

1 can tuna
1/3 cup mayonnaise
½ cup bread crumbs
3 Tbsp. chili sauce
1 egg
lemon juice

salt
pepper
garlic powder
onion powder or green
onion, chopped
celery, chopped

Mix well and make into 4 patties. Fry in skillet with just a little bit of oil.

Bullheads, marinated and "barbecued"
By Richard Blunt

6-8 whole bullheads, 10-12 inches or 4-6 catfish fillets, 6-8 oz. each

Mustard marinade:
¼ tsp. salt
½ tsp. freshly grated white pepper
1½ tsp. Dijon mustard
½ tsp. dried thyme leaves
½ tsp. freshly grated nutmeg
1/8 tsp. allspice
½ tsp. ground ginger
1 clove finely minced garlic
1 tsp. vegetable oil

B.B.Q. sauce:
1 tsp. vegetable oil
¼ cup finely minced onion
1 clove finely minced garlic
¾ cup apple cider
¼ cup fish stock
½ cup light red or rosé wine
1 Tbsp. Worcestershire sauce
3 Tbsp. white vinegar
5 Tbsp. tomato paste
2 Tbsp. brown sugar

In bowl, combine and mix all mustard marinade ingredients.

Rub this marinade on fish and set aside for ½-1 hour.

Over medium heat sauté onion and garlic in vegetable oil until soft but not browned.

Combine cider, fish stock, wine, Worcestershire sauce, vinegar, tomato paste, and brown sugar.

Mix and add to sautéed vegetables. Bring mixture to light boil over medium heat and reduce to low.

Simmer, stirring occasionally until sauce thickens, about 20-30 minutes, but longer if a thicker sauce is preferred.

Set aside to cool for 30 minutes.

When sauce has cooled, arrange fish on greased baking pan.

Brush each portion on both sides with sauce and place in preheated 400° oven to bake.

Bake for about 5 minutes and baste again with barbecue sauce. Continue to cook until fish flakes easily at the thickest part. This should be in 15-20 minutes.

Blunt's fried panfish
By Richard Blunt

6-8 panfish, less than 1½ inches thick (bullheads, trout, perch, bluegills, crappie or any other fish this size)
vegetable oil (enough to cover bottom of skillet with ¼ inch of oil)

1 cup all-purpose flour
½ tsp. salt
¼ tsp. freshly grated black pepper
¼ tsp. dried basil leaf
¼ tsp. dried thyme leaf
1/8 tsp. garlic powder

Cover bottom of skillet with oil at least ¼ inch deep.

Preheat pan over medium heat.

Wipe fish with paper towels to remove excess moisture.

Create a seasoned flour by combining flour, salt, pepper, basil, thyme, and garlic powder in a bowl.

Coat fish on all sides with seasoned flour, and place in heated pan.

Cook for about 5 minutes on 1 side and turn to cook on other side. This should take about 3 additional minutes.

Remove from pan and place on paper towels to drain for a couple of minutes.

Soups

Basic chicken broth
By Richard Blunt

1 5-6 lb. stewing hen or
  roasting chicken
6 qts. cold water
2 medium onions, peeled
  and cut into quarters
1 celery rib with leaves
  attached
1 whole carrot

2 bay leaves
8 whole black peppercorns
3 whole cloves
1 piece peeled fresh ginger
  about 1 inch long,
  chopped
1 tsp. kosher salt

Place chicken and water in a 10 or 12-qt. stockpot. Place pot on stove over low flame and let water come to a gentle boil. A froth will appear on top. This will take from 45 minutes to 1 hour. Carefully skim off froth as it rises to surface. Do not, for any reason, stir pot after froth first begins to appear.

The froth will continue to form on top of broth for about 1 hour. When it stops foaming, let broth simmer for about 30 minutes, then add onions, celery, and carrot.

Let pot return to simmer while carefully skimming off any more sediment that rises to surface. Add bay leaves, peppercorns, whole cloves, ginger, and salt.

Reduce heat to a point where broth is barely simmering. Continue to simmer, uncovered, for 1½ hours. If you are using a roasting chicken or capon, remove it at this point and let the stock simmer for another hour. If you are using an old stewing hen (fowl), leave it in the pot until the end.

Turn off heat, remove stewing hen, if necessary, and let broth settle and cool.

Strain broth into another pot through several layers of cheesecloth and place pot in refrigerator. This is the fastest and safest way to cool a perishable hot food like chicken broth. You can safely let the stock cool, unrefrigerated, for up to 90 minutes before placing it in the refrigerator. If you live in a northern climate, during the winter you can take a pot of hot stock on a cake rack and place it on your back porch for super-fast cooling.

Chicken and dumpling stew
By Richard Blunt

Stew Ingredients:
1 cooked, skinned, and boned 5-6 lb. chicken (cut meat into ½-inch pieces)
8 cups fresh chicken broth
1 bay leaf (dried or fresh)
2 ribs celery, diced medium
½ tsp. dried sage leaves
½ tsp. dried thyme leaves
3 Tbsp. margarine or butter
1 large or 2 medium yellow onions, diced
1 lb. fresh carrots, peeled and cut into medium-sized chunks
¼ cup cold chicken broth
4 Tbsp. all purpose flour
kosher salt to taste
freshly ground black pepper to taste
1 recipe dumpling dough
1 cup frozen peas, thawed

Dumpling Ingredients:
1 cup all purpose flour
1½ tsp. double acting baking powder
¼ tsp. baking soda
½ tsp. kosher salt
2 Tbsp. unsalted butter
2 medium eggs, slightly beaten
1/8 cup buttermilk or low fat plain yogurt

Skin and bone chicken, then dice meat. Hold diced chicken in refrigerator until you are ready to use.

Put 8 cups fresh broth in Dutch oven—or other heavy-bottomed pot large enough to comfortably hold all of ingredients—along with bay leaf, celery, sage, and thyme. Place pot on medium flame, bring to boil and simmer until broth is reduced to about 6 cups. This will take about 20 minutes.

While broth is reducing, melt margarine in cast iron skillet, or other heavy-bottomed skillet. Sauté onions until medium brown. Stir onions frequently to prevent burning. If oil in pan evaporates before onions are done, add a Tbsp. of simmering broth to pan.

Deglaze skillet by adding 1 cup of simmering broth to browned onions. Simmer onions until pan is completely deglazed and broth has turned a light brown color. What we have done here is create a flavor enhancer by subjecting the onions to a controlled high heat. Food scientists call this a Maillard reaction or browning reaction. The process creates a rich flavor and color similar to the crust of fresh baked bread, coffee beans, and the roasted malt used in dark beers and ales.

Add flavored onion mixture and fresh carrots to broth. When broth returns to simmer, combine cold chicken broth with flour and mix until there are no lumps. Slowly stir paste into simmering broth. Continue stirring until mixture shows signs of thickening, which will only be slight. Continue simmering until carrots are tender. This is a good time to make your dumplings if you didn't before you started the stew. (Instructions below.)

Add dumplings to simmering broth mixture. Simmer dumplings until they are raised, and cooked through.

Gently stir in chicken meat, thawed peas, salt, and pepper. Simmer stew until chicken and peas are heated through. Serve immediately.

Dumplings:

Combine flour, baking powder, baking soda, and salt in a bowl and stir until well-blended.

Cut in unsalted butter with pastry blender until flour resembles coarse cornmeal.

Combine slightly beaten eggs with buttermilk or yogurt. Using a wooden spoon, quickly stir egg mixture into flour, using as few strokes as possible.

Lightly flour work surface, and turn dough onto it. Sprinkle a little flour on dough to prevent it from sticking to your fingers.

Gently flatten dough with heel of your hand, sprinkling a little more flour if it sticks to hands or the work surface. Fold dough in half, and gently press it flat again. Repeat this gentle flattening and folding process until the dough is just smooth. Do not try to knead the dough as you would bread dough. Overworked dumpling dough becomes tough and will not rise properly.

Roll dough on well-floured board to ¼-inch thickness. Cut into strips that are 1-inch wide and 2-inches long. Set dumplings aside until needed.

Basic meat broth
By Richard Blunt

2 lbs. meaty beef bones
(fresh or frozen)
3 qts. cold water
1 lb. lean brisket or stew
beef cut into cubes
2 medium carrots peeled
and sliced
2 large unpeeled yellow
onions, washed and cut
into quarters

2 celery ribs, cut into chunks
pinch kosher salt
1 unpeeled garlic clove
1 bay leaf
10 whole black peppercorns
2 whole cloves
½ tsp. dried thyme

Put meat, meat bones, and water into deep soup kettle that will readily hold all the ingredients. Place kettle over low heat and let water heat. It is not necessary at this point to boil the water. In about 45 minutes a scum will start to form on top as water heats. Remove scum as it forms. From this point on, do not stir the kettle.

The scum will continue to form for about a ½ hour. When it stops forming, adjust heat and bring broth to a simmer for about 1 hour.

Add vegetables along with a pinch of salt, raise heat to medium low, and bring mixture back to a slow simmer. Adjust heat as necessary to maintain simmer. The addition of vegetables will create more scum on surface, which should be skimmed off as it rises.

When scum stops forming, add garlic clove, bay leaf, peppercorns, whole cloves, and thyme. Again, adjust the heat to maintain broth at a slow simmer. Continue simmering for a least 3 hours or until stock reaches the desired flavor intensity.

When finished, ladle stock through a triple thickness of moistened cheese cloth. Cool stock, uncovered, as quickly as possible. One way to do this is to place the pot in a sink filled with cold water, changing the water as necessary until the broth is cooled.

Refrigerate the amount of stock that you intend to use within 24 hours and freeze the rest.

Senate bean soup
By Richard Blunt

1 lb. dried Great Northern or navy beans
8 cups cold water to soak the beans
3 smoked pork hocks
2 qts. cold water to cook with
1 qt. meat broth
1½ yellow onions, chopped fine
2 cloves fresh garlic, minced
1 cup rutabaga, peeled and diced fine
1 cup celery, diced fine
1 cup plain, fresh mashed potatoes
¼ tsp. freshly ground black pepper
1 tsp. chopped green onions (without the white part) to be used as a garnish

Combine beans with soaking water and soak for 12 hours or overnight.

Drain beans, discard soaking water and rinse with plenty of fresh water.

In large soup kettle (5-qt. minimum size) combine beans, smoked pork hocks, cooking water, and meat broth. Bring mixture to a boil, reduce heat and simmer beans for 1½ hours. Skim off any scum that rises to the surface.

Add onions, garlic, rutabaga, celery, and mashed potatoes to pot and continue to simmer for another hour or until beans are tender.

Remove pork hocks from soup, dice meat, discard bones and return diced meat to pot.

Serve soup directly from pot into heated bowls and garnish with diced green onion.

Fish stock
By Richard Blunt

2 lbs. fresh fish frames and heads with the gills removed
4 ribs celery with the tops coarsely chopped
1 large yellow onion, peeled and coarsely chopped
pinch kosher salt
½ tsp. lemon juice
1 cup dry white wine (optional)
2½ qts. water
1 peeled garlic clove, crushed
1 bay leaf
4 whole black peppercorns

Rinse fish frames and heads in cold water to remove any slime. Chop frames into 2-3 inch lengths.

Combine washed fish frames and heads with remaining ingredients in a stock pot that will hold all of the ingredients readily. Bring mixture to boil, lower heat to a point where stock comes to a simmer. Simmer stock for 1 hour, carefully skimming off any scum that appears on surface.

Remove pot from heat and let stock rest for 30 minutes. Strain stock through a triple fold of moistened cheese cloth. Strip any cooked flesh from the bones and heads before discarding the bones. Save this treasure and add it to your chowder.

Cool stock quickly, using the cold water bath method, then refrigerate or freeze until ready to use.

Fish chowder
By Richard Blunt

3 lbs. firm-fleshed white fish,
  cut into 1-inch pieces
2 Tbsp. peanut oil or any oil
  of your choice
3½ cups yellow onions,
  diced medium
2 lbs. potatoes, peeled and
  diced

1 qt. fresh fish stock
2 Tbsp. butter or margarine
2 Tbsp. all purpose flour
1 qt. whole milk
kosher salt and fresh ground
  pepper to taste

In large skillet, heat oil over medium heat. Add onions and sauté until lightly brown.

Combine onions, potatoes, and fish stock in pot that will hold all of ingredients comfortably. Set pot over medium heat and bring mixture to gentle boil. Reduce heat until mixture reaches a slow simmer. Continue to cook mixture until potatoes are done.

While the above mixture is cooking, start a roux by melting butter or margarine over medium heat in a small pan. Stir in flour and cook mixture for about 2 minutes, stirring constantly. This roux should be a pale brown when ready.

Remove roux from heat and let cool for 1-2 minutes, then gently stir into the mixture in the pot.

Add fish pieces to pot and cook slowly for about 10 minutes, or until fish is just cooked. Remove mixture from heat.

When you are ready to serve the chowder, place pot over medium heat, add milk, and heat mixture through gently. Do not let the chowder boil.

Jambalaya stew
By Richard Blunt

Special Equipment:
1 seasoned 5-qt. Dutch oven with lid

Ingredients:
2 Tbsp. peanut oil
3 oz. smoked sausage, chopped medium (Andouille, Kielbasa or other smoked sausage)
6 oz. smoked country ham, chopped medium
12 oz. boneless pork, cut into ½ inch cubes
1 medium green pepper, seeded, deveined and diced medium
2 medium onions, diced
4 ribs celery, diced (about 1½ cups)
1 tsp. dried cilantro (1 Tbsp. of fresh cilantro if you can find it at a decent price)
2 bay leaves
1 tsp. cayenne pepper
1 tsp. dried oregano
1 tsp. dried thyme
½ tsp. ground cumin
1 tsp. kosher salt
1½ tsp. freshly ground black pepper
¼ tsp. freshly ground nutmeg
4 cloves fresh garlic, diced fine
1 28 oz. can Italian plum tomatoes (drained and chopped)
¾ cup juice from the tomatoes
2 cups Basmati rice, rinsed in cold water and drained
2 cups fresh chicken stock (or 1 cup canned chicken stock and 1 cup of water)
½ cup scallions, chopped
8 oz. bay scallops (optional)

Special Note: Do all of your measuring and dicing before you start cooking. You will then be able to devote all your attention to the progress of this delicate dish.

Heat peanut oil over medium heat, add sausage and ham, and cook until well-browned. You will notice considerable shrinkage, but don't be alarmed. This is meant to add flavor and color to the stew, not bulk.

Raise heat and add pork and sauté until pork loses its pink color and starts to brown.

With heat still raised, add green pepper, onions, and celery and sauté until onions become translucent. Stir frequently with a good wooden spoon, scraping bottom to prevent anything that sticks from burning.

Reduce heat to medium and add herbs, spices, salt, and garlic. Continue cooking mixture for 1 minute. Add chopped tomatoes and continue cooking until pork is cooked through and tender. This should not exceed 10 minutes because pork, by its nature, is not a tough meat.

Add tomato juice, rice, chicken stock, and scallions and allow mixture to come to a boil. Reduce heat to bring mixture to a slow simmer. Put lid on Dutch oven and allow rice to cook for exactly 10 minutes. Remove lid from Dutch oven and place scallops on top of mixture; replace lid and continue to cook stew for exactly 2 minutes, and remove from heat.

Allow pot to sit covered for 15 minutes before serving, then remove lid and gently fold scallops into stew.

Lentil and meat stew
By Habeeb Salloum

4 Tbsp. butter
½ lb. beef, cut into ½-inch cubes
2 medium onions, chopped
4 cloves garlic, crushed
1 small hot pepper, finely chopped
1 cup lentils, rinsed
5 cups water
4 medium potatoes, peeled and diced into ¾-inch cubes
4 medium tomatoes, chopped
1½ tsp. salt
1 tsp. cumin
½ tsp. pepper
½ tsp. turmeric

Melt butter in a saucepan; sauté beef for 5 minutes. Add onions, garlic, and hot pepper, then stir-fry for another 10 minutes. Add remaining ingredients and cook over medium heat until meat and lentils are well-done, adding more water if necessary. Serve hot with cooked rice.

Brunswick stew
By Richard Blunt

4 lbs. chicken thighs with skin removed
flour for dredging
1/3 cup peanut oil
4 cups fresh unsalted chicken stock—or 2 cups canned chicken stock and 2 cups of water
1 cup dry fruity white wine—or 1 cup English pale ale
1 28 oz. can diced plum tomatoes (without the juice)
2 medium potatoes, peeled and cut into ½ inch cubes
2 cups yellow onion, diced medium
3 medium carrots, peeled and cut into 2 inch chunks
3 ribs celery, diced medium

2 cups fresh or frozen butter beans (use baby limas if you can't find butter beans)
2 cups fresh or frozen corn kernels
2 dried bay leaves (If they have been in your kitchen for more than six months, get some new ones)
½ tsp. dried rosemary
1 tsp. dried thyme
1 tsp. cayenne pepper
½ tsp. fresh ground black pepper
1 medium yellow summer squash, split along the vertical and cut into 1-inch chunks—or ½ cup fresh or frozen okra
3 cloves fresh garlic, minced

Place flour in large paper bag. Add skinless chicken thighs and secure bag at top to prevent flour from escaping. Shake bag until all of the chicken is coated evenly with flour.

Heat peanut oil in Dutch oven over medium heat. Shake any excess flour from chicken pieces and place pieces in the oil, without crowding, and brown evenly on both sides. You will find it necessary to do this in 2 batches, adding additional oil as necessary. Take care to periodically scrape bottom of pot to prevent any sticking matter from burning. After browning, set chicken aside on paper towels to drain.

Deglaze bottom of pot with 2 cups of chicken stock, then add remainder of chicken stock, wine, and chicken pieces. Bring stock to a boil, then reduce heat to a point that will maintain stock at a slow simmer. (Slow simmer means no bubbles popping at the surface.) Cover pot and simmer chicken until tender, between 45 minutes and 1 hour.

Turn off heat and remove chicken to a platter to cool. Carefully remove all fat and scum that is floating on the surface of the stock. Return stock to a boil over medium heat, and add diced tomatoes, potatoes, onions, carrots, celery, butter beans, corn, and seasonings. Return stew to a slow simmer until vegetables become tender, about 45 minutes. While vegetables are cooking, remove bones from cooled chicken.

Return chicken to stew, along with squash and garlic, and continue simmering until squash is tender, but not mushy. Adjust seasoning with salt and freshly ground black pepper. Turn off heat, cover stew, and let sit for at least 1 hour before serving. Slowly reheat if necessary.

Elk stew with mushrooms
By Jackie Clay

2 lbs. lean cubed stew meat (or 1 qt. if home-canned)
¼ lb. margarine
2 medium onions, coarsely chopped
1 lb. sliced mushrooms (or 1 pint if home-canned)
1 qt. beef stock or equivalent

6 medium carrots, scraped and cut (or 1 pint)
8 medium potatoes, peeled and cut (or 1 pint)
1 clove garlic
1 Tbsp. brown sugar
salt & pepper to taste

Melt the margarine in heavy Dutch oven and brown meat on all sides. Add mushrooms and onions, sautéing until barely browning. Add beef stock, vegetables, brown sugar, salt, and pepper. Simmer slowly until everything is very tender, adding water to keep juice covering stew.

When done, add flour to small bowl and enough water to make a smooth paste. Then add enough water to make the paste thin enough to pour. Pour into stew, while gently stirring. Heat enough to thicken the gravy and serve.

Humble stew
By Richard Blunt

1 cup dried red beans
6 cups plus 8 cups cold
  water
3 cups fresh beef, chicken,
  or vegetable stock
½ cup dry red wine
8 Tbsp. margarine or butter
8 oz. onion, peeled and
  diced medium
4 oz. celeriac, coarsely grated
4 cloves fresh garlic, peeled
  and minced
4 Tbsp. flour
4 medium carrots, peeled
  and cut into 1/2 inch pieces

4 small to medium fresh
  beets (without greens),
  peeled and cut into ½ inch
  chunks
½ lb. peeled rutabaga cut
  into ½-inch pieces
4 medium parsnips, peeled
  and cut into ½-inch pieces
1 tsp. dried basil leaf
½ tsp. dried oregano leaf
kosher salt to taste
freshly ground black pepper
  to taste
¼ tsp. cayenne pepper
  (more or less according to
  taste)
2 cups canned whole plum
  tomatoes (with the juice),
  diced medium

Soak beans in 6 cups cold water for at least 4 hours. Drain and
rinse beans, discarding soaking water. In a large sauce pot combine
beans with 8 cups fresh water and bring to a boil. Reduce heat and
allow beans to cook slowly for about 45 minutes. Rinse partially
cooked beans in cold water to cool, drain and set aside.

Combine stock with wine and heat almost to the boiling point over
a medium heat.

Melt butter in a large sauce pot, and add onion, celeriac, and garlic and sauté for about 2 minutes or until onion becomes translucent. Stir in flour and continue cooking mixture over low heat for
another 2 minutes. Add hot stock to this roux while stirring with a
wire whisk. Cook over medium heat until sauce thickens.

Add remaining vegetables, beans, basil, oregano, salt, black pepper, cayenne pepper, and plum tomatoes. If you have a large earthenware casserole, transfer vegetables into casserole, cover and
place in a 350° oven for 45 minutes to 1 hour. Or simply cover the
sauce pot, reduce heat to low, and cook vegetables on top of stove
about 45 minutes, or until everything is tender.

Potato soup
By Alice Brantley Yeager

4 cups peeled, diced Irish
(white) potatoes
1 medium onion, coarsely
chopped
3 Tbsp. flour
1 Tbsp. butter or margarine

1 qt. whole milk
1 egg, beaten
salt and pepper to taste
green onions, parsley, and
grated carrots for garnish

Boil potatoes and onion in just enough water to cover. When tender, add milk, salt, and pepper and reheat.

In small skillet, brown flour in butter and slowly blend into potato mixture. Add a bit of water to beaten egg and slowly stir into soup. Let simmer a few minutes to thicken. Stir often to keep from sticking. (I like to transfer this soup to a double boiler when it begins to simmer, as there's less danger of sticking.)

Garnish bowls of soup with chopped green onions, parsley, or grated carrots to add a touch of color.

Curried root soup
By Richard Blunt

Ingredients:

3 medium beets (separate the greens and save), peeled and diced medium
1 lb. carrots, peeled and diced medium
8 oz. parsnip, peeled and diced medium
1 lb. rutabaga, peeled and diced medium
8 oz. russet boiling potatoes, peeled and diced medium
4 medium leeks (white part only)
2 qts. fresh vegetable, chicken, or beef stock (if you don't have fresh stock, low salt canned stock can be substituted)
5 Tbsp. unsalted butter

2 cloves fresh garlic, minced
¼ tsp. ground cumin
¼ tsp. cayenne pepper
1/8 tsp. ground ginger
1/8 tsp. mustard powder
1 pinch turmeric
¼ tsp. powdered coriander
2 Tbsp. flour
2 Tbsp. fresh lemon juice
reserved beet greens, chopped
Add kosher salt and freshly ground black pepper to adjust seasoning.

Topping ingredients:

1 medium onion, peeled and chopped fine
¼ cup flat leaf parsley, chopped fine
2 cups plain yogurt

Separate the greens from the beets, wash, drain, and chop greens and set aside.

Slice leeks in half lengthwise and dice into ½-inch pieces.

Combine vegetables with stock in a large pot and bring to a boil. Reduce heat and cook until all vegetables are just tender. Remove from heat and strain stock into another container. Set stock and half of the cooked vegetables aside.

Puree the other half of the vegetables in a blender or food processor and set these aside.

Melt butter in a large heavy-bottomed pot, add garlic and sauté over a medium heat for about 1 minute. Add spices and flour while stirring with a wire whisk. Cook this seasoned roux over low heat, to prevent browning, for about 2 minutes.

Slowly add stock to roux while stirring with a wire whisk to prevent lumps from forming. Heat mixture to a slow boil while stirring constantly. Cook over low heat until stock shows signs of thickening, then add chopped beet greens, lemon juice, and diced vegetables. Continue to cook for about 10 minutes or until greens become tender.

Remove soup from heat and add pureed vegetables, stirring gently with a wooden spoon to mix.

Adjust seasoning with kosher salt and fresh ground black pepper to suit your taste.

To serve, combine chopped onion and parsley in a serving bowl and yogurt in another bowl and bring to the table as condiments. Heat soup to a serving temperature of 165-175°. Do not boil again. Sprinkle a little parsley and onion on each serving along with a dollop of yogurt.

Basic vegetable soup
By Alice Brantley Yeager

1 qt. green beans, snapped
1 qt. tomatoes, peeled and chopped
2 cups sweet peppers, coarsely chopped
2 cups onions, chopped
2 cups carrots, chopped
2 cups okra, sliced in ¼-inch rounds
1 cup sweet basil, chopped
1 large clove garlic, minced

1 jalapeño pepper, finely chopped
1 qt. beef or chicken stock
1 qt. chopped, cooked beef or chicken meat
6 oz. broken spaghetti, elbow macaroni, or your favorite type pasta
salt to taste

Put all vegetables and meat in a large pot and cover them with water. Add meat stock, cover pot, and bring to a boil. Add pasta and reduce heat to simmer. Cook until vegetables are tender—about 20-30 minutes. Stir occasionally. If soup seems too thick due to absorption of water by pasta, add a bit more water until you have your desired consistency.

Soups

Spicy New England holiday stew
By Richard Blunt

4 lbs. stew beef, cut into
  1-inch pieces
vegetable oil to brown meat
¼ cup onion, diced medium
1 carrot, diced medium
1 celery rib, diced medium
1 14 oz. can diced tomatoes,
  with the liquid
3 cups fresh or canned beef
  stock
3 cups red zinfandel or other
  good young red wine
1 16 oz. can whole-berry
  cranberry sauce
1 cup grated horseradish,
  drained

1 cinnamon stick
8 whole cloves
5 whole black peppercorns
2 bay leaves
1 tsp. dried thyme
12 small white onions,
  peeled
4 medium carrots, peeled
  and cut into 1-inch pieces
  (about 2½ cups)
3 cups white turnip, cut into
  1-inch pieces
6 medium red skinned potatoes, cut into quarters

Remove all excess moisture from diced beef with paper towels (Wet meat will not brown).

In a heavy-bottomed stock pot or Dutch oven add 2 Tbsp.oil. Over medium-high heat add enough of the diced beef to cover bottom of pan. Brown beef on all sides. Do this in several batches if necessary. Set browned beef aside.

Add another 2 Tbsp. oil to pan and, over medium heat, sauté diced onions, carrots, and celery until vegetables are lightly-browned.

Combine tomatoes, beef stock, and wine. Add this mixture to vegetables and bring to a slow simmer.

Add cranberry sauce, horseradish, and spices and herbs to the simmering stock; increase heat to medium-high, and return browned beef to pot. When mixture returns to a slow simmer, reduce heat low enough to maintain this simmer, and loosely cover pot.

Cook stew at a slow simmer until meat is very tender, about 1½ hours.

While stew is simmering, steam remaining vegetables—white onions, carrots, turnip, and potatoes—individually, until tender, and set aside.

When meat is tender, remove stew from heat and gently fold in steamed vegetables. If you intend to serve the stew right away, return it to the heat and bring to serving temperature. Otherwise, refrigerate until ready to use.

Celery and potato soup
By Alice Brantley Yeager

2 cups coarsely chopped celery	salt and pepper to taste
4 cups diced potatoes	3 Tbsp. flour
1 medium onion, chopped	1 Tbsp. butter or margarine
1 qt. milk	1 egg, well-beaten
	parsley for garnish

Boil celery, potatoes, and onion in a small amount of water until tender but not mushy. Add the milk, salt, and pepper (to taste) and slowly reheat.

Using a small skillet, brown the flour in the butter and blend it slowly into the potato mixture. Add a little water to the beaten egg and stir into the soup. Let it simmer for a few minutes stirring occasionally to keep it from sticking. If you have problems, you may want to use a double boiler. Serve with a garnish of freshly chopped parsley.

This recipe may be varied by adding other chopped vegetables such as carrots, broccoli, sweet peppers, etc. If you'd like to convert the recipe to a delicious chowder, try adding a small can of flaked tuna or minced clams.

Vegetable soup
By Alice Brantley Yeager

1 large beef soup bone with substantial meat left on it
3 qts. water
2 tsp. salt
½ cup brown or white rice
6 medium tomatoes, peeled and cut in small pieces
1 medium onion, chopped
1 large Irish potato, diced
2 carrots, diced

2 medium sweet peppers, chopped
2 cups green beans, snapped
2 cups whole kernel corn
1 cup celery, diced
½ cup fresh herbs (sweet basil, parsley, etc.), chopped
1 small hot pepper, minced

In large heavy pot simmer the soup bone in water with salt until meat is easy to remove—probably about 1½ hours. Take the soup bone from pot, let it cool enough to handle and remove the meat from bone. Chop the meat into small pieces and give the bone to Rover.

Put the rest of ingredients including the meat in a pot with the beef broth and bring to a simmer. (You may want to add more water.) Cook until the vegetables are done. This is a basic recipe and other vegetables may be used. Broken pieces of spaghetti or macaroni may be substituted for the rice. Other meats may be used instead of beef. Chicken and turkey make a lighter type of soup.

Hungarian venison stew
By Tom R. Kovach

1 lb. (or a little more) of chopped venison (ground venison works, too)
3 slices of bacon, chopped
1 medium green pepper cut into 1-inch pieces
½ cup onions, chopped
4 cups chopped, cooked potatoes
1 clove garlic, minced
1 16 oz. can tomatoes, cut up (or fresh or frozen)
1 10¾ oz. can condensed tomato soup
1 tsp. sweet or hot Hungarian paprika
dash of salt
dash of pepper

In a large skillet (a 4-qt. Dutch oven will work), cook venison, bacon, green peppers, and onions until meat is browned and vegetables are tender. Boil the potatoes in a pan on the side until done. Stir in remaining ingredients and bring to a boil, then reduce heat. Simmer uncovered for about 5 minutes or until heated through. This makes about 4 servings

Venison stew with nopalitos
By Jackie Clay

1 lb. lean venison stew meat
shortening for browning
2 medium onions, chopped
1 cup nopalitos, sliced about green bean size
1½ pints tomato sauce
5 medium potatoes, diced medium
1 cup cooked sweet corn
3 long, fresh carrots, diced
1 tsp. salt
1 tsp. black, coarsely ground pepper
1 tsp. medium chili powder (powdered chilies, not mixed spices)
1 Tbsp. honey

Brown stew meat in shortening, then add onions and continue stirring until they are transparent. Add the rest of the ingredients and simmer gently in a large, heavy pot until the meat is very tender. Cover, but add water if necessary. Serve with hot corn bread or corn tortillas.

French onion soup
By Richard Blunt

4 Tbsp. butter or margarine
1 tsp. peanut oil
2½ lbs. (approximately 7 cups) onions peeled and thinly sliced
½ Tbsp. sugar
2 cloves fresh garlic (finely minced)
2 Tbsp. white flour
1 cup white vermouth (or other dry white wine)
6 cups chicken stock

4 cups beef stock
1 bay leaf
salt to taste
freshly ground black pepper
8-10 slices French bread (½ inch thick)
6 Tbsp. butter or margarine (melted)
12-16 slices Emmenthal or other Swiss cheese sliced ⅛-inch thick (or 1½-2 cups shredded)

Peel onions, then cut in ½ and thinly slice, cutting across the grain. In 4 qt. saucepan, heat oil and margarine/butter over low heat. Stir in onions and cook, partially covered, over low heat for about 10 minutes or until onions are translucent and tender.

Stir occasionally to prevent sticking.

Remove the cover, add sugar and stir to blend. The sugar serves 2 purposes. One is to help the onions brown and the other is to increase the sweetness. If you are making this soup in the spring, with a fresh batch of onions from the garden, this is the time of year when onions are at their sweetest, so omit the sugar.

Leaving cover off pot, turn up burner to medium heat. Add garlic and continue to sauté onions until golden brown. Stir frequently to prevent burning. Reduce heat if any signs of burning show. The browning process takes about 20 minutes.

Sprinkle flour in with browned onions while stirring constantly. Continue to cook for another 2 minutes. This additional cooking of the flour prevents it from leaving a raw taste and powdery texture in the soup.

Remove pot from heat and allow to cool for a couple of minutes. Return pot to medium heat and add wine. Bring to a boil, and cook until wine is reduced by ½. (This boils off all the alcohol.)

Reduce heat and add beef and chicken stocks along with bay leaf. Allow soup to simmer very slowly, uncovered for 1½ hours. Add salt and freshly ground black pepper during the last 15 minutes of cooking.

While soup is simmering, preheat oven to 325°. Lightly coat both sides of French bread slices with melted butter or margarine. Place bread on cookie sheet and put in oven to brown. When the up side of the bread has browned, turn it over and brown the other side. When completely browned remove from oven and set aside.

To serve, place a crouton into each serving bowl and ladle in soup. Pass grated Parmesan cheese separately.

For another way to serve this soup, you can heat oven to 370°. Ladle soup into oven-proof soup tureen or individual oven-proof soup bowls. When using the individual bowls, place 1 crouton in each bowl. With the tureen or an oven casserole, use as many croutons as it takes to cover the entire surface of the soup. Cover with a layer of sliced or shredded cheese. Place in oven and bake for 10-15 minutes, or until cheese melts and starts to turn brown. It will be easier to get the individual bowls in and out of the oven by placing them on a cookie sheet.

Blunt's beef stew
By Richard Blunt

2½ lbs. lean beef, diced into 1½-inch cubes (I use chuck, top round, or bottom round as these cuts don't fall apart during cooking)

¼ cup (more or less) cooking oil

1 clove fresh garlic, peeled and minced

2½ qts. fresh brown stock (see recipe on page 299)

1½ cups peeled and seeded fresh plum tomatoes

2 ribs of celery, diced ¾ inch

1 small white or yellow turnip, diced ¾ inch

12-16 fresh white pearl onions, peeled

3 medium red skinned potatoes, unpeeled and diced ¾ inch

¼ tsp. dried thyme leaves

¼ tsp. dried basil leaves

salt and freshly ground black pepper to taste

Dry diced beef with paper towels. Wet meat will not brown properly.

Heat oil in stew pot or large frying pan. Add meat in small batches and sauté until browned. (You brown the meat in small batches because trying to brown it all at once results in leeching the liquid from the meat, and you wind up parboiling and drying it out instead of searing it. Browning in small batches allows the meat to retain more of its juices and more of its flavors. This is why you should also pat it dry before browning it.) If oil becomes low during browning, add more. A few minutes before the last batch is ready, add minced garlic.

If you did your browning in a frying pan, you should now transfer the meat to your stew pot, then use a cup of brown stock to deglaze the frying pan.

When browned meat is in stew pot, add stock (including stock used to deglaze the frying pan, if you used one), and tomatoes. Bring to a boil, reduce heat and simmer until meat shows signs of tenderness. This usually takes about 1 hour. While simmering, have the lid about ¾ of the way covering the pot.

When meat starts getting tender, remove lid from pot and add all carrots, celery, and turnips. Continue simmering until celery shows signs of tenderness. Add thyme and basil.

Add onion and potatoes and simmer until tender. Add salt and freshly ground black pepper to taste.

Basic brown stock
By Richard Blunt

5 lbs. raw beef bones (it helps if some of them are meaty)
5 qts. cold water
2 large carrots, chopped
3 ribs of celery, chopped (if you decide to use the leaves, avoid the green ones, because they turn bitter with long cooking, but the yellow leaves in the middle are fine)

1 medium onion, chopped
1 cup fresh tomato, chopped
1 small white turnip, chopped
6 whole black pepper corns
4 sprigs fresh parsley
1 clove unpeeled fresh garlic
1 tsp. dried leaf thyme
1 bay leaf
6 whole cloves

Preheat oven to 450°.

Mix chopped onion, carrots, and celery and place beef bones along with 1 cup of this chopped vegetable mixture in a roasting pan. Arrange bones and vegetables into a single layer. Place in upper part of oven to brown. Turn bones and vegetables a few times to ensure even browning. Browning should take 30-40 minutes.

Transfer browned bones and vegetables to stock pot and discard all the extracted fat.

Add the water, along with remaining chopped vegetable mixture and other ingredients, to the stock pot. Transfer about 3 cups of the water to roasting pan, after you have discarded the fat, and bring this to a slow simmer on top of stove. While this is simmering, scrape bottom of roasting pan with a wooden spoon until all brown glaze on bottom has dissolved into water and transfer this liquid to the stock pot.

Bring stock to a boil over high heat then immediately reduce to a slow simmer. Remember to remove the grey mass as it appears.

Place a lid on the stock pot so that it covers about ¾ of the pot. Continue the slow simmer for about 4-5 hours.

Remove stock pot from heat and taste stock. If it isn't flavorful enough, return to a simmer and reduce some more. When it tastes good, strain and cool it.

Stewed venison
By Richard Blunt

2 lbs. venison (chuck or rump) trim off and discard all excess fat and dice meat into 1½ inch cubes
¼ cup (or more) peanut oil
1 cup onions, diced
1 cup celery, diced
1 clove garlic, peeled and minced (this is the first garlic in the recipe)
1½ cups fresh brown stock
½ cup fresh chicken stock
¾ cup white zinfandel or other young red wine
1½ Tbsp. soft butter or margarine

2 Tbsp. flour
1 Tbsp. lemon juice
4 whole cloves
1 medium bay leaf
½ tsp. dried thyme leaf
1/8 tsp. cayenne pepper (¼ tsp. if you like spice)
½ tsp. salt
Braised vegetable ingredients:
6 large garlic cloves, peeled
12 whole medium mushrooms
1 Tbsp. butter or margarine

Dry venison with paper towels. Heat oil in frying pan then brown venison, a few pieces at a time, turning each piece to brown on all sides without burning. As each batch of meat finishes browning, place it into a 4-5 qt. oven casserole.

When all meat is browned, discard all but 3 Tbsp. of oil. Return oil to pan at medium heat. Add onions, celery, and minced garlic. Sauté until onions and celery are soft.

Add both stocks and wine and bring liquids to a simmer while scraping the bottom of the pan to free the brown glaze that was left by sautéing the venison.

Mix flour with softened butter (or margarine) to form a smooth paste without lumps. Blend this with simmering stock mixture, stirring constantly to prevent lumping. Continue simmering until mixture starts to thicken.

Add cloves, bay leaf, thyme, cayenne, salt, and lemon juice. Continue simmering for 5 more minutes.

Combine this sauce you have now made with the meat in the casserole. Cover and place in a 325° oven and bake for 2 hours or until venison is tender.

Place 6-8 large peeled whole garlic cloves in a small pan with 1 Tbsp. melted butter or margarine. Cover and cook over low heat for 5 minutes then add mushrooms and cook for another 5 minutes. Ten minutes before removing stew from oven for serving, add garlic, mushrooms, and liquid to stew and blend.

Hamburger soup
By Darlene Campbell

1 lb. ground beef
4 carrots, cut in 2-inch
  chunks
3 potatoes, quartered
1 onion, chopped
½ bell pepper, sliced
1 16-oz. can tomatoes

1 6-oz. can tomato paste
1 cup water or stock
1 tsp. thyme
¼ tsp. each black pepper
  and garlic powder
1 bouillon cube

In a large soup pot, cook the ground beef over medium heat until brown and crumbly. Drain off excess fat. Add remaining ingredients and simmer, stirring occasionally, until vegetables are fork tender. I do not use salt in this recipe, but if you omit the bouillon cube, you may add salt to taste.

For variety, substitute stewed tomatoes for regular canned ones, or add celery or corn. Serve with hot biscuits.

Quick tofu-corn chowder (for 2)
By Rodney Merrill

1 cup skim milk
1 can cream-style corn
1 large (2 small) potatoes
1 medium onion

¼ cake tofu, frozen then
  thawed
1 tsp. poultry seasoning

Wash potatoes and dice (skins on) into ¼ inch cubes. Put diced potatoes in a small saucepan and add just enough water to cover them. Bring to a boil and simmer until tender. Dice onions and tofu into ¼ inch cubes while potatoes are boiling. When potatoes are tender, add milk and cream-style corn, then add tofu, onions, and seasoning. Simmer until onion pieces are tender.
  Good served with fresh bread or biscuits.

Easy Brunswick stew
By Lucy Shober

1 can lima beans
1 can corn
1 can chicken broth
1 can chicken, or 1 lb. fresh
  cooked chicken
**(all cans are the 16 oz.
  size)**
2 large onions, chopped

2 cans chopped tomatoes
3 cooked, peeled, and
  chopped potatoes
a dash pepper, garlic, brown
  sugar, and salt
cooking oil
hot sauce to taste

Put the onions and a tad of oil into the pot first and cook them until they turn clear, then add all the rest. Depending on the amount of juice from the vegetables, you might have to add a little water. Keep it bubbling, and stir it for about 20 minutes.
  Two or three eastern communities with the name of "Brunswick" like to claim this stew as their own concoction, but generally, Brunswick County, Virginia, is given the credit.

Succulent venison stew
By Edith Helmich

3-4 lbs. fat-trimmed venison, cut into 2-inch cubes
Marinade:
2 thinly sliced onions
1 thinly sliced carrot
2 stalks celery, cut in large chunks
1 garlic clove, crushed
2 cups red wine
½ cup salad oil
¼ tsp. thyme
1 tsp. salt
2 bay leaves
10-12 black peppercorns
2 cloves

Stew:
½ cup salad oil
1 cup diced salt pork
1 large onion, chopped
2 carrots, sliced
1 lb. mushrooms, sliced
2 Tbsp. brown sugar, packed
3 Tbsp. flour
1 clove garlic, chopped or pressed
½ cup red wine
2 cups reserved marinade
salt & pepper to taste

Place cubes of venison in a non-metal container, pour uncooked marinade over the meat, and refrigerate for a full 24 hours.

About 2½ hours before serving, drain and save marinade, discarding vegetables. Dry meat gently on paper towels. Continue with the following recipe for the stew.

Sauté oil and salt pork until lightly browned. Add onion and carrots and cook until moderately browned. Sprinkle brown sugar over vegetables, stir well, and remove from pan.

In the same pan, sauté mushrooms until lightly cooked and remove from pan.

Still using the same pan and adding a little more oil (if necessary), brown stew meat. Sprinkle meat with flour and continue cooking until flour is also brown. Add wine and marinade (and additional water, if necessary) to cover meat. Cover pan and simmer on very low heat for 1-1½ hours. Add the reserved vegetables and cook for an additional 30-40 minutes.

Serve over rice and sprinkle with chopped parsley. A blend of wild and white rice is very good with this dish.

Soups

Vegetables

Butterpeas
By Alice Brantley Yeager

3-4 strips of cured, sliced
  bacon
1 qt. shelled and washed
  butterpeas
1 medium onion, coarsely
  chopped

1 medium bell pepper,
  coarsely chopped
½ tsp. salt (optional)
⅛ tsp. black OR cayenne
  pepper

Fry bacon until done but not crisp. Save drippings and cut bacon into small pieces. Put butterpeas in a saucepan with enough water to cover them well. Add rest of ingredients plus about 3 Tbsp. of the bacon drippings. Cover saucepan, bring contents to a boil and then simmer about 20 minutes or until butterpeas are tender. Serves 3-4 persons depending on other side dishes.

Sweet potato pudding
By Larry Cywin

6 medium sweet potatoes
1 cup milk
1 cup sugar

3 eggs
1 Tbsp. lemon juice
1 tsp. cinnamon

Peel the potatoes and boil until tender. Mash potatoes with the milk until smooth. Add the remaining ingredients and beat until well-mixed.

Pour into shallow, lightly-greased dish. Bake at 375° for 30 minutes.

Baby bok choy with tofu
By Leland Edward Stone

3 cups baby bok choy, cut in half lengthwise or veggies of your choice, thinly sliced
1 cup chicken or vegetable stock
1 lb. tofu, sliced or cubed
½ cup sliced water chestnuts (canned is OK)
2 Tbsp. cornstarch, stirred into ½ cup stock or water

2 Tbsp. soy sauce
2 Tbsp. oil
1 Tbsp. fresh ginger, cut into thin "coins"
1 Tbsp. sugar
1 tsp. salt
1 tsp. five-spice powder
½ tsp. pepper
red chilies (optional)
crushed garlic (optional)

Heat oil and sauté the sliced bok choy or other vegetables. Add the chilies and ginger when the veggies just wilt. Stir in the dry seasonings, frying for about another 2 minutes. Add the stock, garlic, water chestnuts, and tofu. Then reduce heat and simmer until hot. Stir in the cornstarch mix and serve immediately, accompanied by rice or noodles.

Fried celery
By Alice Brantley Yeager

celery cleaned and cut into 3-inch pieces
Batter:
1⅓ cups flour

2 tsp. baking powder
salt and pepper to taste
1 egg, well beaten
⅔ cup milk

Sift dry ingredients. Gradually add milk and egg. This is a good batter for frying almost any garden vegetable—squash, green tomatoes, eggplant, and others.

Cut crisp, clean celery stalks in 3-inch pieces. Parboil until tender crisp and drain. Sprinkle with salt and pepper, dip them in batter, and fry in deep hot fat, then drain on brown paper.

Cajun-baked turnip
By Richard Blunt

2 lbs. white turnip, peeled
and diced
6 Tbsp. unsalted butter
¼ cup red bell pepper, diced
medium
1 tsp. whole grain mustard
2 Tbsp. brown sugar
½ tsp. kosher salt

¼ tsp. garlic powder
1/8 tsp. ground nutmeg
1/8 tsp. cayenne pepper
¼ tsp. dried thyme leaf
¼ tsp. dried basil leaf
¼ cup distilled apple cider
¼ cup whole wheat bread
crumbs

Cook turnip pieces in lightly-salted water until just tender. Drain and set aside.

Melt butter in heavy-bottomed skillet, add diced bell pepper, and sauté until the pepper is tender.

Combine mustard, brown sugar, salt, garlic powder, nutmeg, cayenne pepper, thyme, and basil with the apple cider and blend with a fork. Add this mixture to the sautéed bell pepper.

Toss mixture with the blanched turnip in an oven casserole. Sprinkle the whole wheat bread crumbs on top and bake in a 375° oven for about 20 minutes, or until the top is lightly browned and the turnip is to a desired tenderness.

Stewed winter greens
By Richard Blunt

8 oz. dry cured lean salt
   pork
2½ qts. water
1 medium onion, sliced
2 lbs. fresh collards, kale, or
   cabbage (If you use kale,
   choose only young leaves.
   Kale becomes bitter as it
   matures.)

2 fresh hot chili peppers cut
   in half, seeded and deveined.
freshly ground black pepper
   to taste.
kosher salt to taste

Cut salt pork into 8 pieces and sauté over medium heat in heavy-bottomed skillet until lightly browned. Combine pork, water, and onion in a very large pot and bring mixture to a slow boil. Reduce heat, cover pot, and allow pork to cook for about ½ hour at a very slow boil.

Wash greens in plenty of cold water, cut away any tough stems and cut greens into ¾-inch strips.

When pork has simmered for ½ hour, raise the heat to bring broth to a medium boil; add greens and chili pepper and bring mixture back to a boil. Reduce heat to slow simmer and cook greens until tender. Cooking time will vary depending on the type of greens. Young kale takes only about 20 minutes. Hardier greens like collards and cabbage will take up to 1 hour.

A few minutes before removing greens from heat, taste the broth and adjust the seasoning with salt and pepper.

Sweet and sour green beans
By Alice Brantley Yeager

¾ lb. fresh green beans,
washed and cut in 1-2 inch
lengths
4 slices cured bacon, sautéed and drained

1 Tbsp. bacon drippings
3 Tbsp. vinegar
3 Tbsp. sugar
salt to taste

Steam or cook beans in a small amount of water until tender-crisp. Drain. Break bacon into small pieces and mix beans, bacon and rest of ingredients. Simmer in skillet until liquid has evaporated and beans are lightly sautéed.

German green beans
By Alice Brantley Yeager

1 lb. green beans, washed
and snapped
4 slices cured bacon
½ cup vinegar

¼ cup sugar
1 small onion, chopped
3 cups cabbage, shredded
salt and pepper to taste

Steam or cook beans until tender-crisp in small amount of water. Sauté bacon until crisp and set aside. Add vinegar, sugar, onion, and cabbage to drippings in skillet. Cover and simmer for 5 minutes. Stir in drained green beans. Season with salt and pepper to taste. Cook an additional 5 minutes and serve topped with crumbled bacon.

Vegetables

Green beans with mushrooms
By Alice Brantley Yeager

1 lb. fresh green beans,
washed and snapped in
2-3 inch lengths
1 small garlic clove, minced
4 oz. small fresh mush-
rooms, washed and sliced
1 small onion, chopped

1 Tbsp. butter or margarine
¼ tsp. white pepper or freshly ground black pepper
1 tsp. dried dill weed
2 Tbsp. toasted almonds or
pecans, coarsely chopped
(optional)

Steam or cook beans in small amount of water until tender-crisp.
Drain. While beans are cooking, sauté garlic, mushrooms, and onion
in butter about 4 minutes. Combine mushroom mixture with beans,
add pepper and dill weed, and put in warm serving bowl. Garnish
with nuts.

Succotash
By Alice Brantley Yeager

3-5 large ears fresh corn (2
cups when cut from cob)
2 cups fresh butter beans
(limas)

5 Tbsp. butter
salt and pepper to taste

Boil corn in water about 7-10 minutes until corn is just tender.
Remove ears from water and cut off kernels as close to cobs as
possible. (The cobs lend flavor, so you may want to boil them with
the corn and beans and discard cobs before serving.)

Cook beans in just enough water to cover. (Should require about
20 minutes.) Combine corn and beans, butter, and seasoning and
reheat. Serve hot.

Asparagus au gratin
By Jackie Clay

2 lbs. tender wild asparagus
   spears
1 cup sharp cheddar
   cheese, grated
2 Tbsp. butter
2 Tbsp. flour

1 tsp. salt
pinch black pepper
1 cup buttered crackers or
   dry bread bits
1 cup milk or cream

Butter a baking dish, put in whole asparagus spears or cut pieces in layers, sprinkling grated cheese between the layers.

In a small saucepan, melt the butter and stir in the flour. Cook a minute. Add the milk (or cream), salt, and pepper. Stir well until thickened to a medium white sauce. Pour this over asparagus. Cover with crumbs and grated cheese. Bake at 300° until nicely browned.

Green beans with potatoes
By Alice Brantley Yeager

1 lb. green beans
1 medium onion, coarsely
   chopped
3 medium Irish potatoes,
   peeled and cut in half OR
   about 8 "new" potatoes

1 cup diced, salt or cured
   bacon
salt and pepper to taste

Wash and snap green beans, discarding any blemished spots, ends or strings. Put all items listed in a good-sized saucepan and cover with water. Bring to a boil and then cut heat back so contents will simmer. (Check occasionally to be sure pot does not boil dry.) When potatoes are done, beans should be ready to eat, too.

Summer squash stir-fry
By Alice Brantley Yeager

1 medium onion, coarsely chopped or 3-4 green onions cut into 1-inch pieces
1 Tbsp. bacon drippings
4 medium zucchini sliced in ¼-inch rounds
5 medium yellow straightneck squash sliced in ¼-inch rounds

1 medium green bell pepper and 1 medium red bell pepper thinly sliced crosswise or lengthwise
salt & pepper to taste
2 tsp. dried dill weed (optional)

Using a heavy iron skillet, sauté onions in bacon drippings until just past firm stage. Add rest of ingredients and mix with onions. Stir-fry until vegetables reach desired state of doneness. Some folks like to use a lid on the skillet to prevent evaporation of juices. Others prefer to use an open skillet and have a less juicy mixture.

Stuffed winter squash
By Alice Brantley Yeager

3 medium winter squash
1 cup finely chopped onion
4 Tbsp. butter or margarine
1 cup cooked brown rice
1 cup cooked, crumbled sausage
¾ cup chopped pecans or walnuts

2 large eggs, beaten
1 tsp. salt
½ tsp. freshly ground black pepper
½ tsp. ground nutmeg
2 cups grated cheese
honey (optional)

Halve squash lengthwise and discard strings and seeds. Bake covered at 375° about 25 minutes or until tender. Remove flesh leaving a shell. Thoroughly mash squash. Lightly sauté onions in butter or margarine and combine with all ingredients except cheese.

Put mixture into squash shells and bake at 350° about 20 minutes until hot throughout and set. Top with grated cheese and return to oven to melt. If you'd like a bit of sweetness added to this dish, dribble a bit of honey over each squash half as it is brought hot from the oven.

Pot of greens
By Alice Brantley Yeager

greens
turnips, cleaned and diced
green onions, cleaned and
  chopped

bacon or other cured meat
salt and pepper as desired

Gather a good quantity of greens as they will cook down considerably. I prefer a mixture of greens as the blend of flavors is delicious. Turnip greens, mustard, mustard-spinach, radish, beet—whatever you have that is tender and not past its prime.

Inspect greens for any insects and remove tough stems. This is easily done by stripping the stems from the greens wherever the tough stem begins. Wash the greens thoroughly in cool water and drain in a colander. While greens are draining, fry several pieces of bacon until almost crisp and cut in small pieces. Set these aside along with some of the drippings to combine with greens.

Put greens in a stainless steel or porcelain pot (don't use aluminum) and add about 2-3 cups of water. Add chopped onions, turnips, bacon, and drippings and bring to a simmer. Greens will wilt as they cook. Stir occasionally to keep them from forming a mass. They will probably be tender in 20-25 minutes. Taste to see if you might like a bit of seasoning added. Lift greens from pot, draining away liquid and serve hot. Greens should never be served without corn bread, and the crispier, the better.

Fried zucchini with pomegranate
By Habeeb Salloum

¼ cup olive oil
1 medium-sized zucchini
(about 8 inches long and 3
inches diameter), cut into
half then sliced into ½-inch
thickness
1 Tbsp. pomegranate con-
centrate, diluted in 2 Tbsp.
water

2 Tbsp. very finely chopped
fresh coriander leaves
½ tsp. garlic powder
½ tsp. pepper
½ tsp. paprika
1/8 tsp. cayenne

Heat oil in a frying pan, then fry zucchini slices until they turn
golden brown, adding more oil if necessary. Remove and place on a
flat serving platter.

Prepare a sauce by combining remaining ingredients, then spoon
sauce over zucchini slices. Allow to stand for an hour before serving.

Cooked fresh asparagus beans
By Alice Brantley Yeager

1 lb. asparagus beans,
rinsed and snapped. (If
some have grown beyond
the tender snapping stage,
shell the beans and dis-
card the pods.)

2 slices cured bacon, fried
and cut in small pieces.
Reserve bacon drippings.
1 small onion, chopped
¼ tsp. salt
1/8 tsp. freshly ground black
pepper

Put beans in 2-quart pot and cover with water. Bring to a boil and
reduce heat to simmer. Add other ingredients, including 1 Tbsp. of
bacon drippings, and cook about 25-30 minutes or until beans are
tender. Avoid overcooking as beans could become mushy.

Serve as a side dish with other food or serve as a main dish with
your favorite bread or corn bread.

Fried green tomatoes
By Alice Brantley Yeager

4 medium-sized, firm tomatoes—green with just a
tinge of red

1 large onion
½ stick margarine or butter
salt and pepper

Thinly slice onion and fry in margarine until tender. Remove from pan and reserve to put over tomatoes. Slice tomatoes in ¼-inch thick slices and fry in margarine about 1½ minutes on each side. Sprinkle with salt and pepper while cooking. Remove from pan, place on serving dish, and cover with reserved onions.

Another version: Dip tomato slices in your favorite batter and fry. Batter may be enhanced with the addition of dried herbs such as sweet basil, thyme, etc.

Microwave zucchini-corn blend
By Sandra L. Toney

2 cups shredded zucchini (if
frozen, thaw completely;
discard the excess liquid)
1/3 cup diced onion
¼ cup diced green pepper
2 Tbsp. butter or margarine

1 cup whole kernel corn
(drained, if from a can)
½ cup shredded American
cheese
3 Tbsp. chopped pimento
(optional)
½ tsp. pepper

In a 1-quart casserole dish, combine the zucchini, onion, green pepper, and butter. Cover the casserole and microwave the mixture on high for 5 minutes (or until tender).

Mix in the corn, cheese, pimento, and pepper. Cover the casserole and microwave on high for another 2 minutes. Stop, and stir the mixture. Microwave the covered mixture on high for 2 more minutes (or until heated completely through). Serves 4.

Parmesan-zucchini fritters
By Sandra L. Toney

2 cups shredded zucchini (if
frozen, thaw completely;
discard the excess liquid)
2 eggs

½ cup pancake mix
¼ cup Parmesan cheese
½ tsp. salt
2 Tbsp. vegetable oil

In a medium-size bowl, mix the zucchini, eggs, pancake mix, Parmesan cheese, and salt with a fork.

Heat skillet and add oil. Drop the zucchini mixture by tablespoons into the hot skillet. Fry the cakes on both sides until they are brown. Serve them hot.

Makes about 15 3-inch fritters.

Glazed carrots with peas and onions
By Richard Blunt

1½ lbs. sliced fresh carrots
1½ cups chicken or beef
broth
6 Tbsp. butter
½ cup diced fresh onions
1 tsp. brown sugar

2 tsp. honey
1½ cups fresh or frozen
peas
½ tsp. salt
½ tsp. freshly ground black
pepper

Simmer the carrots in the broth over medium heat until just tender. Drain and reserve the broth.

Melt the butter in a skillet and sauté the onions over medium heat until tender.

Add brown sugar, honey, and ¼ cup of reserved broth and stir until sugar is dissolved. Add carrots and peas and continue to sauté until the vegetables are glazed.

Add salt and pepper and serve.

North African vegetable mix
By Richard Blunt

5 small red skinned potatoes
cut into 1/6
1 Tbsp. salt
1½ cups fresh peas (or
sugar snap peas)
1 cup fresh green beans, cut
into thirds
1 cup fresh carrots, cut into
1 inch chunks
1½ cups fresh zucchini, cut
into 1 inch chunks
4 Tbsp. extra virgin olive oil
1 cup diced onion
4 cloves fresh garlic, finely
minced

2 tsp. ground cumin
1 Tbsp. ground coriander
1½ tsp. freshly ground black
pepper
¼ tsp. cayenne pepper
(more or less to taste)
juice of ½ medium lemon
1½ cups fresh plum toma-
toes, peeled, seeded and
diced
½ cup chicken stock
2 tsp. chopped fresh mint
1½ Tbsp. chopped fresh
cilantro

Bring a large pot of water to a boil and add 1 Tbsp. of salt. Add potatoes and cook until tender but still crisp. Remove with a slotted spoon and cool potatoes under running water.

In same water, boil peas, green beans, carrots, and zucchini, in separate batches, being careful not to overcook any of the vegetables. These vegetables only require about 1 minute each in the boiling water.

Heat 4 Tbsp. olive oil in a large sauté pan or wok over medium heat. Add onions and cook until tender. Stir in garlic, cumin, corian-der, black pepper, and cayenne pepper and cook for 2 minutes.

Combine tomatoes, chicken stock, mint, and cilantro. Add to onion, garlic, and spice mixture and simmer for about 2 minutes.

Add cooked vegetables and stir gently until all vegetables reach serving temperature.

Stir-fried vegetables
By Richard Blunt

2 carrots, peeled
2 cups fresh broccoli
2 cups fresh cauliflower
1 large sweet red pepper
4 oz. fresh mushrooms
2 cloves fresh garlic
½ cup snow peas
¼ tsp. minced fresh ginger
2 Tbsp. peanut oil for frying
Sauce:
1 Tbsp. bean sauce
1 Tbsp. Hoisin sauce
1 Tbsp. soy sauce

¼ cup chicken broth, fresh
  or canned
1 Tbsp. dry sherry
1 tsp. sugar
½ tsp. rice vinegar
¼ tsp. freshly ground black
  pepper
½ tsp. fresh chopped lemon
  grass (optional) or ¼ tsp.
  ground dried lemon grass
Thickener:
2 Tbsp. cornstarch
2 Tbsp. water

Slant cut the carrots 1/8 inch thick and set them aside.

Remove broccoli flowers from the main stem. Cut 4 inches from the stem and slant cut the remainder of the stem and set aside. Cut the flowers in half and set aside.

Break off cauliflower flowers and cut to the same size as the broccoli and set aside.

Dice red pepper in ½-inch pieces and set aside. Slice mushrooms and set aside. Peel and mince garlic, set aside. Wash and remove stems from snow peas, set aside. Combine all sauce ingredients.

Mix corn starch and water. Remember to remix before use.

Place wok or sauté pan on medium heat. Add 2 Tbsp. oil along with the ginger and heat. Do not allow to smoke. Add carrots and garlic. Stir-fry for 1 minute. Add broccoli and cauliflower and stir-fry for about 3 minutes. Add snow peas and stir-fry for 1 minute. Add mushrooms and peppers and stir-fry for 1 minute. Add sauce mixture, bring to a boil and cook for 1 minute.

Remix thickener and add to mixture. Stir until sauce thickens. Transfer to a heated serving dish and serve immediately.

Zucchini with green chilies
By Pat Ward

2 lbs. zucchini, cubed into
  ½-inch thickness
1 large onion, diced
2 Tbsp. olive oil

1 6-oz. can of diced green
  chilies
salt and pepper to taste
1 lb. jack cheese, sliced in
  ¼-inch thick slices

In a frying pan, cook the zucchini and onion in olive oil until most of the moisture has been cooked out of the zucchini. Pour off any excess liquid. Add the green chilies, salt and pepper and stir well. Use the slices of jack cheese to cover the squash, then cover the fry pan and let it sit until the cheese has melted, and serve.

Zucchini melts
By Pat Ward

2 eggs
¼ cup milk
1 large zucchini
1 cup flour
olive oil for frying
1 large onion, sliced ¼-inch
  thick

2 large tomatoes, sliced
  ¼-inch thick
1 lb. cheddar cheese, sliced
  ¼-inch thick

Preheat oven to 350°. Gently beat the eggs and milk together until blended. Slice squash into ½-inch slices and dip slices in egg-milk mixture then coat each one with flour. Fry these slices in the oil, a few at a time, until they're tender. Place the fried slices on a cookie sheet and on the top of each piece place a slice of onion, a slice of tomato, and a slice of cheddar cheese. Place the cookie sheet in the oven and heat until hot and the cheese has melted.

Apples and sweet potatoes
By Anne Westbrook Dominick

3 apples, peeled, cored, and sliced
1 Tbsp. lemon juice
1½ lbs. sweet potatoes, peeled and sliced
¼ cup apple juice, cider or vinegar
1 Tbsp. melted butter or margarine

Mix apples and lemon juice. In a baking dish place a layer of sweet potatoes then a layer of apples. Continue until apples and sweet potatoes are finished. Pour in the apple liquid and dribble melted butter over the top. Cover casserole and bake in a 350° oven for 1 hour. Uncover and bake another 15 minutes. Serves 4-6.

Apple-stuffed winter squash
By Anne Westbrook Dominick

2 acorn or medium-sized butternut squash
1 Tbsp. butter or margarine
3 cups apples peeled, cored and diced
½ cup onion, diced
2 cups cottage cheese
¾ cup grated cheddar cheese
¼ cup lemon juice
¼ tsp. cinnamon

Cut squash in half, remove the seeds and bake cut side down in a 350° oven until just tender, about 30 minutes. Melt butter or margarine in frying pan and sauté apples and onion until the onion is transparent. In a bowl, mix the apples and onion with the last 4 ingredients. Fill the squash cavities with the apple mix, return to baking pan and cover with foil. Bake another 20 minutes in a 350° oven. Serves 4.

Chili potatoes
By Richard Blunt

Main ingredients:
8 size A red skinned potatoes (about the size of a
tennis ball. This is about
2½ lbs. of potatoes)
1 medium egg
1 Tbsp. extra virgin olive oil
5 cloves fresh garlic, minced
1 tsp. fresh ginger, minced
2 medium sweet red bell
peppers, seeded, dev-
eined and julienned
1 medium sweet yellow bell
pepper, seeded, deveined,
and julienned
1 medium onion, diced
medium

Dressing ingredients:
¼ cup extra virgin olive oil
1 Tbsp. fresh basil leaves
chopped
2 tsp. fresh spearmint leaves
chopped
2 tsp. kosher salt
1 tsp. Dijon style mustard
1 tsp. freshly ground black
pepper
2 Tbsp. favorite vinegar
1½ Tbsp. finely minced pickled jalapeño peppers
1 Tbsp. juice from pickled
peppers
Garnish:
6 radishes, thinly sliced
2 Tbsp. parsley, chopped

Cut the potatoes into 6 or 8 pieces each and cook in lightly salted boiling water until just tender. Do not overcook. Drain well and set aside.

Cook egg in boiling water until hard cooked. Cool, peel, dice medium, cover and set aside. (If you plan to serve this dish hot, skip the egg.)

Heat olive oil in heavy-bottomed skillet and sauté garlic and ginger over medium heat for 2 minutes (just enough time to release the flavors without browning). Add peppers and onions and continue to sauté until peppers are just tender, while maintaining a little crunch. Combine vegetables with potatoes and egg in large bowl and set aside.

Combine dressing ingredients, blend with a whisk, then toss with the potato mixture.

If you are serving cold, garnish with 6 thinly sliced radishes and 2 Tbsp. of fresh chopped flat leaf parsley. Chill for at least 2 hours.

If you are serving this hot, place mixture in oven casserole, set in 350° oven for about 30 minutes. Sprinkle with 2 Tbsp. fresh chopped flat leaf parsley on top before serving.

Penne with Provencal eggplant and peppers
By Tim and Anna Green

2 medium-sized eggplants,
  unpeeled and cut into 1
  inch cubes
1 cup olive oil
salt
2 medium onions, sliced
3 red, gold, or green sweet
  peppers, thinly sliced
4 cloves of garlic, finely
  minced or pressed

¼ cup freshly squeezed
  lemon juice
2 tsp. dried herbes D'Anna
  (marjoram, basil, rose-
  mary)
1 lb. penne pasta
1½ cups firmly packed
  chopped fresh basil
basil garnish

Place eggplant in a shallow baking pan, toss with ½ cup olive oil, sprinkle with salt to taste and bake at 400° until cubes are soft but hold shape (30 minutes). Set aside to cool.

Heat ¼ cup olive oil in large heavy frying pan. Add onions and sweet peppers; cook over low heat until vegetables are tender and slightly carmelized (35-40 minutes). Stir in garlic, salt and pepper to taste, cook 5 more minutes.

Combine the remaining ¼ cup olive oil, lemon juice, and herbes D'Anna, and salt and pepper to taste. Whisk and reserve.

Cook pasta in 4 qts. boiling water until very al dente. Drain and rinse well in cold water; drain again. Diagonally slice each piece of pasta in half. Toss in a large bowl with onion mixture and reserved dressing. Toss eggplant and chopped basil with pasta. Garnish with basil leaves. Serves 6-8.

Texas caviar-pickled black-eyed peas
By Sharon Thornbury

4 cups cooked, dried black-
  eyed peas
1 cup salad oil
¼ cup wine vinegar

1 clove garlic
½ cup onion, diced
½ tsp. salt
black pepper to taste

After cooking peas, drain the liquid. Mix together all other ingredients thoroughly and then add peas. Store in covered container in refrigerator, removing garlic clove after 1 day. Wait 3 days before serving peas, chilled and arranged in an attractive bowl for a buffet supper.

Mustard greens as a stir-fry
By Anne Westbrook Dominick

1 lb. mustard greens
1-2 Tbsp. olive oil
1 clove garlic, minced
1¼-inch thick slice of ginger
  root, minced

¼ tsp. sugar
1 tsp. cornstarch
2 Tbsp. water

Rinse and drain mustard greens and cut into bite-sized chunks. Heat oil in skillet and fry garlic and ginger root for a few seconds. Add greens and stir to mix. Cover and cook, stirring occasionally, until barely tender, just a few minutes. Add a bit of water if mustard greens start to stick. Mix sugar, cornstarch, and water and add to mustard greens. Stir-fry until sauce thickens, another minute or so.

Index of recipes

328

My favorites

Notes

Notes

Other books available from *Backwoods Home Magazine*

* The Best of the First Two Years
* A Backwoods Home Anthology—The Third Year
* A Backwoods Home Anthology—The Fourth Year
* A Backwoods Home Anthology—The Fifth Year
* A Backwoods Home Anthology—The Sixth Year
* A Backwoods Home Anthology—The Seventh Year
* A Backwoods Home Anthology—The Eighth Year
* A Backwoods Home Anthology—The Ninth Year
* A Backwoods Home Anthology—The Tenth Year
* A Backwoods Home Anthology—The Eleventh Year
* A Backwoods Home Anthology—The Twelfth Year
* A Backwoods Home Anthology—The Thirteenth Year
* A Backwoods Home Anthology—The Fourteenth Year
* A Backwoods Home Anthology—The Fifteenth Year
* A Backwoods Home Anthology—The Sixteenth Year
* A Backwoods Home Anthology—The Seventeenth Year
* A Backwoods Home Anthology—The Eighteenth Year
* A Backwoods Home Anthology—The Nineteenth Year
* Emergency Preparedness and Survival Guide
* Backwoods Home Cooking
* Can America Be Saved From Stupid People
* The Coming American Dictatorship, Parts I-XI
* Chickens: a beginner's handbook
* Starting Over: Chronicles of a Self-Reliant Woman
* Dairy goats: a beginner's handbook
* Self-Reliance: Recession-proof your pantry
* Making a Living: creating your own job
* Harvesting the Wild: gathering & using food from nature
* Hardyville Tales
* Growing and Canning Your Own Food
* Jackie Clay's Pantry Cookbook